CW00517067

Tensions in Bengal Rural Society

Landlords, Planters and Colonial Rule
1830–1860

Chittabrata Palit

Sangam Books

SANGAM BOOKS LIMITED
57 London Fruit Exchange,
Brushfield Street
London E1 6EP U.K.

By arrangement with
Orient Longman Limited
3-6-272 Himayatnagar, Hyderabad 500 029

© Orient Longman Limited 1998
First published by Progressive Publishers 1975
First published by Orient Longman Limited 1998

Published by
Sangam Books Limited 1998

ISBN 0 86311 603 5

Typeset by
OSDATA
Hyderabad 500 029

Printed in India at
Indcom Press
West Mambalam
Chennai 600 033

Preface to the First Edition

Agrarian society in Bengal for some four decades after the Permanent Settlement of 1793 remained a petite culture dominated by a hierarchy of rent-receivers. Traditional structures of power and modes of production were little affected. From the 1830s, however, the agrarian system came under pressure. The official opening of India to Free Trade and to European planters strengthened the linkage of Bengal to the world market and the movement from subsistence to cash crop agriculture. At the same time, the administration was also tightened to preserve the mechanism by which the trade in plantation products was used to remit Home-Charges, to secure larger revenues from the Bengal countryside and to release its productive energies by curbs upon landlordism.

The European planters appeared to be the most significant agricultural innovators in Bengal for their pioneering attempts at capitalist farming of cash crops. By providing new sources of cash and alternative centres of power, they seemed likely also to be subverters of the established rural political order. But they lacked the capital resources to carry through an agricultural revolution. They were content to manipulate the petite culture, to collaborate with the landlords and to take a short-term profit. When they ceased to be useful to the landlord class, as either political or economic allies, they were driven from Bengal by that class, despite the official favour they enjoyed.

The new bureaucratic intervention in agrarian relations was most clearly seen in the land resumption programme begun in the 1830s and in the Rent Act of 1859. They first monetised the semi-feudal economy considerably by bringing rent-free tenures under assessment, increased the government tax resources and constituted the first serious interference with landlord powers. The second, a logical corollary, created legal occupancy rights and sought to regulate the distribution of agricultural profits between the rentiers and the entrepreneurial occupancy farmers to allow capital formation in the latter's hands for agricultural development on a wider scale. In more general terms, the government also sought to tighten the administration of justice and police so as to reduce landlord power based on coercion. In every case, however, the landlords were successful in thwarting or blunting government intentions.

The most crucial decades in the first century of British rule have thus been examined to measure agrarian change or otherwise. I have taken pains to determine the interactional position of social, economic and political forces in the social syndrome of the period. The relation of the units of the study to the overall theme may not be obvious. But they are seminal for an analysis of the social system.

This work is a slightly modified version of my thesis submitted earlier to Cambridge University for the degree of Doctor of Philosophy. I have worked mainly on the records of the India Office Library, the British Museum, the Public Records Office, the Scottish Record Office, Edinburgh, the University Library and the Centre of South Asian Studies at Cambridge. I have indicated all sources of my information in the footnotes and more adequately in the bibliography at the end.

I have tried to underline as few revenue and judicial terms as possible to keep the text tidy. Their English equivalents have been given in the text when possible. A fuller glossary has been provided at the end. I have sought to maintain the standard transliteration but variations in spelling might have occurred without my knowledge. Colonial spellings have been retained in quotations as well as when reference is made to offices and positions of the colonial period (e.g., collector of Midnapore). As far as possible, standard Indian spelling has been used in the text (e.g. Midnapur) for words transliterated from Indian languages. The outline of the thesis has been given in the introduction that follows.

I am deeply indebted to Professor Eric Stokes of St Catherine's College, Cambridge, for his painstaking and kind supervision. I wish to record my debt to late Professor N K Sinha of Calcutta University for initiating me into research. I am grateful to Dr Tapan Roy Choudhury of Oxford University and Dr Ranajit Guha of Sussex University for their help. I wish also to thank Mr B Farmer and Mr A J N Richards, the Director and the Librarian respectively, of the Centre of South Asian Studies, Cambridge for their kind hospitality and help. Professors Nemai Sadhan Bose and Amitabha Mukherjee, my colleagues in the department have been a source of constant encouragement to me. To Dr Sunil Sen of

Rabindra Bharati University, my debt is overwhelming. But for his initiative, the publication of my thesis could have been indefinitely delayed.

Finally, it remains for me to acknowledge my debt to my wife for the care she has taken to prepare the typescript and sustain me while the work was in progress. My little daughter provided all my recreation during this period of all work and no play.

Department of History   Chittabrata Palit
Jadavpur University
Calcutta
1975

Preface to the Second Edition

This book is basically a study of the political and economic pressures
unleashed by the Raj on Bengal rural society to break its feudal bind and
release its productive energies through the Permanent Settlement (1793),
land resumption measures (1828–36), enfranchisement of planters as
pioneers of commercial agriculture, Rent Act (1859) and the framework
of law and order. All these cumulatively produced a mild push which
tautened the socio-economic structure to some extent and caused extraction of some rural surplus in the form of revenue and cash crops. Social
equations also underwent some transformation. The new zamindars rose
and declined and the jotedars prospered and maintained their newly
acquired status and power over the market economy. But in the end, the
status quo prevailed. Feudalism was not undermined. The ever increasing
size of our population scrambled for a minuscule share of a receding rural
surplus, both the top and bottom halves of the society caught in an
economy of no outlets. On the whole, it was a transition from relative
prosperity to misery after the fat of the land was taken out by vulgar
commercialism under the colonial aegis. The British authorities were
content with manipulating the petite culture without any genuine desire
to contain the zamindars who were the cheapest and the safest agents for
revenue collection and the pacification of the countryside. Initially the
planters and increasingly the jotedars were utilised as spearheads of the
push factor causing such outbreaks as the Indigo Revolt of 1860 and the
Pabna Uprising of 1873. But they were minor tremors lacking the potency
to upset the equilibrium. This is, in short, the nature of the tension
generated by the British rule in the nineteenth century.

The book when first published raised a few significant issues. Foremost
among these was the question of continuity of agrarian structure since

precolonial times. It was stated that the Permanent Settlement constituted no watershed in agrarian history as all old zamindaris did not go to the hammer for default of arrears. While Rajshahi, Cossijora, Rokanpur and Birbhum fell or passed to the zamindars' nearest relatives and the staff of their establishment, Dhaka, Murshidabad, Paikpara, Nadia and Burdwan survived the shock. The parvenu zamindars were also mostly the rural gentry. There was no major migration of capital from business to land. In this sense, there was continuity. Of the old zamindars, the Muslims were not the main victims (Akhtar 1986).

The whole book has been viewed as an early demonstration of the now raging theme of continuity in Indian history, especially as it highlights the successful landlord opposition to all government measures threatening to undermine their status. My concern was not to show that the pious intentions of the government were frustrated by the zamindars. Feudalism was not effectively undermined by the colonial government which only sought to maximise its gain from revenue, security, extraction of cash crops and exploitation of the peasantry by minimum intervention and expense through the agency of the zamindars. There was mutual accommodation of interest between the government and the zamindars resulting in slow transition. This is the core of my thesis of continuity. I only demonstrated that all insincere attempts at so-called improvement failed because of the inadequacies of the new utilitarian framework which allowed it to be appropriated by the rural elites. Yet some tactical breaches were made in the feudal structure by the ruling class, just enough to syphon off a sizeable rural surplus, agitating the economy to a pitch and leaving it impoverished. This continuity of feudalism is precolonial only in form and not in content as one may find in the works of Bayly (1988) or Yang (1989).

The second issue of consequence emerging out of this is the concept and agency of improvement. Improvement was the manifesto of the Whig liberals in England who came to dominate Westminster around the time of the Permanent Settlement. It had its impact on the framers of the revenue policy in Bengal. In the debates over this issue, Thomas Law, Pattullo, Philip Francis *et al* put their physiocratic and liberal Whig arguments in favour of Permanent Settlement of revenue leaving the future generation of rural surplus in the hands of the regulation landlords to invest in the infrastructure of capitalist agriculture like drainage, irrigation and soil conservation for successful commercial agriculture. This stake in estate would assure all round improvement of the neighbourhood and help in the extraction of cash crops for international markets. The British landlords were respected members of the House of Lords and had a say over the legislations affecting them. No such representation was available for Bengal zamindars to safeguard their interests except through their own Landholders' Society and its successor, the British Indian Association. The Landholders' Society fought land resumption and the latter, Sale Laws and Rent Acts encumbering their freehold, road cess, income tax and revenue demand to reclaim some portion of the rural surplus granted to allow capital formation for improvement of agriculture. The creation of land market under the Sunset Law and the Sale Laws led to the elimination of resident landlords and the formation of patchwork estates stretching from Barisal to Benares owned by absentee landlords, the creatures of circumstance who had to depend on their petty peons for collection of rent and prompt payment of revenue. They turned into mercenaries and not 'improving landlords'. The rule of property of 1793 was therefore not really a watershed though some historians have over-emphasised its importance (Guha 1963; for contrary opinion, Islam 1979).

This brings us to another lively debate on the nature of resumption of rent-free tenures which is a core chapter of this work. These tenures were of two kinds, one given to Mughal officials in lieu of salary and the other genuinely for religious, scholarly and charitable purposes. There were also forged titles. *Lakhiraj* of the second type was also utilised for non-cultural purposes and sold for profit. The alien government was trying to resume these feudal vestiges and monetise them by making them revenue-bearing estates and commodities in the land market. It was a mild push suspended in the face of landlord opposition. In many cases, genuine cultural endow-ments were ruthlessly escheated back to the estate. This argument has not been queried by any scholar since it was broached in this book, though some quantification of *lakhiraj* had been made in an earlier unpublished thesis and the problem discussed in some published works. The issue has been thoroughly researched in a recent work on waqfs and idgahs in the northwest provinces in which an attempt has been made to relate it to the cultural decline of the Muslim community (Wahiduzzaman 1969, Stokes 1978, Akhtar 1986, Kozlowski 1985). The fact that has been ignored is that the Hindu *lakhiraj* property was similarly affected leading to their cultural crisis but they tided over it. The major controversy in the agrarian history of Bengal in recent years has been over the role of the jotedars or rich peasants as controllers of agricultural production vis-a-vis the zamin-dars who exercised only land control for rent. This semi-capitalist role of the jotedars in their production relations with the sharecroppers was the core of the Tebhaga struggle and discussed thoroughly by one of the participants (Sen 1979). The historical roots of the jotedars and their changing role in agrarian Bengal since the beginning of the nineteenth century has been worked out in detail in almost all the chapters of the book. While the research for this work was in progress in Cambridge and brainstorming sessions accompanied it, a parallel work for the period immediately before it was being undertaken by another scholar tracking the *jotedar* since Plassey. The role of the jotedars as the real rural magnates since precolonial times till the twentieth century was emphasised in this other work. This part of the finding was published by that author in two papers before this book was put in print (Ray and Ray 1973 and 1975). This again was incorporated in her book published in 1979. This later thesis was, however, cast in a different mould, which has come to be known as the new Cambridge orthodoxy of continuity, deconstructing the colonial framework (Ray 1979). The view expressed in my book still holds good. In a period of hectic reclamation and scarce labour in the late nineteenth century, the *jotedar* or the pioneer farmer and his colony of sharecroppers were much-solicited, elusive customers for the zamindars having *jungleburee* or forest estates like in Buchanan-Hamilton's *Dinajpore* and *Rungpore*. They were, no doubt, all powerful, having a hard bargaining power backed by the threat of desertion. This desertion is obviously different from the simple formulation of leaving one's hearth and home due to rackrenting during a famine (Zilli-Nagchowdhuri 1982). But to say that the zamindars of 1793 might have been the creatures of the Raj and yet that they were at the mercy of the primordial jotedars who continued to enjoy such power and control over productivity till 1947 is unhistorical. As a careful reading of contemporary records shows, the *jotedar* had some economic power over the mode of production but the territorial authority of the zamindars remained unimpaired. The zamindars, by coercion or conciliation, managed to get their due share of the rural surplus. In fact, the jotedars collaborated with the zamindars to exploit the lesser peasantry as shown in this work and elsewhere (Palit 1980). The bargaining power of the *jotedar* was considerably reduced from 1793 due to the increasing coercive authority of the zamindars under the Permanent Settlement and an adverse land–man ratio. The Whig experiment with the idea of the 'improving landlord' was carried out for sometime without the requisite infrastructure. Next, European planters were sent into the countryside as the new improving agents. They also degenerated into rentiers and the government began enfranchising the submerged jotedars by the Rent Act of 1859 for the same improving role of procuring cash crops from the hinterland. While this restoration of the jotedars was going on, the zamindars were not really undermined. They continued their *lathi raj* with impunity (Palit 1980).

The return of the *jotedar* thus had a context substantially different from his role as a precolonial pioneer farmer, which set in motion considerable rural differentiation and dynamics of downward mobility beneath an apparent equilibrium.

The *jotedar* debate has recently been extended by another scholar who has deflated the jotedar's perceived economic and political power. A zonal distribution of jotedars in Bengal has been mapped out and their variation in the respective zones in the denotative sense from rich to small peasant categories is shown to illustrate their lack of homogeneity as an economically and politically powerful class. It has been further shown that international market forces unleashed by British rule determined the destiny of the jotedars and the economic depression of 1930 sapped whatever power base the *jotedar* had at the beginning of the twentieth century (Bose 1986 and 1993). I had used the term *jotedar* in a connotative sense to mean a rich peasant-turned-landlord combining semi-feudal and semi-capitalist levers of control to extract cash crops from a small peasant economy. He reinforced it by moneylending, grain dealing, milling and transporting of cash crops. The nomenclature could be anything ranging from *khudkasht, asullee praja, gantidar, haoladar, lotdar, thikadar* to yeomanry, substantial ryot, ryot-purchaser or the term *jotedar* itself. They were obviously a dominant minority in a community of small peasants (Palit 1982). The north and the east zones had more of them. On another count, it can be argued that the world capitalist system did not directly affect their position in Bengal. The Depression of 1930 did not upset their apple cart. It is evident from the Report of the Land Revenue Commission (1940). The jotedars controlled 20 per cent or more of all arable land in Bengal and in some districts over 30 to 40 per cent. Its recommendation was, therefore, to give tenancy rights to sharecroppers and fix their share at two-thirds of the harvest. As this was shelved repeatedly due to the Second World War and the famine of 1943, the sharecroppers rose in revolt, led by the CPI in 1946–47 (Palit 1882, Sen 1979).

A more recent debate concerning the continued substantive power and solvency of the landlords throughout the nineteenth century raised by the Japanese scholars in the field, and first formulated by K K Sengupta, does not seem convincing either. It was argued in this book that high landlordism was being eroded by tenancy laws and various government cesses on the one hand and the production control by the rising jotedars on the other. In fact, a class of indigent zamindars was emerging who had to sell parcels of their estates or give away valuable property in perpetual leases to this rising class of ryot-purchasers (Sengupta 1965, Kawai 1986–87, Nakazato 1994 also, Sen *et al* eds, 1982).

This work generated the most heated controversy over the interpretation of the nature of the Indigo Revolt (1860) and the Pabna Uprising (1873). It was stated that the Indigo Revolt was led both by zamindars like Ramratan Roy of Narail and the Palchowdhurys of Ranaghat and jotedars like the Biswases of Poragachha, at the head of the peasantry, in a bid to extrude the common enemy—the indigo planters. This was against the widely held view that it was a spontaneous groundswell. As for the Pabna Uprising, it was shown to be a tug of war between the zamindars and jotedars for cornering the growing rural surplus, when the informal basis of such adjustments through levies of additional cesses was rationalised by the government by proposing a consolidated rent for the tenantry. The uprising was led in the field by petty zamindars and jotedars like Ishan Chandra Roy and Khudi Mollah and the court cases were fought by their mukhtears. The peasantry, no doubt, participated en masse in this movement but the leadership remained in the hands of this combination of rural sub-elites all of whom had to bear the brunt of this enhancement of rent in some form or other. This was in refutation of Sengupta's earlier version of the uprising as the movement of an undifferentiated tenantry against the new Rent Act and its implementation by the zamindars. Guha follows the same line in his recent work, without meeting this argument, but Nakazato incorporated it without due acknowledgement (see Chattopadhyay 1985 and Guha 1983 for Indigo Uprising, Sengupta 1965, Benoy Chaudhuri 1973, Palit 1982 and Nakazato for Pabna Uprising 1994).

Department of History   Chittabrata Palit
Jadavpur University
Calcutta
1997

References to the Preface
(Second Edition)

Akhtar, S   *The Role of Zamindars in Bengal 1707–1772*, Dhaka, 1986

Bose, S   *Agrarian Bengal: Economy, Social Structure and Politics, 1919–1947*, Cambridge, 1986

Bose, S   *The Peasant, Labour and Colonial Capital: Rural Bengal since 1770*, Cambridge, 1993

Chattopadhyay, M   *From Petition to Agitation*, Calcutta, 1985

Choudhuri, B   *Peasant Movements in Bengal in Nineteenth Century Studies*, vol. 1, Calcutta, 1973

Guha, R   *A Rule of Property for Bengal*, Paris, 1963

Guha, R   *Elementary Aspects of Peasant Insurgency in Colonial India*, Delhi, 1983

Islam, S   *The Permanent Settlement in Bengal: A Study of its Operation, 1790–1819*, Dhaka, 1979

Kawai, A   *Landlords and Imperial Rule: Change in Bengal Agrarian Society, c. 1885–1940*, vols i–ii, Tokyo, 1986–87

Kozlowski, G C   *Muslim Endowments and Society in British India*, Cambridge, 1985

Nakazato, N   *Agrarian System in Eastern Bengal, c. 1870–1910*, Calcutta, 1994

Palit, C   *New Viewpoints on Nineteenth Century Bengal*, Calcutta, 1980

Palit, C   *Perspectives on Agrarian Bengal*, Calcutta, 1982

Palit, C (ed.),   *Agrarian Bengal under the Raj*, Calcutta, 1987

Ray, R and R Ray   'The Dynamics of Continuity in Rural Bengal under the British Imperium', *Indian Economic and Social History Review*, 101: 2 (1973)

Ray, R and R Ray   'Zamindars and Jotedars: A Study of Rural Politics in Bengal', *Modern Asian Studies*, 9:1 (1975)

Ray, R   *Change in Bengal Agrarian Society, 1760–1850*, New Delhi, 1979

Sen, S   *Agrarian Struggle in Bengal (1946–47)*, New Delhi, 1979

Sen, A *et al* (eds.)   *Perspectives in Social Science*, vol. ii, Calcutta, 1982, for essays by Ashok Sen and Partha Chatterjee

Sengupta, K K   *Pabna Disturbances and the Politics of Rent, 1873–1885*, New Delhi, 1965

Stokes, E T   *The Peasant and the Raj*, Cambridge, 1978

Wahiduzzaman, A M   *Land Resumption in Bengal, 1819–1846*, Unpublished Ph D Dissertation, London University, 1969

Zilli-Nagchowdhuri, A   *The Vagrant Peasant*, Wiesbaden, 1982

Abbreviations

as.	annas
BBIS	Bengal British India Society
B.C.J.C.	Bengal Criminal and Judicial Consultations
BIA	British Indian Association
BIS	British India Society
B.J.C.	Bengal Judical Consultations
B.M. Addl. Mss.	British Museum Additional Manuscripts
B.R.C.	Bengal Revenue Consultations
C.O.W.R.	Court of Ward Reports; full title: Report on the Wards' and Attached Estates in the Lower Provinces
IESHR	Indian Economic and Social History Review
IPA	Indigo Planters Association
I.R.C.	Indian Revenue Consultations
LHS	Landholders' Society
P.P.	Parliamentary Papers [i.e., P.P. vii (1857–58) refers to vol. 7 of the year in brackets]
P.P. xliv (1861) R.I.C.	Report of the Indigo Commission in the Parliamentary Papers. Shortened to only R.I.C. after its first use in full
PSA	Principal Sadar Amin
SA	Sadar Amin
SAB	Statistical Account of Bengal
SDA	Sadar Diwani Adalat
Settlement Report	Final Report on the Survey and Settlement Operations in the district of (for example, Bakarganj)
SP	Superintendent of Police
UGC	University Grants Commission

Contents

Introduction

In the early nineteenth century, the term 'Bengal Presidency' included the whole of eastern India. Bengal in this study stands for Bengal proper or the Lower Provinces as official records described it in those days. It excludes Bihar, Orissa and Assam. A more atomistic study down to the district or village level could not be made for lack of sufficient information in contemporary documents and printed accounts. Yet in the revenue and judicial proceedings of Bengal, piecemeal information on districts is available which, if carefully handled, can make a fairly reliable local history of Bengal. One has to be content with the art of the possible and this is precisely what has been attempted here. One has the consolation of being more cautious than those who make the inadequate study of a few villages or districts the basis of their sweeping conclusions about the whole province, or even India.

Bengal historical studies are either based on the Bengal records of the period 1765–1793 or the period after the 'Mutiny'. The early period is largely available in print, thanks to the labours of Firminger and Hunter. The government took the decision to print the proceedings of the post-1857 period. The chosen period of this study (1830–1860) remained a notable gap in historical studies because of the difficulty it presents to scholars, in weaving scattered information from mostly manuscript source materials.

Yet, this was the period of the first confrontation of two alien systems of political economy. British rule was fairly well consolidated on the foundation of the Permanent Settlement to make its impact felt on the rural society. The government made a serious attempt to transform a semi-feudal social system into a 'money economy' by resuming the rent-free service tenures which sustained it. The period also marked the mounting of a major offensive by the government to control agrarian relations (through the Act X of 1859) and release the productive powers of the land by rent control and protection of the small rural entrepreneurs, that is, the occupancy ryots. It also saw the infiltration of planters into the interior in larger numbers, as the officially sponsored 'agents of improvement'. They constituted the most formidable attempt to open up an otherwise insulated agrarian system and make it yield the much needed cash crops in larger quantities than before to feed Free Trade.

The importance of the period cannot be exaggerated. But it is usual to regard a period of convulsion like the interregnum of 1765–1793 or the 'Sepoy Mutiny' or the famines as the only epochs deserving a historian's attention. Such episodes were sensational but their symptoms cannot be generalised for less spectacular periods of real history. The present study focuses attention on a less sensational but more crucial period of throbbing possibilities in the annals of Bengal, for which no integrated and analytical history exists.

As the title indicates, it seeks to examine the role of British rule in general and the planters in particular as catalysts of agrarian change. It looks at the genesis of capitalist farming. It traces the quest for the rural entrepreneur as it threads through the whole period under review. It does not take for granted that the British rule brought in the land market, property in land, a swing to cash crops and an alteration in agrarian relations for the first time. In short, the coming of the British is not equated with agrarian change resulting from de-industrialisation of a communal system of agriculture and handicrafts. While it does not dote on a pre-British paradise lost, neither does it ignore that colonial rule accelerated the process of commercialisation of a semi-monetised, semi-feudal society in a critical stage of evolution.

The Permanent Settlement was an attempt at providing an economic and political framework for the creation of a land market. The zamindars were recognised as a special category who would manage estates as large farms and government revenue demand was perpetually fixed to allow capital formation for agricultural development. The estate-holders, however, had to be given up as an agency of improvement as they concentrated on rental profits, favoured by the existing economic situation. The government next tried to subvert the fabric of landlordism and take up the mantle of improvement temporarily by resumption measures. The planters were allowed to take over as entrepreneurs, following mismanagement of the *khas* mahals. But they seemed to make little headway and the task was finally assigned to rich peasants. But hopes were again belied. The answer to these recurring failures has been sought in this book.

Modern research has made it obvious that careers of governor-generals and statute books by themselves represent very little of the history of the country they addressed. It was more often a confrontation than a mere unilateral impact that caused a social ferment. The word 'impact' gives the impression of a hammer and anvil. Societies, after all, are not dead metals. Much depends on the reaction and response of the receiving side. The words 'confrontation' and 'tension' convey more of the bilateral interface than facile impacts and changes. This study is a measure of the confrontation between the new economic and political forces and the existing political economy of the country, controlled by landlords.

Chapter 1 sets out to define the character and composition of landlords after the Permanent Settlement as they were the rural elite who lorded over the social system and were inveterate enemies of any attempt to undermine their position. It is strictly devoted to their evolution as a class through interaction between their old and new attributes. It makes the point that progressive rental profits effectively barred them from undertaking any other enterprise whole-heartedly.

Chapter 2 takes up the first of a series of definite pressures on a rural society to make it amenable to the western concept of land economy. Land resumption was an attempt to pirate upon the landlords' unearned increment since Permanent Settlement. It was also a war on feudal privileges. The feudal economy was considerably monetised as a result. The official interference in permanently settled areas and the ryotwari settlement of resumed land were steps towards a major agrarian change. The landlords resisted it to maintain the status quo. The chapter disputes the notion that *lakhiraj* or rent-free holdings were only charity grants and investigates the extent of its abuse as a cover for large scale appropriation of resources by the rural elite. It records the political mobilisation of landlords and the measure of their success in thwarting bureaucratic aggression.

Chapter 3 looks at the spread-effect of the British system of justice and police over a period of fifty years from 1793, especially when it was tightened up between 1828 and 1838. How far did the rule of law affect the traditional processes of power and undermine the rule of force? Who benefited from the new source of power and opportunity? Was the administrative framework adequate for social engineering by regulations?

Chapters 4 and 5 are devoted to an analysis of the most serious challenge to the economic and political fabric of the country. This was the non-official intervention of the planters into the interior of Bengal to bring about change from within the social system. They enjoyed official patronage and posed the most formidable threat to the landlords' power and position. Their threefold impact on men, money and material, smacked of an economic transformation. After the degeneration of the hoped for 'improving' landlords into mere rent-receivers, the government pinned their hopes on these capitalist farmers for rural entrepreneurship. The demands of remittance and Free Trade put a premium on the growth of cash crops. The existing mode of production under the withering touch of the landlords, appeared incapable of delivering the goods. The planters were looked upon as new economic messiahs.

Chapter 4 is an assessment of the reception of this new external factor into the insulated politico-economic system. It attempts to explore the multidimensional character of the planters' pressure on the indigenous social system.

Chapter 5 deals with the brewing confrontation and final showdown between the planters and the landlords. It analyses the factors behind the confrontation and the assimilation of planters into the iron frame of landlordism.

Chapter 6 traces the genesis of the Rent Act of 1859 and its aftermath. This was the most inspired piece of social engineering by regulation. The government sought to regulate agrarian relations and the distribution of agricultural profits after a long period of *laissez-faire*. The government supported the occupancy ryot when the planters petered out as an entrepreneurial agency in the *mofussil*. Agricultural development was no longer equated with the achievements of a few planters or with the prospect of a crop showing diminishing returns. Expansion of Free Trade demanded firmer and closer linkages with the empire. Even the remotest corner in Bengal had to be harnessed to produce for the world market and receive western wares. Capital formation at the grassroots level was a necessity to help the small rural capitalist to develop resources for export on a national scale and to restore purchasing power to the countryside. The occupancy ryots who formed less than 50 per cent of the peasantry were chosen as the new agency for a silent agrarian revolution. On a review of the protracted policy of *laissez-faire*, the government found that it had led to polarisation of agricultural profits in favour of the non-productive sector of society. The Act X of 1859 reflected the need and official resolve to intervene in agrarian relations, in order to leave a fair margin of profits to the yeomanry to carry on agriculture. A rightful participation in the fruits of their labour was likely to rally the yeomanry to the new commitment desired by the government and undermine the hold of the landlords. The chapter discusses the limitation clauses of the Permanent Settlement as the precedent of rent control, their lapse into *laissez-faire* and resuscitation in 1859 in stricter form and substance. The long period of *laissez-faire* has been examined in some detail to study the consequences of exposing an agrarian society of teeming millions to market forces. It brings out the whole gamut of agrarian problems under colonial rule and tries to place the Rent Act in its historic setting. The chapter finally evaluates the measure and the landlords' tactics to stem this potential agrarian revolution.

Chapter 7 sums up the various pressures generated by an alien rule on a semi-feudal, insulated society and on its wardens, the landlords. How far did these pressures contribute to continuity or change? Did they undermine landlordism or add to it? What were the impediments to development from below? What caused the frustration of all agencies – the landlords, the government, the planters and the occupancy ryots – in bringing about agrarian change? Why did the tension subside into a political and economic equilibrium? In the final analysis, an answer has been sought to all these questions.

One

Landlords after the Permanent Settlement

The term 'landlord' has been used in the text to include all rent-receivers above the actual cultivator who did not sublet. The term 'zamindar' would have excluded all other grades of rent-receivers who represented land-lordism no less than the estate-holders. Sub-infeudation in its spread-effect strengthened landlordism. It saved a superstructure like the Burdwan Raj and made it possible for a strong *patnidar* or intermediaries like the Mukherjees of Hooghly to emerge as major landlords in our period. The intermediaries accounted for the staying power of the semi-feudal social structure and agrarian system in a large measure. In their political confrontation with the state and economic bargaining with the primary producers, all grades of rent-receivers seemed to uphold the institution against its possible subversion or transformation. Sub-infeudation hardly affected the traditional processes of power and mode of production. In the scramble for rent and power the interactional position of landlords might have upset the hierarchy in some districts but it did not undermine the social system as a whole. In Rangpur and Dinajpur, the powerful zamindars were, to some extent, dependent on the jotedars for reclamation and cultivation of their comparatively arid and sparsely populated estates. It was in their interest to keep the rich and contented farmers on their estates for better use of land. But the jotedars were the privileged section of the tenantry. The same privilege of low rent was not extended to other weaker and poorer sections. The *jotedar*, though a ryot in the zamindar's rent-roll, was the immediate landlord of his *korfa* under-tenants and sharecroppers.

He personified the more ruthless kind of landlordism—its milder form being practised by his overlord.[1]

There can also be a horizontal classification of landlords into big and small, or strong and weak. The actual cultivator was none the better for it. In Sylhet and Chittagong, the estates were so numerous and small that the districts virtually had a ryotwari settlement. But small resident landlords had a far greater local influence and a tighter grip on the under-tenants than many big and absentee landlords had on their unwieldy estates.[2] Absenteeism, however, was not axiomatically a sign of weakness. Many absentee landlords had a regular administration on the spot and it was subject to strict, periodic supervision. It can be regarded as an efficient management on the basis of the Court of Wards reports of estates like Paikpara or Nadia.[3] Moreover, absenteeism was not 'disadvantageously prevalent in Bengal'. The great majority of zamindars lived on or near their estates.[4]

All these differentiations in landlordism have been noted to demonstrate that there was unity in diversity in the final impact of landlordism on the rural society. If the zamindars figure more prominently than the interme- diaries in it, it is because they were the rural elites par excellence and contemporary sources usually mentioned them and held them responsible for the good or ill of the agrarian system. The 59 estates under the Court of Wards between 1873 and 1878 accounted for a sixteenth of the landed property in Bengal and collected between Rs 53 and 61 lakh as rent. Their under-tenures contributed about Rs 5 lakh to the sum. If this could be the general pattern for Bengal, the role of the intermediaries would appear inconsequential in agrarian relations.[5] Last but not the least, it is hard to

1. F Buchanan-Hamilton, *A Geographical, Statistical and Historical Descrip- tion of the District or Zillah of Dinajpore in the Province or Soubah of Bengal (1808)*, Calcutta, 1833, (hereafter, *Dinajpore*) pp. 235–36, 240, 251–52; also Mss. Eur. F. 86/165, Temple Collection, Substantive Law for Determination of Rent (1876), Answers to Circular, from E V Westmacott, collector, Dinajpore to commissioner, Rajshahi for a later picture
2. *Decisions of Zillah Courts of the Lower Provinces (1846), Sylhet*, Calcutta, 1846, pp. 20–21 for Case no. 157 of 1845 giving an intimate account of rent and power distribution among zamindars, jotedars and adhiars in the district; for Chittagong, see Chapter 2, pp. 81–82
3. *Report on Wards' and Attached Estates in the Lower Provinces* (hereafter, C.O.W.R.) (1875–76), Calcutta, 1877, pp. 13–15
4. *Bengal Administration Report (1874–75)*, Calcutta, 1875, p. 15
5. C.O.W.R. (1877–78), Calcutta, 1879, pp. 3–8

differentiate between the person at the top and the lessee holding the former's land. Even a cursory look at the Court of Wards records suffices to show that a big estate was really an aggregate of estates and various tenures, including a *jote* or a ryot's holding. For example, the Paikpara estates consisted of 79 large and small zamindaris, 11 patnis, 121 *mukarrari* jotes, 45 *ganti* jotes and 43 *lakhiraj* holdings.[6] A zamindar was in most cases the sub-holder under another zamindar. They were the monopolists of the land market and cornered whatever tenure was available on sale or lease. The landlords, apparently, were much more homogeneous than they are supposed to have been. When they formed the Landholders' Society in 1837 and began their politics of interest as a fairly centralised pressure group, they bore the characteristics of a class. In their individual and collective attitude and action vis-a-vis the government, the planters and the primary producer, they showed an unmistakable class bias. Referring to the Landholders' Society, the *Friend of India* remarked in 1840:

> It would be preposterous to make an irresponsible oligarchy of landholders in Calcutta the sole channel of communication with the entire agricultural community of the country.

The landholders remained tightly knit as a class even when they re-grouped in 1851 under a more pompous name—the British Indian Association. A writer in the *Calcutta Review* observed in 1857:

> Why do not these gentlemen who write pamphlets against the Sale Law and who opposed the revenue survey, find for themselves some less ambitious and more apropriate title? Their claim to stand forth as the exponent of all classes is not generally recognised.[7]

Permanent Settlement and after

Too much has been written on the idea of Permanent Settlement to obscure the fact that it was essentially a pragmatic measure by a foreign minority government to secure revenue from the native people. The settlement had to be concluded with zamindars as they were already found entrenched in the old order and it was difficult for the government to supersede them. W Thackeray, the Bengal civilian of the pre-Permanent

---

6. C.O.W.R. (1874–75), Calcutta, 1876, p. 14
7. *The Friend of India*, 9 January 1840; *Calcutta Review*, vol. xxix, July–December (1857), 'Life in the Rice Fields'

Settlement period who moved to Madras in time to defend a ryotwari settlement, wrote to Bentinck in 1806:

> They had zemindars in Bengal, in the Circars and some other places and the opposition which they made to the collectors was one reason for putting them in, perhaps the strongest reason.[8]

Boughton Rous had written in identical terms in 1771 on Natore.[9] The zamindari settlement was clearly unavoidable. The decision was also deliberate. It was not an official blunder, born of haste and misunderstanding of the local situation. Various experiments had been carried on for twenty years to collect accurate information of the value of land and the agrarian system.[10] The zamindars were the official favourites in 1793 as they were the cheapest, safest and smallest agency through which the past government had, and the present government could, collect revenue and control the masses. With discreet use of authority and tact, the government could make them agreeable. These factors, more than any theoretical bias towards landlords, decided the issue. The English notion of landlordism lent its weight to the idea of perpetual limitation of the estate demand. The purpose was to leave a surplus as capital for the 'improving landlord'.

The tendency to describe landlords after the Permanent Settlement as 'regulation landlords' or creatures of law, is to deny their whole background and basis of power. The Permanent Settlement was not hailed as a boon by all landlords. The raja of Cossijora, accustomed only to paying a tribute, refused to engage for a regular *jumma*.[11] The Dhaka landlords found the assessment too heavy to discharge and did not come to terms until concessions were made.[12] In Rangpur, landlords connived with their ryots in hiding the resources of the estates from official scrutiny. This was achieved by allowing ryots to hold their land at a quit-rent for a low valuation of the estate while the ryots agreed to make up the loss of rent by payment of abwabs. The intrigue worked. Barring a few estates of

8. P.P., vii (1812), *Fifth Report of the Select Commitee to the House of Commons* (hereafter, *Fifth Report*), Appendix no. 31; *Fort St George Revenue Consultations*, 9 April 1806, Thackeray to Bentinck

9. *Proceedings of the Controlling Council of Revenue at Murshidabad*, vol. vi, Calcutta 1919–24, pp. 139–40

10. *Fifth Report*, Appendix no. 5, Cornwallis Minute of 3 February 1790

11. A Mitra ed., *Midnapore District Records (New Series), 1777–1800*, Calcutta, 1962, pp. 607–8

12. F D Ascoli, *Dacca Settlement Report (1910–1917)*, Calcutta, 1917, p. 54

known assets, most of the estates escaped with a light assessment. Low rent was continued to delude the officials in future and illegal exactions were unleashed on areas enjoying low rent.[13] To frustrate the purpose of the Sale Law of 1845 and obtain a reduced *jumma*, many estates in several districts were allowed to be auctioned off and were then re-purchased *benami* by their proprietors. A re-settlement was made with their benamidars at a *jumma* acceptable to them. The raja of Burdwan had the largest transaction of this kind. He transferred almost the whole of his zamindari to his lawyers and amlahs and re-purchased it *benami*.[14] Some of the easy-going rajas of old estates like Rajshahi, Dinajpur, Nadia and Cossijora could not, however, cope with the exactitude of the new revenue system and were victims of the rigorous Sale Law.

The frequent sales for arrears of revenue in the first decade of the Decennial Settlement was not always a sign of distress befalling landlords. In 1789, Mandalghat *pargana* of the Burdwan Raj was sold (*jumma* Rs 2,10,749). This was perhaps the exchange of an unprofitable *mahal* for a profitable one as in 1791, the maharaja (still in arrears) was found purchasing the mahals of Barahazari and Karisunda of the Bishnupur Raj, assessed at a revenue of Rs 2,14,147.[15] The Bengal government in their Home Despatch of 23 September 1798 noted that the raja bought in to the amount of Rs 6,14,410 out of the total sale of Rs 6,44,325 and concluded that the purpose was to quash under-tenures and in some cases, to withhold revenue for more profitable business.[16] We have the evidence of Thomas Fortesque before the Select Committee in 1832 saying that sale did not imply destruction of property and of the ancient families holding it. It was a convenient mode of getting rid of undesirable lands and acquiring profitable ones. Holt Mackenzie corroborated this analysis with an example drawn from Midnapur where on one occasion, the revenue of estates notified for sale was Rs 60 lakh and that of estates actually sold after the expiry of notice was only a few thousand rupees.[17] The nature of land sales seems to have remained unaltered throughout the period under study. The table illustrates the situation in Midnapur.

---

13. Mss. Eur. D. 75, F Buchanan-Hamilton papers on Rangpur, vol. ii, pp. 108–15
14. A Mitra and R Guha, ed., *Burdwan District Records, (New Series)* (*1780–1800*), Calcutta, 1956, Introduction, pp. xxiii–iv
15. K A L Hill, *Burdwan Settlement Report (1927–34)*, vol. i, Calcutta, 1940, p. 20
16. P.P., xi (1831–32), Appendix no. 31
17. P.P., xi (1831–32), Minutes of Evidence, pp. 192–3 and p. 218

Midnapore (1837–1850)

Year	No. of estates sold for arrears of revenue	Mutation by private sale
1837	73	1
1838	16	18
1839	63	102
1840	33	34
1841	43	71
1842	36	61
1843	35	41
1844	21	29
1845	21	58
1846	15	62
1847	19	66
1848	24	65
1849	27	31
1850	26	33

Source: H V Bayley, History of Midnapore, Calcutta, 1902, p. 91

Even the old estates like the Dinajpore[*] Raj survived the initial shock and later rallied to a great extent. Bell reports in his Settlement Report that tauzis (lots) 1–12 were purchased *benami* from the sales of 1797–99 in the name of Rani Tripurasundari and her son. Tauzis 70, 80, 81, 84 and 210 were added in the nineteenth century.[18] Obviously estates of known assets had been among the worst affected by the settlement. But lightly assessed estates became sources of enormous profit for the holders in future.

The Permanent Settlement is, perhaps, wrongly supposed to have been severe in the first twenty years. The affected estates probably suffered more due to mismanagement than high assessment. The collectors' reports in 1802 give a clear picture of the increasing population and the extension of cultivation as a result. The land–man ratio was thought by Colebrooke as early as 1794 to have reached the optimum point including the vast stretch of wasteland.[19] In a settled district like Hooghly, estate Kalora

---

[*] British colonial spelling has been retained in quotations and in cases where positions/offices refer to those of colonial times (e.g. Dinajpore Raj). In other cases accepted contemporary transliteration has been used (e.g. Dinajpur)

18. F O Bell, *Dinajpur Settlement Report (1934–40)*, Calcutta, 1941, p. 69
19. *Fifth Report*, Appendix no. 10; also H T Colebrooke, *Remarks on the Husbandry and Internal Commerce of Bengal*, Calcutta, 1806, (hereafter, *Remarks*) p. 27

(Boro no. 2), having a *jumma* of £261 14s 0d, yielded a collection of
£830 2s 0d in 1795 and £1833 6s 0d in 1804 and £3368 8s 0d in 1873.[20]
Rent was doubled in Burdwan between 1800 and 1810 without any
change in the crops cultivated as reported by W B Bayley, then magistrate,
Burdwan in a private letter to J H Harrington, judge of the *sadar adalat*.[21]
Everywhere in general, landlords virtually doubled their collection as population rose and cultivation was extended. This is borne out by the following
list showing the district-wise break-up of aggregate government *jumma*
and actual collection of all the estates under the Court of Wards in 1830 (in
sicca Rs):

District	Government revenue	Farmers' rent	Zamindars' profit
Birbhum	14,508	23,871	9,363
Bhagalpur	9,958	14,820	4,862
Burdwan	27,360	34,652	7,297
Dacca	2,248	3,225	977
Dinajpur	66,562	1,10,041	43,479
Jessore	1,10,224	2,25,037	1,14,813
Jungle Mahals	3,654	19,677	10,023
Midnapur	5,045	12,906	7,861
Murshidabad	1,01,882	1,89,631	87,749
Mymensing	1,15,941	3,16,732	2,00,791
Nadia	23,823	43,204	19,381
24 Parganas	6,625	8,601	1,976
Rajshahi	40,474	84,263	43,789
Rangpur	25,656	57,587	31,931
Tippera	20,464	31,828	10,664
	5,74,424	1,1,75,375	6,00,951

Source: H Mackenzie, *Answer to Q. 2929 in P.P., xi (1831–32)*

20. W W Hunter, *Statistical Account of Bengal* (hereafter, *SAB*), vol. iii,
    Hooghly District, London, 1876, p. 382; from papers filed by zamindars
21. J H Harrington, *Minute and Draft of Regulation on the Rights of Ryots in
    Bengal*, Calcutta, 1827, pp. 22–23

In estates supposed to be in distress, the rent was generally double the revenue on an average. Considerable enhancement of rent was a contributory factor to this increase apart from extension of cultivation. The Court of Wards report for the next ten years shows that at the end of the period, the rent was still double the revenue.[22] The estimate for the period 1873–77, after all deductions, gives the same margin of profit for the landholders.[23] The lightly assessed *jungly* estates turned into a gold mine at a later date. Rangpur provides a good example of the result of reclamation. Glazier gives the following information on three estates in the district in the 1870s.

Estate	'Jumma' at Permanent Settlement	Zamindar's collection
Baharbund	Rs 81,160	Rs 3,12,133
Patiladaha	40,555	3,06,124
Saruppur	22,521	62,562

Source: E G Glazier, *Further Notes on Rungpore Records, vol. ii*, Calcutta, 1876, p. 43

The profit went on soaring until it reached the following astronomical figures in Bakarganj at the beginning of the twentieth century:

Estate	Rate per acre at Permanent Settlement	Profit at settlement (1900–1908)
Selimabad	6 annas 10 pice	108 per cent
Chandradwip	10 annas 4 pice	185 per cent
Syedpore	1 anna 7 pice	536 per cent
Ratandi Kalikapur	12 annas 2 pice	26 per cent
Krishnadebpur	0 annas 5 pice	1,600 per cent
Tappa Haveli Selimabad	9 annas 6 pice	500 per cent
Idilpur	10 annas 0 pice	500 per cent

Source: J C Jack, *Bakarganj Settlement Report, 1900–1908*, Calcutta, 1915, p. 96

22. Bengal Revenue Consultations (hereafter, B.R.C.), 25 August, 1840, no. 92
23. C.O.W.R. (1877–78), Calcutta, 1879, pp. 3–8

Besides, many estates had extensive *khamar* and *lakhiraj* lands to fall back upon for personal maintenance in the event of ryots' defaults and sale for arrears of revenue. Much of the reclaimed land was converted into *khamar* or personal farms by zamindars who got them cultivated by hired labour or sharecroppers. The Dinajpore Raj had an estimated income of Rs 41,502 from *khamar* before the Permanent Settlement.[24] *Lakhiraj* or rent-free holdings were a real safety valve and saved estates like Rajshahi, Bishnupur, Nadia and Chandradwip from liquidation.[25]

It is clear from the above that the Sale Law (1845) did not work the ruin of estates. Though a few old estates were initially hard hit, the majority of them became a source of prosperity to their holders.

The staff

Upto 1802, sale proceedings indicated that sale was confined among thirty families approximately.[26] They were the same rural elites with minor variations of vertical mobility. The rural parvenus were mostly the petty landholders and amlahs of the zamindari and government collectorate. For Burdwan in 1797,

estates changed hands from one group of zamindars to another. Thus the principal purchasers of the lands of the Rani of Burdwan were Dwarakanath Sinha of Singur, Chhaku Sinha of Bhastura, the Mukherjis of Janai and the Banerjis of Telinipara.[27]

Chandradwip *pargana* of Bakarganj district was sold in 1799 to Rammanik Mudi, a shopkeeper and *gomasta* of the raja of Chandradwip, Messrs Panioty, a Greek merchant and one Dal Singh.[28] The majority of the landholders of purchased estates in Dinajpur were found by Buchanan-Hamilton in the early nineteenth century to be agents of old landholders, officers of the government, local merchants and manufacturers.[29] Bell traces

24. N K Sinha, *Economic History of Bengal*, vol. ii, Calcutta, 1962, Appendix A
25. See Chapter 2 for details
26. M S Islam, *The Permanent Settlement and the Landed Interests in Bengal (1793–1819)*, unpublished thesis, London University, 1972, pp. 233–37, 282
27. A Mitra and R Guha ed., *Burdwan District Records (New Series), (1780–1800)*, Calcuta, 1956, Introduction, p. 1xxiv
28. H Beveridge, *The District of Bakarganj: Its History and Statistics* (hereafter, *Bakarganj*) London, 1876, pp. 390–91
29. F Buchanan-Hamilton, *Dinajpore*, Calcutta, 1808, pp. 250–52

one family from the brother of *Dewan* Ramkanta Roy of the Dinajpore Raj and another from its *naib* or cashier.[30] The police report of the Lower Provinces for 1842 mentions one district (Nadia?) where about a dozen landholders held the whole of the land with the exception of a few rent-free tenures. Their fathers had been servants of the old landlords.[31] Writing about another district (which appears, from its description, to be Jessore), the author of an article in the *Calcutta Review* in 1859 describes how 317 estates of 1793 multiplied into 4,550 estates in 1858 but added that 'rural families of respectability and worth could not be wiped out and ownership still runs in the old channels'.[32] In the Hooghly district, 34 old and established families controlled virtually all the estates in 1856.[33] Thus, for more than half a century after the Permanent Settlement, there was no appreciable change in the composition and character of the rural hierarchy. It is not difficult to understand why this should be so. It was nearly impossible for an outsider to establish himself as the auction purchaser of an estate in the teeth of violent opposition from the ex-holder of formidable local influence. The raja of Chandradwip could successfully withstand the Dhaka purchasers of his estate for a long time.[34] Dwarakanath Tagore had to seek official help repeatedly to gain possession of his purchased estate of Shajadpur in Rajshahi district.[35] In Midnapur, the former landlord of Jellasore and Dantoon had so much hold over his ryots as to enable him to resist his creditor from executing his decree for eleven long years.[36] The opposition also came from the ryots refusing to pay rent to the outsider. An Armenian landlord, Owen John Elias had to institute a thousand summary suits to get the legitimate rent from his ryots.[37] The existing landholders, the zamindari and collectorate amlahs were the fittest persons to buy estates and keep them. They had local influence, experience, information, money and cunning, all in their favour to monopolise the land market.

30. F O Bell, *Dinajpur Settlement Report (1934–40)*, Calcutta, 1941, pp. 73–75

31. *Calcutta Review*, vol. i, (1844), 'The Rural Population of Bengal', p. 193

32. *Calcutta Review*, vol. xxxii, (1859), 'The Owner of the Soil', pp. 4–5

33. *The Friend of India*, 8 May 1856, Editorial on the Nobles of Hooghly

34. H Beveridge, *Bakarganj*, pp. 80–88, 199; also M S Islam, *The Permanent Settlement and Landed Interests in Bengal*, p. 90

35. B. R. C., 19 September 1837, no. 10

36. H V Bayley, *A History of Midnapore*, Calcutta, 1902, p. 24

37. P.P., xxxi (1852–53), Minutes of Evidence before the House of Lords, Answer to Question 6289

As time wore on, the reshuffling of estates showed three basic trends: (*a*) the old giant estates, except for one or two, continued in a partially truncated form and, over the whole of the nineteenth century, regained some of their lost territories. The Dinajpore Raj provides the best example of such a process; (*b*) many of the small estates grew into vast estates due to successful land speculation by their business-like proprietors. The Kandi and Kashimbazar estates illustrate this trend;[38] (*c*) the majority of the estates were, however, small or medium sized and were managed by capable holders. Most of the large estates were propped up by numerous under-tenures of various grades. The picture that emerges at the end of our period is somewhat as below:

Estates of various sizes (1873)

(Class I: Over 20,000 acres; Class II: Between 500 and 20,000 acres; Class III: Under 500 acres excluding *lakhiraj* under 20 acres)

District	Class I	Class II	Class III
Burdwan	6	36	2,804
Bankura	4	48	481
Birbhum	7	213	275
Midnapore	22	800	1,983
24 Parganas	11	330	1,476
Nadia	47	569	1,137
Jessore	23	335	1,877
Murshidabad	8	378	2,449
Dinajpur	22	467	251
Maldah	7	169	371
Rajshahi	15	385	1,165
Rangpur	20	283	246
Pabna	6	187	674
Dacca	8	476	7,324 *Contd..*

38. L N Ghose, *The Modern History of the Indian Chiefs, Rajahs, Zamindars*, (hereafter, *The Modern History*), Calcutta, 1881, Part II, *The Native Aristocracy and Gentry*, pp. 334–36 and 396–7; for more on the Kandi or Paikpara Raj family, *Calcutta Review*, January 1874, 'The Territorial Aristocracy of Bengal: The Kandi Family', pp. 95–120

District	Class I	Class II	Class III
Faridpur	7	164	2,817
Bakarganj	46	664	4,618
Mymensing	40	428	5,829
Sylhet	14	556	53,368
Chittagong	1	671	3,577
Noakhaly	14	106	1,346
Tipperah	14	305	1,512

Source: D J McNeille, *Memorandum on the Revenue Administration of the Lower Provinces (1873), Appendix 1,* Calcutta

The small proprietors were in reality stronger than the holders of vast estates insofar as they exercised direct control over their estates on the spot. As early as 1794, Colebrooke gave a very favourable opinion of these small proprietors:

Having their whole property within the reach of their own super-intendence, being minutely acquainted with the circumstances of every part of the estate, if they did not altogether disuse the practice of under-farming, they at least exercised judgment in the conduct of it and mostly gave some attention to the remedying of abuses.[39]

Buchanan-Hamilton had the same kind of impression about Dinajpur lotdars:

I must, however, say that their lands are in general better cultivated and the appearance of the people not so miserable as on some of the estates that have belonged to one family for several generations.[40]

Westland also noticed small and viable new estates in Jessore showing signs of prosperity and their holders frequently buying new parcels of land strewn all over the country.[41]

The Permanent Settlement, therefore, hardly constituted a watershed in the agrarian history of Bengal. It was concerned more with recognition of existing landlords than their creation. The Sale Law (1845) did not work

---

39. H T Colebrooke, *Remarks*, p. 88
40. F Buchanan-Hamilton, *Dinajpore*, Calcutta, 1833, pp. 250–52
41. J Westland, *A Report on the District of Jessore*, Calcutta, 1874 (hereafter, *Jessore*), p. 143

for their ruin. Because of their command of the local situation, the
landlords could twist the Sale Law and the settlement itself in their favour.
The incidence of revenue was made to fall lightly on them. It did not sap
their financial strength. The landlords, after 1793, seemed to enjoy a life
of sheltered ease. A keen observer noted in 1859:

> The Permanent Settlement has very largely increased the value of
> property and has invested the original zamindaries now split up into
> scores and hundreds with a far greater measure of security than is
> commonly believed.[42]

As there was very little change in the personnel, the landlords retained
their semi-feudal, local influence in their family. Added to it was the power
derived from regulations. Thus, Regulations 7 of 1799 and 5 of 1812 gave
them power of distraint over ryots and Regulation 8 of 1819 allowed them
to lease out estates in times of crisis.

The rights of the tenantry were kept undefined and unprotected from
considerations of security of revenue through the agency of landlords. The
new Sale Laws of 1841 and 1845 considerably modified the rigours of the
Sunset Law. Finally, the institution of the Court of Wards worked for the
salvation of even moribund estates. It saved them often from the verge of
collapse, managed their estates efficiently, cleared their debts and
launched a minor with a fortune on his attaining majority. The Nadia Raj
is a striking example of such rescue operations.[43] The law courts, police
stations and the collectorate were to become the landlord's agents of power
in time. They were far more equipped with wealth and education than the
rest of the community to use or misuse them.[44]

The landlords of the 1830s

The new generation of the 1830s can be especially marked off from their
predecessors on several counts. They combined the semi-feudal power of
the past with the power derived from the regulations in a far greater degree
than their fathers. They were better educated, better acquainted with the
rules and the rulers, and better organised. Landlordism had become a

42. *Calcutta Review*, vol. xxxii (1859), 'The Owner of the Soil', p. 310
43. K C Roy, *Autobiography* (in vernacular), Calcutta, 1956, pp. 161,
    175–179; also, C.O.W.R. (1874–75), Calcutta, 1876, p. 15 and C.O.W.R.
    (1875–76), Calcutta, 1877, p. 15
44. See Chapter 3 for details

career, a business more mercenary than it was ever before. The new generation consisted of professional rent-receivers. Their *raison d'etre* was to maximise rent. They thought of their estates in terms of rent and not people and territory.[45] Their entrepreneurship lay in land speculation. They placed their huge unearned income in what had become the safest and most remunerative form of investment. They controlled the land market and purchased all sorts of holdings from the estate to the *jote*. This was their way of territorial expansion. In Murshidabad and Bakarganj, examples were found of estate-holders purchasing under-tenures in order to intercept profit at a lower stage of sub-infeudation.[46] They also managed to get Sunderban grants and promoted reclamation in Jessore and Bakarganj.[47] Prannath Chowdhury, zamindar of Satkhira estate, Khulna, was a notable farmer and promoter of reclamation.[48]

Apart from landholding, these landlords indulged in exclusive money- and paddy-lending. The landlords, both big and small, were in most cases the local mahajans or moneylenders. In 1832, Dampier, the superintendent of police reported that the landlords ran into arrears and almost always availed themselves of the grace period for payment of revenue to enable them to collect the latest interest on money lent by them.[49] It appears to have remained a major occupation for landlords throughout the period under study. Most of the landlords appearing before the Indigo Commission in 1860 admitted that their money- and paddy-lending business clashed with the planters' interest.[50] Quite a few landlords can be picked

---

45. P.P. xiiv (1861), Report of the Indigo Commission, Minutes of Evidence, Joychand Palchowdhury, zamindar, Ranaghat, Nadia, Q. 159–172: Answers

46. *Ibid*, A Grote Q. 1546; Answer, p. 90; for Murshidabad, W W Hunter, *SAB*, p. 117; for Bakarganj, H Beveridge, *Bakarganj*, pp. 196–98; also J C Jack, *Bengal District Gazetteers, Bakarganj*, Calcutta, 1918, p. 93

47. For Jessore, R S Sen, *Report on the Agricultural Statistics of Jhenidah, Magura, Bagirhat and Sunderban Sub-divisions—District Jessore*, Calcutta, 1874 (hereafter, *Report on Jhenidah*), *Report on Baghat*, pp. 2–39; also Westland, *Jessore*, Calcutta, 1874, pp. 152–157; for Bakarganj, see Beveridge, *Bakarganj*, pp. 202–6; for a general picture, F E Pargiter, *A Revenue History of the Sunderbans from 1765 to 1870*, Calcutta, 1885, (hereafter, *Sunderbans*), pp. 11–69

48. C.O.W.R. (1875–76), p. 12; also, L N Ghose, *The Modern History*, London 1876, p. 420

49. Quoted in J C Jack, *Bakarganj Settlement Report (1900–1908)*, Calcutta, 1915, p. 100; also cf. P.P., v (1831), Minutes of Evidence, James Mill, Answer to Q. 3154, p. 295

50. See Chapter 5 for details

up from the Court of Wards reports as moneylenders of some magnitude in various districts. Ganga Gobinda Sen of Tippera was one of them. He lent out a large amount in small sums to his own tenantry mostly and 'went on squeezing the interest out of his debtors for years, always keeping the principal unpaid'.[51] The enquiry into rural indebtedness in 1876 showed the large-scale involvement of all grades of landlords in the *mahajani* business.[52] Together with money- and paddy-lending, many carried on extensive grain trade. The entire rural network of haats or markets was their creation.[53] It was a source of profit as markets fetched high rent and cesses from people using them. But the most significant fact was that the local sale of the surplus crop assured payment of rent. The trader-landlord bought his stock here and stored it in golas or godowns. The one-and-a-half times return of the paddy lent out, added to the stock. The produce was brought to the riverports where the landlord kept warehouses for wholesale business. Traders like the owners of the Nihalia estate in Murshidabad, made advances for the paddy, conducted transport and storage and transacted their business upto the point of the riverport where they had warehouses. The big dealers like the Roys of Narail, Jessore controlled the business from the village to their Calcutta warehouses for export.[54]

A section of landlords made an early debut as indigo-planters— Gopimohan Tagore being the most notable pioneer in the early nineteenth century.[55] Many of them were supplanted by European planters around the thirties.[56] Those who survived the competition became prominent in the fifties. A short sketch of the careers of a few key figures among landlords of the period under consideration is provided here to illustrate the character of the new generation.

---

51. C.O.W.R. (1875–76), p. 32; for others, Estate Chooramon in Dinajpur, p. 24; Sydabad Estate in Murshidabad, p. 19; C.O.W.R. (1877–78), Estate Nischinta in Midnapore, p. 15

52. *Mss. Eur. F. 86/161*, Temple Collection, Demi-official Enquiry into Condition of Peasantry in Bengal (1875), Replies to Circular

53. R S Sen, *Report on Jhenidah*, Calcutta, 1874, p. 73, see Appendix B for a list of haats or markets in Jhenidah subdivision owned by various landlords. There were 101 haats in 900 square miles

54. C.O.W.R. (1875–76), p. 20 for Nihalia Estate and pp. 15–22 for Narail estate

55. *Mss. Eur. D. 75*, Buchanan-Hamilton papers on Rangpur, vol. ii, pp. 56–59

56. P. P., viii (1831–32), Appendix V, no. 74, Court of Directors to governor general, 10 April 1832, para 17 quoting Judge Walters, Dacca; also, *Asiatic Journal*, vol. xix, 1836, 'Indigo Planters', *passim*

Joykrishna Mukherjee of Uttarpara, Hooghly (1808–1888): His father was *banian* to the Fourteenth Regiment (foot). He started his career as a clerk in the Brigade Major's office. He went to the siege of Bharatpur and returned with the Bharatpur prize money. In 1830, Joykrishna became the record-keeper of the Hooghly collectorate. His employment as a record-keeper gave him exceptional facilities for ascertaining the actual condition of all the estates which were brought to sale due to depreciation of land value following scarcity of gold and silver, inundation and resumption. He used the prize money and his official knowledge to purchase estates which were being sold cheap. He thus laid the foundation of his position as one of the largest landholders of the district, paying Rs 90,000 as revenue directly to the government and having patnis and durpatnis under the Burdwan Raj. A resident landlord, he preferred direct dealing with the ryots to sub-infeudation. The rate of rent was high in Hooghly and he did not have to share his profit with intermediaries.

Joykrishna set up indigo factories and raised the plant under the system of advances. His ryots grew indigo and delivered the produce under the same nominal advances as the European planters offered. He confessed that they did it to please him without the hope of profit. He studied the world market and promoted cash crops like jute and sugarcane in 1854–55 during the Crimean War and the crisis in the West Indies.

Joykrishna was also a keen moneylender and grain dealer. He floated one lakh in moneylending at his declared rate of 12–24 per cent. He also lent paddy and kept golas for storage of paddy. Two-thirds of his ryots were in debt.

Joykrishna was not a rustic, money-making landlord. He was educated and well acquainted with the ruling machinery. He was a very active member of the associations of landholders and one of the notable men behind their pamphlets. He wrote effectively against the government handling of the village watch and justice and police in general. He was also a bitter critic of the Rent Act of 1859 and raised the slogan 'Permanent Settlement imperilled' against it. Yet he was the first to offer to raise a battalion of *goala* (milkman caste) lathials to help the government during the Mutiny. He provides the best example of loyalty at a heavy price.[57]

57. L N Ghose, *The Modern History,* Calcutta, 1881, p. 310; also C E Buckland, *Bengal under the Lieutenant Governors*, Calcutta, 1902, vol. i, Appendix IV, p. 1050; G Toynbee, *A Sketch of the Administration of the Hooghly District from 1795 to 1845*, Calcutta, 1888 (hereafter, *Hooghly*), p. 64; P.P., xliv, R.I.C.,Evidence of Joykrishna Mukherjee,

Ramratan and Haronath Roy of Narail, Jessore: The Roys of Narail were the grandsons of Kalishankar Roy who was a notorious dacoit in the eighties of the eighteenth century and later rose to be the *dewan* of the Natore Raj. The servant successfully exploited the difficult days of his master to appropriate much of the latter's estates in his own name at the beginning of British rule to found the Narail estate. His scions inherited his pragmatism and were quite a contrast to the easy-going grandees of Natore and Nadia. They built up a huge estate by judicious purchases and by frequent resort to lathials and law-courts. It consisted of 211 estates and 447 tenures including patnis, durpatnis, jotes and izaras.

They had 24 indigo factories in Jessore, Faridpur and Pabna. Ramratan was perhaps the most successful native indigo planter of his times. But indigo was raised by the same non-remunerative system of nominal advances as by European planters. Territorial influence was used to exploit the small peasant economy. Ramratan was destined to play a key role in the indigo confrontation and the revolt of 1860.

But greater still was the volume of their grain trade which they controlled from the rural base to their warehouses in Calcutta. They had fourteen granaries in Jessore and four warehouses in the suburbs of Calcutta. They advanced paddy to tenants on bonds at an exorbitant interest. The outstanding paddy loans of the House were estimated in 1874–75 to be 3,28,696 maunds. Net profit from one warehouse in the same year amounted to Rs 22,344. Ramratan Roy was an active member of the Landholders' Society and the British Indian Association and frequently petitioned the government for redress of various grievances. Though he stayed for long spells in Calcutta, his absenteeism did not seem to affect his rural activities and local influence. The estate was directly managed without sub-infeudation.[58]

Dwarakanath Tagore (1794–1846) and Prosanna Kumar Tagore (1803–1868) both profited from their connection with the government, the former as the *dewan* of the Salt Board and the latter as the *dewan* of the export-import warehouse and government pleader. They directed their fortune to land. Dwarakanath invested his profits from land in indigo,

---

pp. 256–58; D J McNeille, *Memorandum on the Revenue Administration of the Lower Provinces of Bengal,* Calcutta, 1873, Appendix V; A Mukherjee, *The Annals of British Land Revenue Administration in Bengal from 1698 to 1793,* Calcutta, 1883, p. 71

58. L N Ghose, *The Modern History,* Calcutta, 1881, p. 318; J Westland, *Jessore,* Calcutta, 1874, pp. 146, 150, 158–60; C.O.W.R. (1875–76), pp. 15–17

silk, salt-works and coal. Prosanna Kumar tried his luck for a long time in indigo before giving it up in the mid-1850s. Both inherited paternal estates and added to them enormously by purchases. They were landlords first and businessmen and professionals next.

Dwarakanath owned six indigo factories, the Kumarkhali silk filatures, the Bengal Coal Co., and founded Carr, Tagore and Co. and the Union Bank. He was the first native managing agent of calibre. But he was not an entrepreneur *per se*. He hovered between landlordism and trade. When he was ruined by inoppportune speculations and the cunning of his partners and died in 1846, his son, Devendranath settled down as a landlord and the secretary of the landlords' organisation, the British Indian Association.

Dwarakanath was the principal architect of European collaboration and the fountainhead of all political activities in the first half of the nineteenth century. Prosanna Kumar shares the honours with him in this respect. Both were instrumental in the founding of the Landholders' Society. Dwarakanath was also responsible for the creation of the Bengal British India Society.

Prosanna Kumar efficiently managed his lightly assessed paternal estate of Patildaha in Rangpur to convert it into a virtual gold mine. He had direct dealing with his ryots, the jotedars, without the intervention of intermediaries. The jotedars, however, sublet to their under-ryots. While he built up a considerable legal practice in Calcutta, he also consolidated a vast estate out of his profits from the practice and from the estate of Patildaha. His absenteeism and occasional visits to the estate did not make him a redundant annuitant. He used to pay the sum of Rs 7,91,414 as government revenue and made a total bequest of Rs 6,70,000 to various organisations after providing for his family.

Prosanna Kumar edited *The Reformer*, the mouthpiece of the landlords, and was the secretary of the Landholders' Society throughout its existence. He organised urban politics for the rural elites to put pressure on the government at the headquarters and nip all adverse regulations in the bud. He was an authority on regulations and an asset to the landlords in their legal battles with the government.[59]

---

59. L N Ghose, *The Modern History*, Calcutta, 1881, pp. 201–217 for both, p. 200 for P K Tagore's estates; C E Buckland, R.I.C.Q. 1027, *Bengal under the Lieutenant Governors*, Appendix IV, evidence of P K Tagore, pp. 250–54; Rev K M Banerjee, *A Few Facts and Memoranda with Reference to the Early Career of the Late Hon'ble P C Tagore, CSI*, Calcutta, 1870; K C Mitra, *Memoirs of Dwarakanath Tagore*, Calcutta, 1870

24   Tensions in Bengal Rural Society

These were the leading men of the new generation of landlords. They had a pre-British heritage and post-British accomplishments. They enjoyed the best of both worlds. They blended power from tradition and from regulation. When various pressures which threatened the status quo were mounted on the rural society it seemed that these landlords were here to stay. Holt Mackenzie said about them in 1831–32:

Q: Are they a class of persons who assist to uphold the Government or do they embarrass the Government ?

A: I am not aware of their doing anything directly to uphold the Government; the indirect effect of a large body interested in maintaining the existing state of things may be considerable. But they still generally, I fear, dislike and fear us and they certainly embarrass the Government whenever they think their own interests are likely to be affected by its acts. Thus, they are very much averse to any inquisition into their collection from their tenants and set themselves to baffle the Government in all attempts made to discover the actual condition and rights of the great body of the people, though such attempts are professedly and actually directed to the better administration of justice. They appear to have been very successful in their resistance to all such measures and so far have been, I think, very mischievous.[60]

---

60. P.P., xi (1831–32), Minutes of Evidence, Evidence of Mackenzie, Q. 2632

TWO

Land Resumption and Landlord Resistance

Factors behind land resumption

The zamindari settlement in Bengal became discredited within three decades of its operation. The settlement had been a success only in its immediate goal of getting the zamindars to undertake much of the petty local administration of the country, and pay a moderate revenue punctually. The economic incentive given to zamindars by perpetual limitation of the revenue demand had not made them 'improving landlords'. They thrived on rent as pressure of population on the land pushed it up and reduced agriculture into a subsistence economy. But with the opening of India to Free Trade in 1813, the country was expected to yield more cash crops to meet the import bill than was permitted by the existing mode of production. The problem of remittance and the demands of Free Trade made agricultural development as much a serious concern of the Indian and the home government as the security of revenue.[1]

The commercial need was fed by a secular financial deficit. The average annual deficit for the fifteen years ending in 1828–29 was £12,27,343 amounting for the whole period to £1,84,10,141.[2] The cost of expansion and consolidation of the empire accounted for this mounting deficit. The government regretted its decision to freeze revenue in 1793 and looked

---

1. See Chapter 4
2. P.P., viii (1831–32), Report, p. 33

for a larger share of the rental profits, reaped by the landlords. The success of the ryotwari settlement in Madras, which produced an increasing revenue, prejudiced the Fifth Report (1812) against the zamindars. The official criticism of landlords found its classic expression in Mill's *History of India* (1818) where they were depicted as the drones of society, fleecing the ryots and living parasitically on rent. The criticism never ceased thereafter. The answer to agrarian and fiscal stagnation appeared, to the official experts in the India House, to lie in the subversion of landlordism and in the sub-ryotwari settlement of estates acquired by the state. This was a recurring theme in home despatches to Bengal especially between 1814 and 1830.[3]

By 1830, after half a century of minimal government, the British began to gain control of the administrative problem. The official favour shown by the home government to the active type of administration set up in the northwest provinces must inevitably have rebounded on the Bengal government. The Bentinck administration (1828–34) reflected the need for economy in the appointment of the Finance Committee and the resolve for strong government in the union of the offices of collector and magistrate.[4] Bentinck also gave a thrust to the process of land survey on orders from the home government to improve administration and collection of revenue. He laid down in his minutes of 3 September 1829, the broad principle of plane table and traverse surveys and presided over a conference of revenue officers and surveyors at Allahabad in January 1833 which effected a great acceleration of the surveys and reduction of their costs. The year 1830 saw the historic beginning of the great Trigonometrical Survey under Everest from its Calcutta base line.[5] All these developments were indicative of the government's desire to draw the zamindar's teeth a little.

The new bureaucratic offensive was directed against allegedly invalid rent-free tenures—*lakhiraj*. In his reply to a query by the Select Committee as to the possible ways of augmenting revenue in Bengal, Holt Mackenzie, secretary to the government, made the most precise reference to *lakhiraj* and wastelands. Mackenzie was the author of Regulation 3 of 1828 which unleashed the resumption of *lakhiraj* in Bengal.[6] *Lakhiraj* was made the

---

3. P. P., xi (1831–32); appendices 7–22, 87; also P.P., vi (1830); evidence of Mangles referring to ryotwari settlement of Krishnarampur bordering Sunderbans; P.P., v (1831), evidence of James Mill, Q. 3145–50, 3159–66

4. E T Stokes, *The English Utilitarians and India*, Oxford, 1959, (hereafter, *English Utilitarians*), pp. 150–168

5. R H Phillimore, ed., *Historical Records of the Survey of India*, vol. iv, (*1830–43*), Dehradun, 1959, pp. 1, 262

6. P.P., xi (1831–32), Q. 2677

special target as its resumption appeared the least exceptionable new resource in a period of financial crisis. Additional taxation could justifiably be raised from those who paid no taxes at all. Fraudulent rent-free tenures were notorious as the device by which landlords obtained a reduced assessment on their estates. Such evasions, as we shall see in the next section, were whittling away state resources. By resumption alone could the government carry out its cherished idea of a sub-ryotwari settlement of the *khas* mahals, so acquired. Through this measure again, the government could hope to regain its right to investigate the permanently settled estates and obtain a closer grip on local administration and agrarian relations.[7] Any agricultural and administrative improvement was linked with this inventory of estates. Land resumption therefore, has to be seen, to some extent, as simply one aspect of a general tightening up of local administration. Finally, *lakhiraj* was a feudal relic, an anathema to capitalist agriculture. It tended to concentrate land in the hands of the priestly class and other non-cultivating people who kept such holdings under-utilised. It also limited the scope of the money economy.[8]   In effect, resumption of *lakhiraj* was packed with dynamite. Contemporary journalists believed that the government was out to smash the zamindars.[9]

Lakhiraj land

Lakhiraj tenures were legion in description. Some of them could be easily identified as service tenures of a semi-feudal society, such as *nankar, chakran, paikan, ghatwali* and others. The first was a means of subsistence for a collector of rent in lieu of salary, the second mainly for watch and ward, the third for supply of troops and the last for security of the border.[10] The second set may be called community tenures, given to occupational

---

7. P.P., xi (1831–32), Holt Mackenzie, Q. 2632; also P.P., v (1831), Mill, Q. 3280–81, 3299; cf, G Toynbee, *Hooghly*, Calcutta, 1888, p. 64

8. B.R.C., 24 November 1820, no. 35, Halhed's Report on the Rent-free Establishment Relating to U. P; also, B.R.C., 29 May 1828, no. 3; Metcalfe's Minute; *The Englishman*, 16 November 1838, Letter by Gauntlet (i.e., R D Mangles as identified by T Dickens in the issue of 25 December); B K Sinha, 'Attitudes of the Christian Missionaries towards Land Problems of Bengal in the first half of the 19th Century', *Journal of Indian History*, 15 August 1968, *passim*

9. *The Englishman*, 19 June 1837, Editorial; *The Friend of India*, 12 April 1838, Correspondence

10. S Mukherjee, 'A Note on Lakhiraj Lands', *Indian History Congress Proceedings*, 1958, pp. 425–30

groups for their services to the community and to the grantor. In this way, potters, blacksmiths, goldsmiths, barbers, physicians (vaidyas)—all held land and they clearly paid a labour rent.[11] The remaining tenures may be grouped under the heading of religious and charitable grants. In Bengal, these were the largest group. But in a *jajmani* system, the maintenance of religious worship was also to be seen as one of the essential services to the community. Thus *aima* (for the *imam*), *bhatottar* (for the *bhat* or bard), *brahmottar* (for brahmins), and *devottar* (for the temple), belonged to this category. Certain other grants like *vritti, mahattran, millaki* and *waqf* were given to learned men for imparting education to the community. All *lakhiraj* grants were, therefore, service tenures.[12] In Mughal times, charity lands were generally resumable. *Madad-i-maash* (subsistence grants) had been subject to renewal and even in Shah Jahan's time, they were greatly reduced. Grants by subordinate officials were mostly resumable by higher authorities.[13] *Aima* tenures granted by the Afghans were subjected to light assessment after the Mughal conquest of the province.[14] According to precedent, it then appears that the retention of *lakhiraj* was more a matter of executive indulgence than right. But as long as the area involved was not large and it was utilised to serve the community, the practice was generally not objected to.

But under this ostensibly humanitarian cover, there had been large-scale appropriation of revenue by zamindars of big estates. Most of these had been effected in the period of interregnum to delude the new British government and leave something to fall back upon in case the zamindari was terminated. Thus, Maharaja Krishnachandra of Nadia Raj estate handed over to his youngest wife and their son, Raja Sambhuchandra, fifteen grants totalling 20,000 bighas under the denomination of *vritti, brahmottar* and *devottar lakhiraj*.[15] Further enquiry in 1838 was to reveal that these lands were all farmed out to relatives at low rates for which

11. T Roy Choudhury, *Bengal under Akbar and Jehangir*, Calcutta, 1953, pp. 33–35
12. A M Wahiduzzaman, *Land Resumption in Bengal (1819–46)*, unpublished thesis, 1969, London University, (hereafter, *Land Resumption*), pp. 15–16 for varieties of *lakhiraj*
13. I Habib, *The Agrarian System of Mughal India*, London, 1963, pp. 307–315
14. A M Wahiduzzaman, *Land Resumption*, p. 8
15. K C Roy, *Kshitishavamsabalicharita* (in vernacular), *A History of the Nadia Raj*, Calcutta, 1932, pp. 11–12; also R Saha, *British Administration in a Bengal District—Nadia (1785–1835)*, unpublished thesis, 1973, Calcutta University, (hereafter, *British Administration in Nadia*), pp. 184–192

heavy fines and anticipated rents had been taken for years. They were not devoted to religious services and had been fraudulently appropriated before the Decennial settlement to preserve the most valuable possessions within the estates. Three-fourths of the total *lakhiraj* in the district was claimed by the Raj.[16] In Burdwan, 5,68,736 bighas were appropriated and distributed among 70 people. The possessors were the minions and mutsuddis of the official landholder 'whose acquiescence to such collusive benefices under the sanctified appellations of religious and charitable gifts at different times became necessary as they were in their nature wholly fraudulent and sure to be resumed if made known to the Mussalman Government'.[17] The Natore Raj had lands fraudulently appropriated to brahmins, holding them collusively for its own benefit. The total appropriation in the Raj amounted to 4,29,149 bighas in 1778 and a lakh worth of *devottar* estates was given over to Sibnath, younger son of Raja Ramkrishna.[18] The Bishnupur Raj held 1,06,934 bighas as *lakhiraj* and 1,36,971 bighas as *chakran* by such collusive transfers.[19] The Amini Commission in its report of 1778 observed that zamindars 'trusting to the

Rajshahi	4,29,149 bighas	
Birbhum	1,08,771 "	1,27,117 chakrans
Jessore	87,350 "	
Bankura	1,06,934 "	
Chittagong	2,73,202 "	
Dacca	6,15,468 "	
Rangpur	1,46,072 "	
Nadia	3,78,904 "	
Hooghly	1,16,545 "	
24 Parganas	3,34,960 "	
Midnapore	2,01,863 "	
Mahmudshahi	1,36,790 "	
Total	2,9,36,008 bighas	

Source: Amini Commission Report (1778) p. 9; B. M. Addl. Mss. 29086

16. B. R. C., 11 December 1838, no. 46
17. P.P., vii (1812), *Fifth Report*, Appendix 5, J Grant, 'A View of the Revenues of Bengal' (hereafter, Grant, *View*), pp. 402–406
18. *Ibid*, p. 349; also L S S O'Malley, *Bengal District Gazetteers, Rajshahi*, Calcutta, 1916, p. 172
19. Grant, *View*, pp. 394–5

want of information of government have alienated vast estates,' and supplied the table (p. 29) of appropriations in various districts (1 acre = 3.5 bighas approximately). The enquiry was not quite complete at that time. The Commission recommended resumption of at least the late grants and measures 'to check the growth of a practice so alarming and injurious to the public revenue'.[20] The practice went on unabated. The collectors reported that high appropriation had taken place even between 1765 and 1788. In Rajshahi, appropriations since the 1778 report amounted to 23,205 bighas.[21] The moderate estimate of Shore in 1789 of the total appropriation in round figures was 71,71,095 bighas and at his rate of 8 annas per bigha, resumption was likely to fetch Rs 35 lakh a year as revenue.[22] The Landholders' Society, in their petition in 1838, admitted that the *lakhiraj* grants had continued since 1765 and 'extensively increased ever since'. Their plea was that the revenue was paid by the grantor.[23] R D Mangles, secretary to the government, estimated in 1837 that two million bighas were given away as grants in Nadia alone.[24] The process did not end there. In 1851–52, H V Bayley discovered 2,500 bighas of confirmed *lakhiraj* land in Midnapur, fictitiously held back by a former treasurer of the collectorate as provision for his family when his property was sold.[25]

Resumption and resistance (1793–1832)

From the time of the Baze Regulation of 1732, *lakhiraj* was allowed to survive on sufferance because of the official policy of minimum interference in the affairs of Indians. The government did not feel strong or experienced enough to take action against the *lakhiraj* estates or tenures. Thus, grants made before 1765 were held valid while Badshahi grants (by Mughal emperors) and grants below one hundred bighas were also conceded by Act XIX of 1793. But by the Proclamation of 22 March 1793, the government retained the right to investigate and resume all invalid titles. Regulation 19 of 1793 offered 25 per cent commission on the first year's revenue from the resumed land to the collector responsible for resumption. S S Blunt, commissioner of Bishnupur, attempted a major

---

20. *B. M. Addl. Mss. 29086*, Amini Commission Report, 1778, pp. 5–7
21. *B. M. Addl. Mss. 21548*, pp. 128–37
22. P.P. vii, *Fifth Report*, Appendix no. 1, Shore's Minute, 18 June 1789, p. 181
23. B. R. C., 10 October 1837, no.74
24. B. R. C., 15 January 1839, no. 35
25. H V Bayley, *History of Midnapore*, Calcutta, 1902, p.1

assault on the Bishnupur Raj in 1801. He asked all lakhirajdars to appear with their sanads before him within one month but not a single claimant appeared. Blunt then tried to ascertain them from the zamindar's *baze zamin duftur*, but the records were asserted to have been accidentally destroyed by fire. Finally, a list of hundreds of names was submitted by the zamindar. But Blunt soon discovered that no reliance could be placed on the list. He calculated the total value of resumable grants at Rs 40,000. The sanads were forged on such a scale, Blunt reported, that forgery became a profitable profession. The other strategy was to flood the law courts with taidads or sanads for registration. No less than 70,000 cases were filed in the Burdwan Collectorate within a year. As Blunt observes:

> In fact, the large number of taidads filed between 1800–1802 seems to have had the effect of stopping further action on the part of the authorities.[26]

The official zeal subsided for the time being and Regulation 2 of 1805 allowed sixty years for a tenure to become time-honoured. The right of resumption was reasserted by Regulation 8 of 1811 and the collector was armed with judicial powers. The measure was extended to the ceded territories and the Sunderban wastes in 1817. The wars of Wellesley and Hastings brought about a financial crisis and resumption appeared a means of raising the demand for land revenue on Bengal without breaching the Permanent Settlement, and, in the upper provinces, of raising the collections without increasing the incidence of the demand. Regulation 2 of 1819 was directed against alluvial and concealed lands. D S Scott, commissioner of the Sunderbans, in his attempt to enforce the measure met with stiff opposition from the landlords concerned. He complained in 1818 that the zamindars were against him and chief among them were Rajballav Rai, Ramratan Mitra and Rani Sankari Dasi:

> The landholders declined to produce their documents and when visited with fines, offered copies of the 1,190 (1,794) chittas which were found to be utterly untrustworthy, for not only were the originals often unattested by the signature of any European officer, but they had also been mutilated and tampered with in the Collector's office and false copies had been collusively obtained therefrom. The Amins, too were obstructed in their work and the aid of the police had to be invoked.[27]

---

26. F W Robertson, *Bankura Settlement Report (1917–24)*, Calcutta, 1926, pp. 29–40

27. F E Pargiter, *Sunderbans*, Calcutta, 1885, pp. 11–15

The enquiry into jungle lands in 1819 provoked numerous petitions from the zamindars to the governor-general submitting that such an enquiry was a violation of the Permanent Settlement. The government conceded that permanently settled areas would not be violated.[28] The slogan came to be repeated against any measure affecting landlords' interests. But the defensive attitude was given up very soon and the government seemed determined to go on with resumption. The financial situation turned from bad to worse. With the coming of Bentinck, the government began to trench upon *lakhiraj* in earnest. Regulation 3 of 1828 invested the collector with special legal powers to investigate *lakhiraj* tenures and make summary awards, subject to appeal to special commissioners created for the purpose and to the Board of Revenue. The new summary procedure recognised no grant as hereditary unless specified in the *taidad* or register. Non-registration or failure to notify mutation of title on succession subjected grants to lapse. Appeal was virtually foreclosed by limiting its period to two months and making the plaintiff liable for the cost of the suit if illegal title was proved against him.[29]

Soon after the promulgation of this regulation, three petitions were addressed to the government by zamindars complaining of the severity of the measure: (a) petition from Raja Gangaprosad Roy and 55 others from Barisal (b) petition from Syed Khadim Hussain Khan and others signed by 120 individuals (c) petition from inhabitants of Bengal, Bihar and Orissa signed by Rammohan Roy, Radhakanta Dev, Dwarakanath Tagore, Prosanna Kumar Tagore and Kalinath Chowdhury, leading representatives of the zamindars. The main protest was against summary investigation and award in resumption laws by the collector who combined both administrative and judicial functions. The collector was described as 'incompetent and arbitrary' and appeal within two months to commissioners sitting at a great distance in Calcutta and Patna, virtually ineffectual in 'two cases out of three'. The sore point was, however, the enquiry after the lapse of such a long time when *lakhiraj* had become a *fait accompli*. The cry of 'Permanent Settlement in danger' was raised again and the government procedure decried as a breach of public faith.[30]

The government was labouring under legal constraint. The enquiry was bound to be superficial. It was impossible to trace thousands of petty

---

28. P.P., v (1831), Mill Q. 3280–81; also, B. R. C., 20 June 1837, no. 1.3

29. R Clarke, *Regulations of the Bengal Government Respecting Zemindary and Lakhiraj Property*, London, 1840, pp. 124–873 for all resumption measures

30. B. R. C., 19 May 1829, nos 3–5

lakhiraj tenures with the help of a handful of amins and a few overworked collectors. The Permanent Settlement was a revenue demand arrived at by guess work and not proper survey and settlement operations. Conquest led to revenue demand but often after re-allocation of land to the allottee. The *tauzi* or the rent roll frequently had no relationship with the *ruqba* or land for which revenue was demanded. Resumption presupposed survey and registration. Moreover, the special tribunals created for resumption cases were too inadequate to offer balanced and prompt judgements. The courts were already flooded by a spate of such cases. Finally, Regulation 2 of 1805 exempted *lakhiraj* of sixty years' standing from resumption. It was indeed unjust to call upon the grandchildren of the original grantee to dig out moth-eaten taidads as evidence of validity. A quick summary verdict on such complicated cases could be nothing but perfunctory.

The landlords systematically gained on the government on this score. The local government tried to defend the summary process in 1830 on grounds of 'cheapness and celerity of justice' but the Court of Directors rejected the plea. They admitted that there had been denial of justice in cases that were in arrears for 3–10 years and the judiciary had not been the third party. Even a lapse of sixty years was regarded as being too long for prescriptive rights. Special judges were appointed soon after to demonstrate judicial impartiality.[31]

To sum up, land resumptions between 1819–32 yielded only Rs 12,06,343 in a period of thirteen years while a mass of cases remained in a state of stagnation as the collectors were unable to enquire into them.[32] On 1 January 1832, cases pending for enquiry numbered 4,995 in the Calcutta division and 821 in Murshidabad.[33] The amount of oppression, abuse and mistrust in the government generated by the measure was officially admitted to have been considerably more than the financial gains. The approaching question of the renewal of the charter postponed further official inroads into *lakhiraj* for some time.

Preparations for the final struggle (1833–1837)

The renewal of the charter in 1833 and the approval of the detailed survey and settlement of the northwest provinces by the home government, infused a new spirit in the Bengal administration. Before his final departure in

31. P.P., xi (1831–32), Appendix no. 86, pp. 352–57
32. B. R. C., 10 October 1837, no. 4
33. *Ibid*, no. 11

1833, Bentinck initiated the survey in Midnapur and recruited competent Indians as special deputy collectors, to carry out the investigation and resumption of *lakhiraj*. Metcalfe set the pace of Auckland's all out drive to bring resumption to a quick and fruitful end. The cost of the Afghan war sharpened the need to raise revenue. The extension of cultivation in the Sunderbans, Chittagong and Midnapur beyond the limit of the Permanent Settlement prompted the government to prevent such extensions from being included within the Permanent Settlement. An exact and thorough survey of these areas was ordered by the government from 1830 onwards. Alexander Hodges undertook it in the Sunderbans between 1830–35. Henry Siddons started it in Chittagong in 1834 with new vigour. H V Bayley supervised the work in Midnapur from 1833. Auckland gave it the thrust it needed. The Indian Law Commission at this time demanded a detailed map of the Bengal districts and the Survey Committee (1837– 41) began its work in Calcutta. In 1837, the survey was speeded up in Midnapur and Chittagong. The standard of survey was generally of a higher quality than that in the northwest provinces. The surveyors were given professional control and full charge of the detailed *khasra*, with adequate staff and assistants, Indian surveyors and amins for help. Legal pressure was exerted on zamindars and village headmen to elicit information.[34]

The assault on *lakhiraj* was far more organised than ever before. Auckland had in his command a survey team, a strong executive and a judiciary reinforced by the appointment of special deputy collectors and special judges to cope with the burden of the resumption operation. Auckland and his secretary, Mangles, took pains to explain that their measure was an attempt to free the masses exploited by the brahmin and equalise taxes.[35] The financial constraint was crippling the government's efforts to tighten up local administration. It needed additional funds to conduct an efficient survey and set up a detailed system of local judiciary and police. It was only fair to tax those who had enjoyed exemption for such a long time.[36]

The rigours of the new offensive were beginning to tell upon landlords. They had no doubt that the government meant business this time. They

34. R H Phillimore, ed., *Historical Records of the Survey of India*, vol. iv, *(1830–43)*, Dehradun, 1959, pp. 8–11, 261–297

35. *B. M. Addl. Mss. 37711*, Auckland Papers, vol. iii, Minute on Resumption, 25 January 1839; B. R. C., 10 October 1837, no. 74 for Mangles

36. B. R. C., 15 January 1839, no. 37, Halliday refers to 'burthen of public expenses'; *The Friend of India*, 21 January 1836, supports government on that ground in 1836; cf E Stokes, *English Utilitarians*, pp. 150–68

had too great a stake in *lakhiraj* to let it be resumed without a showdown. It has been seen that large estates contained most of the *lakhiraj* land. The small units of *lakhiraj* did not mean that they involved only indigent people. The Nawab Nazim of Murshidabad had 62,482 bighas of *lakhiraj*, comprising many as small as two bighas which he distributed among his relatives.[37] The final resumption of *jagir* and *nawarra* (granted for supplying boats to the government) lands between 1822–40 revealed that:

> where the lands were distinguishable, proprietors at the time of the Novennial Settlement studiously inserted minute portions of such revenue-free lands throughout their revenue-paying lands in the hope of avoiding detection and consequent resumption.[38]

A matter of graver concern was the attempted resumption of alluvial and wastelands within and outside the Permanent Settlement by the government since 1817. These lands had become highly valuable assets which the local zamindars could not afford to expose to the government. As Hencknell, the earliest settlement officer of the Sunderbans observed in the 1780s, their claims reached the sea, though the jungle lands had not been included in their hustabuds and formed no part of their estates. A *vritti* of Shyam Rai Thakur in Jessore totalling 33,475 bighas was reported to have encroached on the jungle to the extent of 7000 bighas by 1830.[39]

The enquiry was the most hated thing. It had been successfully resisted so far and had not been pressed too hard by the government to ensure the landlords' loyalty in difficult times. There was an unwritten contract that the local landlords were to be allowed to run local affairs as they chose to as long as they paid the revenue and did not create rows. The government's right to interfere in the affairs of the estate, safeguarded in 1793, had been allowed to lapse. Its revival signified the danger of exposing the landlords' illegal gains from *lakhiraj* appropriations and reclamation of forests beyond the limits of the Permanent Settlement. It would give the bureaucrats an excuse to interfere in agrarian relations. This was viewed with great repugnance by the landlords while the government welcomed it as an important step.[40]

---

37. B. R. C., 6 July 1837, no. 81
38. F D Ascoli, *Dacca Settlement Report (1910–1917)*, Calcutta, 1917, p. 58
39. F E Pargiter, *Sunderbans*, Calcutta, 1885, p. 3
40. P.P., iv (1859), Evidence of Mangles before the Colonisation Committee, Q. 1199–A

The landlords also seem to have genuinely feared a possible revocation of the Permanent Settlement. The Manifesto as well as Regulations 10 and 11 of the Landholders' Society mirrored this fear insofar as they proposed 'to safeguard the provisions of the Permanent Settlement against encroachments like the present resumption of land', and 'to act for the extension of the Permanent Settlement in U.P'.[41] The *Bengal Hurkaru*, a pro-landlord journal observed in 1837 how landed proprietors were being reduced yearly and the government was by degrees becoming the holder of an ever-expanding zamindari.[42]

The landholders were clever enough to realise that the task of fighting resumption on the spot would be too difficult and protracted to be effective. The wiser course of action was to strike at the root, to challenge the policy itself. The legal and constitutional battles needed to be fought at the headquarters in Calcutta to put pressure on the government. The journals had long been a forum for airing the political views of the landlords. The *Reformer* (1831) was run by Prosanna Kumar Tagore, one of the signatories of the 1829 petition. The *Bengal Herald* was owned by Dwarakanath Tagore who also bought the *India Gazette* and a share of the *Bengal Hurkaru*.[43] The resumption issue was discussed by them from time to time. As early as 1833, Prosanna Kumar in an editorial of the *Reformer* outlined the future Landholders' Society:

> We earnestly propose to them (landlords) to form themselves into an association the object of which will be to protect their interest by every legitimate and lawful means in their power.[44]

The *Bengal Herald* took up the resumption issue directly and maintained that resumption if undertaken soon after 1765 could have had more validity but after a lapse of seventy years all *lakhiraj* had attained prescriptive rights.[45] The *Reformer* in 1836 squarely condemned the special tribunals and called the special deputy collectors, young, inexperienced

41. Landholders' Society, Rules, Regulations and Report of Proceedings for the first six months, (in vernacular), Calcutta, 1838, *India Office Library* (hereafter, *IOL*), *Vernacular Tract 1900*, pp. 1–10
42. *Bengal Hurkaru*, 14 June 1837
43. B B Majumdar, *History of Indian Social and Political Ideas*, Calcutta, 1967, p. 77
44. *The Reformer*, 16 June 1833
45. *The Bengal Herald*, 20 March 1836, quoted in *The Calcutta Courier*, 21 March 1836

officers with an eye on promotion, unfit to administer impartial justice. The *Reformer,* again in 1837, pointed out the necessity of an organisation as a more effective political platform against resumption than mere journalism:

> Had one-hundredth part of the mischief done by these Regulations been done in England, petitions upon petitions would have been poured upon the legislature.[46]

Their new move was to form a fairly representative centralised organisation for concerted and continuous agitation at the centre.

The Landholders' Society had its inception at a meeting held at the Hindu College on 12 November 1837, mostly attended by the resident zamindars of Calcutta. Prosanna Kumar was himself one of the founders of the Society. Raja Radhakanta Dev, Kalikrishna Dev of Shovabazar, Dwarakanath Tagore, Munshi Kalinath Roy of Taki and Raja Rajnarain of Andul were the other founding fathers. The Landholders' Society was formally launched by a public meeting in the Town Hall on 19 March 1838. The landlords had a powerful and unexpected ally in the European settlers who had become entrenched at different levels of the land system as zamindars or patnidars or izaradars after the open door policy for European settlers was declared in 1835. These Free Traders on the spot and their patrons at home railed at resumption for its depressing effect on the land market. The landlords had not made any efforts to mobilise them as yet. But they welcomed the settlement of Europeans at a Town Hall meeting of 15 December 1829, where Rammohan Roy and Dwarakanath Tagore had eloquently pleaded their cause.[47] This was the beginning of a collaboration which survived beyond the agitation over resumption. In 1838 the landlords supported the settlers in another meeting at the Town Hall to discuss the Black Act question (Act XI of 1836, which brought under the purview of British-born subjects 'native' civil courts). Dwarakanath made a curious speech on the occasion to cement the unwritten alliance which deserves recording here:

> Some time ago, we poor heathens were not permitted to sit on the Jury. How, I ask, did we get in there? Was it not by the exertions of Mr. Dickens and other lawyers who vehemently came forward to make us partake

---

46. *The Reformer,* 27 March 1836, quoted in *The Calcutta Courier,* 29 March 1836 and in *Bengal Hurkaru,* 22 May 1837
47. *Report of Proceedings at a General Meeting of the Inhabitants of Calcutta on the 15th of December* 1829, Calcutta, 1830, (hereafter, *Report of the Meeting in Support of Colonisation*), pp. 4–5

of this important right enjoyed by Englishmen? What, are we to have
no gratitude? What ungrateful wretches must we be, if we, now that
they are to be degraded in the mofussil, do not come forward to
support them.[48]

Rewards were expected, and not in vain, for all these solicitudes. This
was to come on the resumption question. The European settlers had
already supported them in their journals; the *Calcutta Courier* (editor,
George Prinsep), the *Bengal Hurkaru* (Samuel Smith) and the *Englishman* (J Stocqueler and W C Hurry). The *Englishman* strongly criticised
the creation of special tribunals and lamented that the lakhirajdars were
left 'to flounder on in the mire'.[49] The *Bengal Hurkaru* ridiculed resumption measures which were said to be born of greed.[50] Theodore Dickens,
a barrister of the Supreme Court and owner of many indigo factories and
landed estates in Gorakhpur, U.P., in his speech at the inaugural meeting
of the Landholders' Society in 1838 criticised resumption measures as a
violation of the Permanent Settlement, and said that it was directed against
the landed aristocracy to meet the increasing expenses of British conquests. The Society was able to rope in Dickens and George Prinsep as
members of the executive committee and almost all the leading planters
in the *mofussil* as ordinary members. W C Hurry, the editor of the
Englishman became one of its joint secretaries.[51]

The declared objectives of the Society were promotion of landholders'
interests, unity of landed interests irrespective of caste, creed and colour,
information on land profits, arbitration of all disputes and fixation of state
demand. The more immediate ones included repeal of adverse laws,
representation of individual cases in the interest of all, protection of the
provisions of the Permanent Settlement against encroachments like resumption and extension of the Permanent Settlement to the northwest
provinces. The Society was to act as the headquarters for all activities on
behalf of distant landholders in the *mofussil* and was to set up branches in
all districts. This gives a clear idea of the nature of the organisation. Instead
of zamindars and zamindari associations, the terms 'landholders' and
'landed interests' were consciously used to include intermediaries, European settlers and lakhirajdars *per se*. But the membership was restricted

---

48. *Report of a Public Meeting held at the Town Hall, Calcutta on the 24th of
    November 1838*, London 1839, pp. 27–30
49. *The Englishman*, 6 July 1836
50. *Bengal Hurkaru*, 12 February 1836
51. *Report of the Meeting in Support of Colonisation*, Calcutta, 1838, pp. 16–49

by a rather high annual subscription of twenty rupees to exclude many small rent-receivers and lakhirajdars. The inaugural meeting was attended by 'upwards of two hundred of the most respectable Zamindars. The executive committee consisted of Prosanna Kumar Tagore of Pathuriaghata, Calcutta and Rangpur, Satyacharan Ghosal of Bhukailash, Calcutta and Chittagong, Raja Rajnarain of Andul, Raja Radhakanta and Kalikrishna of Shovabazar, Calcutta, Ashutosh Deb of Calcutta, Ramratan Roy of Narail, Jessore, Ramkamal Sen of Calcutta, Munshi Muhammad Amir of Jessore, George Prinsep, editor of the *Calcutta Courier* and a planter and Theodore Dickens, a barrister of the Supreme Court. The list of membership reveals names of leading resident and absentee landlords. Some of the *mofussil* zamindars were represented by their mukhtears. Apart from neighbouring districts like Nadia, Hooghly, Jessore, distant and remote districts like Chittagong, Tippera were also represented. Sub-committees were duly formed to take special care of a group of zillahs in the following order:

Zillah Behar, Patna, Sarun, Sahabad—Ashutosh Deb, Raja Baroda-kantha Roy

Zillah Bhagalpur, Dinajpur, Maldah, Monghyr, Purnea and Tirhut—Kalinath Chowdhury and W Ferguson

Zillah Birbhum, Bogra, Murshidabad, Patna, Rajshahi and Rangpur—Sambhuchandra Mitra and Captain Bint

Zillah Bakarganj, Kachar, Dhaka, Faridpur, Jayanti, Mymensing and Sylhet—Satyacharan Ghosal and Raja Radhakanta Dev

Zillah Chittagong, Noakhali, Tippera—Raja Kalikrishna and W Storm

Zillah Durrang, Goalpara, Kamrup and Nowgong—George Prinsep and Ramkamal Sen

Zillah Barasat, East Burdwan, West Burdwan, Hooghly, Jessore, Nabadwip and 24 Parganas—Ramratan Roy, Munshi Muhammad Amir and Prannath Chowdhury

Zillah Baleshwar, Cuttack, Hijli, Khurda and Midnapur—Radhamadhab Banerjee, Mathuranath Mallik

Prosanna Kumar Tagore and W C Hurry were made joint secretaries and notification was sent to the government of the formation of the Society.[52]

It is clear from the above that the movement against resumption spread through Bengal and was not in the nature of sporadic action in isolated

---

52. *Report of the Meeting in Support of Colonisation*, Calcutta, 1838, pp. 16–49

districts. Nor was it a conspiracy of a few Calcutta based landlords masquerading for the rest of their community. The landlords adopted, as we shall see, a policy of physical obstruction of survey and enquiry and constitutional agitation in Calcutta.

The preliminary round was over for both the government and the landlords and events were headed towards a final showdown.

The climax (1837–1842)

Both the law courts and the actual territory in dispute became the battle-field of this contest. The impact of resumption in its final phase was vividly described in retrospect by a writer in 1857:

> In this sudden start to life of Government which arose like a slumbering giant to require its own, lay the real grievance to owners of real property, which to this day has not ceased to be actually felt.[53]

A. *The bureaucratic aggression*

In Burdwan, the court was flooded by landlords with 70,000 applications for the registration of taidads. It may be noted that upto 1837, there were 4000–5000 cases which were disposed of after enquiry.[54] Special Deputy Collector W Taylor felt that the documents submitted had been pre-pared so as to show the total *lakhiraj* in parts of less than a hundred bighas each in order to qualify for exemption.[55] On 3 May 1837, he disposed of 429 cases *ex parte* in favour of the government. Such a whipcrack was condemned even by his own commissioner, as a 'most alarming and monstrous abuse of power'.[56] Halliday, secretary to the government, however, chose to ignore it.[57] A similar instance was repeated elsewhere. In the single district of Chittagong, 14,855 cases were similarly disposed of between 1830 and 1840. C W Smith, a member of the Board of Revenue on deputation to enquire into the irregularities of the cases, reported in 1840 that many of the titles resumed were actually

53. *Calcutta Review*, xxix (1857), Article IV, p. 372
54. B. R. C., 15 January 1839, no. 34, Petition of the LHS, Forwarding by secretaries
55. B. R. C., 12 March 1839, no. 12
56. *Ibid*, no. 1
57. *Ibid*, no. 21

valid.[58] The following is the detailed list of cases and *ex parte* decisions in all districts:

Period	Districts	Total cases	Decided	Ex parte
June 1835– Nov 1841	Patna	1,583	969	161
-Do-	Purnea and Maldah	2,813	879	134
Dec 1836– Oct 1841	Dinajpur, Rajshahi, Pabna, Bogra, Rungpore	891	371	219
1837–1841	Murshidabad, Nadia, 24 Parganas	1,184	493	215
1837–1841	Birbhum, Burdwan, Bankura, Hooghly	3,503	1,248	933
1837–1841	Dacca, Mymensing	1,159	665	210
1837–1841	Sylhet, Tipperah	3,855	3,427	214
1837–1841	Faridpur, Bakarganj, Jessore	1,565	369	208
1837–1841	Midnapore, Hijli	13,692	6,912	1,461

Source: B.R.C., no. 9 of 17 June 1846

The table shows that almost one-fourth of the cases were decided *ex parte*. In districts like Midnapur, Hijli and Sylhet, the large number of cases were duly decided as people did not contest the claim. In Midnapur and Hijli, it was officially admitted that the difficulty of going to the *sadar* station for a suit had led to surrender. In Sylhet, the surrender was explained by the fact that most of the titles were invalid and did not bear scrutiny. The table shows the huge accumulation of cases by which the landlords sought to clog the process of justice. It testifies that this was the official strategy chosen to combat the situation.

The result of bureaucratic aggression outside the court in the first year (1836–37) appeared 'satisfactory' to the government and the report on resumption for the year said: 'There is no doubt that it will go on improving.'[59]

---

58. B. R. C., 5 May 1840, nos 21 and 23
59. B. R. C., 18 September 1838, no. 91

The table below indicates the index of the growing income from resumption for a period of three years (rupees in round figures):

Year	Total collection	Collection charges	Net receipt
1834–35	1,93,510	9,262	18,247
1835–36	1,86,203	24,382	1,61,521
1836–37	2,13,715	15,300	1,98,415

Source: B.R.C., 18 September 1838, nos 81–83

The two major areas surveyed, Chittagong and Hijli-Midnapur, yielded the highest increase of revenue. The result of the survey in Chittagong can be gathered from the phenomenal enhancement of revenue in the resumed mahals from Rs 12,800 in 1836–37 to Rs 64,339 in 1837–38.[60] The illegal action of Harvey was reported by Commissioner Ricketts. But Auckland ignored it. This led Ricketts to grab land with unprecedented severity. In 1842, the new settlement yielded £16,000 according to one estimate.[61] In Hijli district, 1633 new mahals were resumed in 1837–38 worth Rs. 41,541 in revenue. The Majnumutha estate held 50,000 out of 54,242 bighas of *lakhiraj* in the district which comprised half the measured area. The raja of Majnumutha had appropriated vast tracts of fertile land attached to salt works of the government fraudulently, although he was fully aware of the invalidity of such titles. They were recommended to be resumed at full rates.[62]

The rigours of the aggression can be measured from some extreme cases of resumption of alluvial lands. In Murshidabad, 309 bighas were attached for three years by the collector on alleged alienation. But on enquiry, no appropriation was discovered and the attachment was held illegal. Collector Smelt was censured by the higher authorities for his over-zealousness.[63] Halliday, secretary to the government, had to order

60. B. R. C., 18 October 1838, no. 25
61. B Torrens, Bengal Civil Service to Rt. Hon'ble R V Smith, *IOL Tract*, no. 508, London, 1856, pp. 10–14
62. B. R. C., 29 October 1839, no. 12
63. B. R. C., 19 June 1838, nos 43–44

the release of two farms of 22 bighas and a fraction of a bigha in Chittagong and Hijli respectively, for their ridiculously small size.[64]

The total revenue from resumed and settled mahals in Bengal, Bihar and Orissa was estimated at Rs 59,51,935 in round figures for 85,84,165 bighas in 1846.[65] Mangles, in his evidence before the Colonisation Committee, quoted a parliamentary return of resumption operations in Bengal showing £3,79,850 per annum as the additional revenue in 1847–48 and £14,08,817 as the collection charges for the whole period of 1828–41.[66] Further the all-India character of the operation and its gains elsewhere helped to add to the substantial financial gains of the government.

Of the 5,462 *khas* mahals finally retained by the government in 1849–50, 4,579 were settled ryotwari.[67] This was, however, a mellow fulfilment of a cherished project. The government, anxious to promote cash crops like sugarcane, had tried *khas* mahals as model farms and by keeping the rent low for sugarcane in one government *mahal* under the Chittagong commissioner, had succeeded in doubling the output of the crop in 1837.[68]

It has taken some time to analyse the extensive and intensive nature of the official pressure mounted on the rural society by resumption operations and this account has made the struggle look like a one-sided affair. The following account of resistance should help to make a correct assessment of the final upshot.

B. The opposition of landlords

The resistance, conducted on two fronts, was equally strong. Stiff local resistance was given on the spot whenever collectors and their amins tried to investigate, measure and resume. At the same time, the official policy was brought under the attack of the Landholders' Society at the headquarters through petitions, public meetings and the press.

Chittagong became the major scene of local opposition when J J Harvey, collector of Chittagong, attempted to carry out a survey and settlement of the district with the intention of resuming invalid tenures. In a despatch

---

64. B. R. C., 10 October 1839, no. 26
65. B. R. C., 17 June 1846, nos 2–6 and 24
66. P.P., iv (1859), Q. 1085, p. 57
67. B. R. C., 21 January 1852, no. 13, *Report on the Revenue Administration of the Lower Provinces (1849–60)*, pp. 8–10
68. B. R. C., 27 March 1838, no. 74

to the commissioner, Chittagong division of 10 January 1837, he reported that the landholders were opposing survey operations 'deliberately and obstinately, forcibly and doggedly'. The situation became so desperate that military reinforcements had to be called to maintain authority. The opposition was described as a confederacy of Hindu lakhirajdars and zamindars determined to put a stop to measurement by violence. The opposition first began at Thanas Puttea and Satkania when deputy collectors in charge of the surveys were subjected to violent assaults. Clubs and other offensive weapons were freely used and they were threatened with serious consequences if the authorities proceeded with their measurement and survey. Morton, assistant to Siddons, the surveyor, was the next victim of attack. His field books and instruments were destroyed and he narrowly escaped with his life. Owen, Parker and Mullens were similarly assaulted in other parts of the district. When Harvey came to their rescue, the mob tried to reach him with cries of 'Harvey sahebko maro' (thrash Harvey). The local landlord, Ramkanoo Chowdhury was apprehended along with other rioters at Harvey's summons. But they were snatched away by a mob collected by the beating of drums in Anoopara. Another party of twenty burkundazes and fifteen peons led by a *darogah* was again deforced. Harvey, with another party of about a hundred men, recaptured them, but was chased by a mob of a thousand people, gathered together by drumbeats who attacked them with sticks, bludgeons and clods of earth. He then opened fire, killing two.[69]

There was a little relaxation of resumption measures in view of the bloodshed. But the incident was flashed in the *Friend of India* in strong words:

The first blood has been shed in the execution of the Resumption Laws and we sincerely hope it may be the last.[70]

It suggested a light assessment of *lakhiraj* lands which might have reinforced the idea of a compromise, recommended by the Court of Directors in 1833. Chittagong was chosen as the testing ground of settlement at half rate in 1838.[71]

A second case of local conflict was reported by Bidwell, the special deputy collector of Sylhet and Tipperah (Tippera) in 1841. He tried to identify and trace *lakhiraj* lands in the Bhullooah estate of Rani Kattayani

---

69. B. C. J. C., 24 February 1837, no. 46; B. C. J. C., 24 January 1837, no. 55
70. *The Friend of India*, 12 January 1837
71. B. R. C., 25 August 1840, no. 42

of Kandi Raj. With defective documents as his only guide and the zamindar resisting his operations at every step, he found his job extremely difficult. In many instances, lakhirajdars coalesced with the zamindar and denied the existence of rent-free tenures. Amins and deputy collectors were hindered in their inventory of the estate. Informers became the victims of the zamindar's wrath. Rani Kattayani finally agreed to a compromise at half *jumma* if all claims to investigate *lakhiraj* in her territory were withdrawn by the government.[72]

An enquiry into new accretions in the Tamluk estate of Midnapur in 1839 met with similar opposition. The zamindar first of all countered the claims by pointing out depletions of the estate by diluvion. He was asked to submit papers in proof. He evaded this altogether. The collector, after a fortnight's notice, proceeded with an enquiry on the spot. He found out, with the help of a number of old resident ryots and mukhtears, that no diluvion had taken place and many more formations had been annexed to the estate than claimed by the government. The zamindar had prayed for remission for the alleged dissolution in 1835–36 and loss of rent caused by it. The government had waived the interest and the penalty for the benefit of the ryots. In reality all rents were paid by the ryots for which they had receipts. Still they were subjected to extreme physical torture until the amount of penalty and interest was recovered from them. The zamindar's distaste for enquiry was apparent. It was feared that official witnesses would be fined and their rents enhanced twenty times by him. The collector of Midnapore advised Deputy Collector Beatson, who made the enquiry, to allow relief to peasantry.[73] The frontier areas were traditionally turbulent because of their remoteness from the seat of government. The practice of allowing remission was carried upto the time of boundary delimitation surveys (*thak*) in the 1850s. In the report on the survey operations of the Lower Provinces in 1852–53, the insuperable difficulty of obtaining any information from zamindars without fining them was narrated with concern, and it was suspected that this was due to the fear that survey operations and preparation of a register were preparatory to a revision of the Permanent Settlement.[74]

The landlords, however, concentrated their energies on the constitutional agitation of the Landholders' Society in Calcutta. They felt that there

72. B. R. C., 1 June 1841, nos 6 and 7
73. B. R. C., 30 June 1840, no. 55 (Enclosure)
74. *Report of the Survey Operations of the Lower Provinces 1852–53*, Calcutta, 1853, pp. 7–26

was greater need for concerted action than individual physical resistance in the interior. Landlords like Rani Kattayani of Kandi Raj who had borne the brunt of bureaucratic aggression in their estates in large measure appealed to the organisation for redress of their grievances.[75] In January 1839, the Landholders' Society sent a petition to the government, signed by 20,000 people 'including those of a large portion of the most opulent zamindars of Bengal'. In the forwarding letter, the joint secretaries renewed the attack on the centering of both administrative and judicial functions in 'youngmen (sic) appointed as special deputy collector to seek out cases of doubtful tenure, men in whom the character and interests of informer are combined with judicial powers'. They also pointed out the hasty and irregular manner in which some hundred decrees were passed in a single day without proper notice, obviously referring to the proceedings of Taylor. They took care to expose the weaknesses in the official position by stressing the prescriptive right attached to *lakhiraj* tenures of more than sixty years' standing, as conceded by Regulation 2, para 18 of 1805.[76] The Bengal government was acutely alive to its weak position. Millet, the secretary to the *Sadar* Board of Revenue, had prepared a draft of compromise in 1837 which exempted the *lakhiraj* under one hundred bighas within an estate, ten-bigha independent holdings and endowments, but it was vetoed by Mangles' note.[77] Halliday, who succeeded Mangles as secretary to the government, had urged for a consensus of opinion in 1837 among the special deputy collectors, on a possible compromise to avoid resumption as desired by the Court of Directors in 1833. Many of them thought that a compromise would mean surrender.[78] The Supreme Council had also insisted on a compromise, even at the cost of a loss of revenue, to stop agitation, except Morison, the member from Madras who strongly defended the right of resumption. But he conceded in 1838 that lakhirajdars deserved indulgence because their right had been allowed to lie dormant for a long time. This was to avoid a politically undesirable contest with a 'formidable band of Malcontents open to every impression hostile to their rulers which there are not wanting interested Agents to foment'.[79] Morison was obviously referring to the Landholders' Society formed a few months earlier that year, having European settlers as

75. *The Asiatic Journal*, October 1838, Asiatic Intelligence, Report of LHS Meeting, 9 July 1838
76. B. R. C., 15 January 1839, no. 34–35
77. B. R. C., 10 October 1837, nos 59 and 74
78. B. R. C., 25 August 1840, nos 35–36 and Enclosures
79. I. R. C., 29 April 1839 no. 39

agents in it. Auckland, in his Minute of 25 January 1839, endorsed his view too with the realisation that 'the spectacle of a close and keen contest carried on between a Government and a large class of its subjects cannot but have a very undesirable effect'.[80]

While concessions were being contemplated by the government, the Landholders' Society got unexpected support from the Free Traders in London. The newly formed British India Society in London, looking for an ally in India tapped the Landholders' Society at this very time. F C Brown, honorary secretary, British India Society, in a letter dated 11 May 1839, to T Dickens, chairman, Landholder's Society wrote:

The provisional committee feel persuaded that the formation of this society will have your entire approval and will meet with the hearty aid and concurrence of the Landholder's Society of Calcutta and will secure the active support and encouragement in both hemispheres of every real friend and well-wisher to the connection, the welfare and the prosperity of England and India.

The *Friend of India*, the missionary paper, underlined its importance in an editorial very aptly:

It will not be surprising if we should find the eloquence of George Thompson and the sarcasm of Lord Brougham employed in support of a system of unequal and therefore unjust taxation.[81]

The Landholder's Society looked formidable after this new alliance.

The government of India soon announced concessions through the Bengal government. The terms of compromise were—(a) settlement of *lakhiraj* at half rate with retrospective effect from 1825; (b) resumed land held as *khas* (rent-free land resumed by government and held in official possession) to be returned to *lakhirajdar* on the same terms; (c) exemption of ten-*bigha* tenures held before 1790 without interruption; (d) this applied in perpetuity for the holder and his heirs; (e) no resumption on mere non-registration; (f) no resumption of tenures not specified heritable in the document. This was almost a reproduction of Millet's draft of 1837 which had been put into cold storage by the hauteur of Mangles

80. *B. M. Addl. Mss. 3771*, Auckland Papers, vol. iii, Minute on Resumption, 25 January 1839
81. (a) *Bengal Hurkaru*, 4 September 1839; *Cambridge University Library Addl. Mss. 7450/14*, F C Brown Papers re BIS (1839–41)
    (b) *The Friend of India*, 5 December 1839

and Auckland.[82] The Landholders' Society in their annual meeting of 7 December 1839, however, had resolved to take the issue to England for appeal and had appointed John Crawford as the Society's agent in London.[83] The Society saw resumption primarily as a threat to Permanent Settlement with its enormous profits and immunity from control, and its chief aim was to see the measure repealed and the status quo restored. In a further petition to the government of India dated 19 May 1840, backed by another from 268 lakhirajdars from Bihar, the Landholders' Society argued that the half-*jumma* really meant a 15 per cent remission as 35 per cent was normally given for collection charges and proprietor's allowances. It claimed more concessions for the distress and suffering incurred or, in other words, cost of suit in legal terms and for 'unqualified loyalty shown and all treasures invested in government securities even during a period when the government was at war'. All these were clever bargains.[84]

The petition was the signal for a further fight and this time, in England. Crawford had already been appointed the London agent of the Landholders' Society for an annual retainer of £500. He was 'the channel of communication' between the Landholders' Society and the British India Society and briefed George Thompson and Lord Brougham for their speeches in the Parliament on India.[85] The British India Society through its organ, the *British India Advocate*, mounted an attack on the East India Company and gave unreserved support to the Bengal landlords:

> The fact is indisputable that no sooner does the acquisition of fresh territory or an improvement in fiscal extortion or ingenuity . . . open a new vein of gold . . . than it is forthwith wrung from the hard hands of peasants and appropriated without a shadow of compunction by the unsatiable harpies of the Leadenhall street.[86]

The pressure must have hastened the despatch by the Court of Directors to the government of India dated 17 August 1840 stressing 'the imperative necessity of relaxing the severity of the resumption and of introducing a

82. B. R. C., 25 August 1840, no. 108
83. *Bengal Hurkaru*, 14 December 1839
84. B. R. C., 29 September 1840, nos 22–23
85. J H Bell, *British Folks and British India Fifty Years Ago*, London, 1891, (hereafter, *British Folks*) pp. 88–91 and 97–100 for Free Trader domination of the BIS, London
86. *Bengal Hurkaru*, 29 and 31 May 1841, quoting British India Advocate

much greater degree of lenity and liberality in the enforcement of the claims of the government'. Resumption was ordered to be brought to a quick end and the officers were censured for harsh dealings.[87]

Though the Act contained palliatives, it did not revoke resumption. So the Landholders' Society sought to pressurise the India House into submission. Early in 1842, Dwarakanath Tagore, the pivot of the Landholders' Society sailed for England 'to bring the momentous subject of resumption' to the notice of the government and people of that country.[88] Dwarakanath got the desired reception. He 'was invited to a Mansion House banquet to the Prime Minister, there his health was drunk amid loud acclamation from the city grandees'. It is difficult to estimate the effect of his visit. He was probably much too overwhelmed to talk business. His net achievement was to influence the British India Society and persuade George Thompson to 'engage in propaganda in British India'.[89]

George Thompson arrived in Calcutta in the winter of 1842. This advertised the link with Free Traders in England in a big way and was bound to have an impact on the government. Thompson actively participated in the proceedings of the Landholders' Society in 1843. He made it clear in his speech on resumption that:

> the Landholders' Society had law, justice, good faith and sound policy, all on their side and earnestly hoped that their hopes would be crowned with success in sweeping away the resumption measures and with it the many and monstrous evils to which it had given birth. He assured his full cooperation in its plans for the maintenance of the principles laid down in the acts of the settlement.[90]

A further sign of official retreat was the government order of 26 January 1841 exempting fifty bighas of patchwork *lakhiraj* from resumption.[91] This seemed to be the last limit of concession. The government did not give up resumption but tried to wind up the operation amicably at the earliest possible date. The Landholders' Society suffered a setback at the death of Dwarakanath Tagore in 1846. His death meant the end of the Landholders' Society which he had inspired. But on the ruins of the Landholders' Society grew a more powerful organisation of those landholders who

---

87. B. R. C., 12 October 1841, no. 2
88. *The British Friend of India*, October 1842, vol. 2, p. 239
89. J H Bell, *British Folks*, London, 1891, p. 140
90. *Bengal Spectator*, March 1842
91. B. R. C., 12 June 1845, nos 1–5

could pay fifty rupees as annual subscription. It was pompously named, the British Indian Association, and Devendranath Tagore, son of Dwarakanath, became its secretary.[92] From a petition forwarded by him as honorary secretary, to the government dated 31 December 1851, it appeared that the resumption issue was not forgotten and the landholders were only biding their time. The opportune moment arrived when an appeal taken to the Privy Council by the raja of Burdwan against resumption of his *lakhiraj* was upheld by it on the ground of presumptive rights under Act II of 1805. The petition traced the history of the agitation since 1829 to show how the government had to backslide and briefly related the case in question. It was first decided in favour of the government by the special deputy collector of Burdwan on 24 January 1837 and confirmed by the special commissioner, Murshidabad on 11 August 1837. The party appealed to the Privy Council on 25 June 1851. The British Indian Association demanded that 'all resumption should now be relinquished'.[93] The government of India in its reply dated 29 April 1853 stated that the ruling applied only to the case in question. The general application of the decree was overruled.[94] The debate over Regulation 2 of 1805 was about to be resumed when the resumption operation virtually became a closed chapter.

Conclusion

From the view point of the government, the balance sheet was more or less favourable from the fiscal point of view. A net addition of over 3½ million rupees to the *sadar jumma* was a substantial gain. But we cannot jump to conclusions on the basis of this figure. This was what was left after conceding half-rentals to landlords for all resumed land. A similar amount, if not more, was sacrificed to effect the compromise. In 1846, 85,84,165 bighas were estimated to have been resumed in Bengal, Bihar and Orissa. W N Lees estimated in 1857 that 40 million acres had been added to the cultivated area since 1793.[95] If the figures were compared, resumption would appear to have affected a negligible segment of the territory exempt from revenue demand. Even those 8½ million bighas

92. B B Majumdar, *Indian Political Associations and Reform of Legislature (1818–1917)*, Calcutta, 1965, pp. 34–36

93. B. R. C., 14 October 1852, no. 48

94. B. R. C., 19 May 1853, no. 4

95. W N Lees, *Land and Labour of India*, London, 1867, p. 169

were not finally retained. The terms of compromise allowed much of it to
slip away. One can form an estimate of the area exempted from the
following table, allowing ten bighas for each *lakhirajdar* at the least for
the period 1874–76:

District	Lakhirajdars		Total
	Male	*Female*	
Nadia	1,316	1,163	2,479
Jessore	1,014	333	1,347
Burdwan	1,529	479	2,008
Hooghly	2,094	524	2,622
Dacca	57	80	137
Bakarganj	26	—	26
Faridpur	297	38	335
Mymensingh	11	411	422

Source: W W Hunter, Statistical Account of Bengal, London, 1874–76

Even a sampling of a few (eight) districts at ten bighas per holding
gives about one lakh bighas of rent-free tenures. For the whole province,
a million bighas roughly escaped payment of revenue in this way. Hunter
makes a distinction between zamindars and lakhirajdars. The above account, therefore, does not apply to *lakhiraj* within estates. Most of the
estates retained *lakhiraj* long after resumption operations were over. The
table below shows the profits of some of the estates from *lakhiraj* between
1874–76.

Estate		District	No. of lakhiraj tenures	Profits
Chakdighi	1874–75	Burdwan	100	Rs 1,463
"	"	"	Resumed lakhiraj	Rs 2,661
Kandi or Paikpara	"	24 Parganas	43	N.A.
Naldanga	"	Jessore	2	—
				Contd..

Estate		District	No. of lakhiraj tenures	Profits
Bogchar	"	"	5	—
Ramnagar	"	"	10	—
Pudea	"	Rajshahi	3	Rs 2,303
Sitlai	"	"	1	Rs 178
Estate of Nayantara Choudhurani	"	Chittagong	22	N.A.
" Ganga Gobinda Sen	"	Tipperah	18	Rs 501-11
" Chanchal (1875–76)		Maldah	21,127 bighas	—
" Nischinta (1877–78)		Midnapore	658 bighas	—
" Mahishadal	"	"	846 bighas	—
" Chowgong	"	Rajshahi	—	Rs 1,992

Source: C.O.W.R., 1874–78

Many other estates possessed *lakhiraj* but the reports do not give their number and rentals. It is not true, therefore, that large estates did not seek to keep their petty *lakhiraj* holdings. Their tenures were the residual ones after the bulk to their resumed *lakhiraj* had been settled at half-rate. Besides, Hunter's distinction between the zamindar and the *lakhirajdar* seems to preclude the possibility of their collusion. We have the evidence of F W Prideaux in 1852–53 and Joykrishna Mukherjee in 1860 in support of such collusion.[96]

Finally, *lakhiraj* alienation continued even after resumption was brought to a close. The boundary delimitation survey in Nadia led to the discovery of 3,578 bighas *lakhiraj* in excess in the Nadia Raj estate.[97] The Road Cess returns of the Hooghly district in 1878 showed that the total number of annexed *lakhiraj* was 4,96,706 bighas distributed in 69,612 tenures of under 100 bighas each, one hundred tenures each of 100–150 bighas and six of over 500 bighas. 75,282 tenures covering 1,49,872 bighas were still unassessed.[98] Many concealed *lakhiraj* holdings were

96. P.P., xxviii (1852–53), Evidence of Prideaux, Q. 5267; P.P., xliv (1861), R. I. C., Evidence of Joykrishna Mukherjee, Q. 3829
97. C. O. W. R. (1856–76), Calcutta, 1877, p. 15
98. G Toynbee; *Hooghly*, Calcutta, 1888, p. 69

also discovered in Bankura during the Thakbast survey.[99] In Hooghly, in 1904, a tenure of a 100 acres was discovered as *lakhiraj* alienations by a *patnidar* in Baksha before the *patni* went to sale for arrears.[100] In Midnapur, the practice was found fairly established in 1907–13 in estate Khandkhola where one ex-proprietor after another tried to appropriate *mal* lands into *lakhiraj* in the name of dependents and relatives as their estate went under the hammer.[101]

In the final analysis, much of the institution of *lakhiraj* remained as such and only a little was resumed by the state in terms of its total value. Its utility as a cover for collusive transfers remained undiminished. What was more, most of the resumed estates were given back to landlords at half-rates.

The ryotwari experiment of *khas* mahals proved illusory. The report on management of *khas* mahals for the period 1819–1832 says:

> In the one case, the illicit gains of the native officers and of their nominees, the sezawals, ameens or tehsildars are acquired at the expense of the rentals justly due to Government; in the other, the claims of the state are made the stalking horse for the plunder of the people.[102]

W H Belli, collector of Hooghly, wrote in 1827:

> Khas management, as far as it has come under my experience in this district, has completely failed and I do confess I look upon the ryotwary system as altogether unpracticable here. We have been trying for years to explain the intentions of Government in this matter to the ryots generally . . . but not one individual has yet been induced to engage directly with the Government. In fact, they never seem half so manageable as when left under the control of the Sudder proprietor while the collector with all his power cannot effect in a year what a second class talukdar attains in a month.[103]

---

99. F W Robertson, *Bankura Settlement Report (1917–24)*, Calcutta, 1936, p. 41

100. M N Gupta, *Final Report on the Survey and Settlement of Certain Government and Temporarily Settled Estates and Zamindary Estates in the District of Hooghly*, 1904–13, Calcutta, 1914, p. 29

101. B Sanyal, *Final Report on the Minor Settlement Operations in the District of Midnapore 1907–13*, Calcutta, 1914, p. 6

102. B. R. C., 10 October 1837, no. 4

103. G Toynbee, *Hooghly*, Calcutta, 1888, p. 64

W Taylor, superintendent of the *khas* mahals reported in 1840 that huge balances were outstanding against the resumed mahals. 'The tenures were resumed', he wrote, 'without enquiry, measurement and survey and a considerable time must elapse before the assets could be ascertained. A flat rate of Re 1 per bigha was demanded for all kinds of land which was undoubtedly rather high.'[104] Taylor, as collector of Burdwan, had seen in the case of Government vs. Panawal Huq, that 12,000 bighas resumed in 1827 had remained unsettled up to 1836 due to the machinations of taluqdars and the corruption of investigating officers. Not a farthing was realised. On looking through the records it was discovered that the original papers were being concealed in heaps while the forged ones were on the stack for use.[105]

An old ryot in reply to an enquiry by the Bengal British India Society in 1844 said:

> When the Company resumes the lands for want of payment of the revenue they are held in such a way as we are very sorry for. We never like they should fall into the Company's hands: the Company gives them in farm for 2 or 3 years to some one who knows nothing about us and oppresses us; the old zemindar on the contrary being permanently connected with the land used to say to himself: 'I must use my ryots well for my own sake, the interest being my own and for the sake of the next generation.' But in the Khas lands, there is no feeling of this kind and the ryots are the worst off of all.[106]

Resumption in this respect had lost its *raison d'etre*. In the final phase of resumption, the pious wish of promoting cash crops by rent control was given up and over assessment led to the sale of resumed estates in the Nadia district.[107] The survey and the enquiry, the two mechanisms of official scrutiny, had to be given up after the compromise at half-rate. They were not undertaken seriously again before the Mutiny of 1857. The official attempts at intervention in agrarian relations was adjourned till 1859. The landlord–planter alliance had won the day. The management of the *khas* mahals by the government had proved abortive. The planters

---

104. B. R. C., 21 April 1840, no. 86
105. *The Englishman*, 4 February 1837, News
106. *Bengal Hurkaru*, 12 November 1844, News, Report of the Bengal British India Society Enquiry into the Condition of Ryots in Bengal
107. B. R. C., 10 June 1852, no. 9; *Report on the Revenue Administration of the Lower Provinces for 1850–51*, p. 45

emerged as the official favourites for rural improvement in new glory after 1841. Any further row over landlord rights was avoided to give them a fair trail. But the right to intervene had been most effectively asserted and the level of government activity was destined to rise in future. As J H E Garrett observed in 1910, resumption proceedings enabled the government for the first time to gain a detailed knowledge of the rights and obligations of different classes of landlords and tenants as a background to Act X of 1859.[108]

___

108. J H E Garrett, *Bengal District Gazetteers, Nadia*, Calcutta, 1910, pp. 109–10

Three

Justice and Police in the Interior and the Conflict over Local Authority

Organisation of justice and policy

The policy of land resumption was a sign of an assertive government. The period of minimum interference had slowly been waning since the days of Warren Hastings and by 1793 the government had its feet firmly planted in the alien soil when it began the rule of law. The wars of Wellesley, Hastings and Amherst consolidated British rule. With the arrival of Bentinck in 1828, the period of confidence could be said to have begun. As we have noticed in the earlier chapter, government intervention in local affairs was necessary to end the fiscal and agricultural stagnation that had set in. Bentinck, backed by James Mill in the India House, represented the authoritarian school of Utilitarians and found his theory in consonance with the official mood of the time.

The main task of the government was to subvert the local authority of landlords and establish an environment for economic development. But financial stringency was a serious limitation on government planning. Bentinck had to cut the cost of administration and make it more efficient at the same time. The government had long pursued the policy of working through local institutions, though landlords had been deprived of their judicial and police authorities by Regulation 22 of 1793. The landlords were enjoined by law to become the errand boys of the government. They were to organise the village watch, report crime and apprehend criminals. They were to help run the *dak* system and supply provisions to troops during their march through the estates. The government tried to enforce its authority by fines, imprisonment and punishments for neglect of duty. While the British formally established a monopoly of coercive authority in the districts, they left the landlords with the unpaid duties of watch and ward. They were expected to act like the English Justice of Peace in their localities.[1]

The Bentinck administration sought to widen the role of the government in social change, to enforce the rule of law and play a decisive role in the country's destiny. Bentinck took this opportunity to reduce establishment costs by uniting the offices of the collector and magistrate in 1831. This meant that the Cornwallis era of separation of power was over and the collector was to have tighter control over local authorities. As Eric Stokes puts it, 'Exercising the office and dignity of magistrate, with command of police functions and with summary jurisdiction in rent cases, the collector was now more properly termed the district officer. The double institution of the divisional commissioner and the district officer permanently modified the Cornwallis structure and supplied the orthodox model for the future British colonial administration.' Special deputy collectors were appointed in 1833 to assist collectors with the resumption measures. On a higher plane, the Charter Act (1833) introduced the set-up of governor-general-in-council as the single legislative authority in the country. In 1834–35, Macaulay arrived as the law member of the council to draft the Indian Penal Code as a single system of law.[2] Auckland continued to implement the policies of Bentinck in a similar direction. By Act XXV of 1837, the post of *munsiff* was created to try civil cases in the *mofussil*, for any amount subject to appeal to the *sadar* court directly, for cases above Rs 5000. In 1837 again, the Police Committee sat to review justice and police in the interior. It recommended a new gradation of pay scales for darogahs in charge of police stations and re-allocated jurisdictions of magistrates for more effective control over local affairs. It retained the institution of village watch as the responsibility of landlords but advised greater supervision by magistrates.

The change was however short-lived, insofar as the collector was involved. The resumption measures discredited the union of the offices of the collector and magistrate, as some zealous collectors like Harvey

---

1. R Clarke, *The Regulations of the Government of Fort William in Bengal*, London, 1854, vols i–iii; also, *Police Committee Report on the Reform of Mofussil Police (1838)* with Minutes of Evidence, Calcutta, 1838, (hereafter, *Police Committee Report*), p. 109

2. E T Stokes, *The English Utilitarians*, Oxford, 1959, p. 164

indulged in excesses of power. The landlords, in their petitions and in their evidence before the Police Committee in 1837, strongly criticised the changes. Many officials too felt that the pressure of business on the collector and his supreme commitment to the collection of revenue, made him unfit to continue the duties of a magistrate. Act XXIV of 1837, therefore, revived the post of the superintendent of police and reorganised the separation of power.

But the other changes were accepted. Further, a number of deputy magistrates were placed in charge of the newly formed subdivisions in 1843–46. There were 34 subdivisions in 1845 but a hundred more were gradually created. No further administrative reform was undertaken until Dalhousie showed some initiative in 1854 by creating the office of the commissioner for suppression of dacoity and by sending judges on regular tours of inspection into the interior. At the same time the new Affray Law gave special powers to the magistrates to hold the belligerent parties to penalty. Public works were also seriously undertaken.

The Mutiny made the government conscious of the need for a strong and effective government and the combining of the offices of the collector and magistrate again in 1859 was a step in this direction. But all these alterations were made at the rank of the top executives. There was no administrative reorganisation at the lower level before 1860. The Indigo Revolt of 1859–1860 at the lower level, and the recommendations of the Indigo Commission for further subdivisions and more thanas to bring justice nearer to the scene of the crime, were translated into action. The police force was augmented, the salaries were enhanced and all grades welded under one central command.[3]

The extent of government and its physical limitations

But the administrative network remained hopelessly inadequate for the vast country and its teeming population. The marginal impact of the government in the interior can be measured from the following comparative lists of police establishments as they existed in 1837 and as required according to F J Halliday, secretary to the government of Bengal. The police force in the Lower Provinces in 1837 consisted of 444 darogahs, 473 mohurirs, 580 jemadars, 6,699 burkundazes, or 8,196 men altogether at an annual charge of Rs 6,23,629 for an area of 1,19,013 square miles and a population of 3,12,00,000, that is, one policeman for every fifteen square

---

3. C E Buckland, *Bengal under the Lieutenant Governors*, vol. i, pp. 229–31

miles and for about every 3,900 people. This was at a time when the strength of the police force in Ireland was at a rate of 1 to 875 people and that of the London police, 1 to 363. Halliday wished to have an establishment of 1 superintendent general, 32 sub-superintendents (one to each district), 32 assistant superintendents, 888 inspectors (one to each *thana*), 4440 jemadars (5 to each *thana*), 66,600 burkundazes (75 to each *thana*). He also wanted to dispense with the immense number of effete chowkidars, who were theoretically under the government, but practically bound to the landlords. The scheme was to ensure at least one officer to every 43 people. But the Police Committee, restrained by financial handicaps, could not implement it.[4] The situation remained unchanged for the next two decades. Though Dalhousie caused some re-shuffling at the top level in the fifties, the police force was still not equal to its task. In 1857, seventy magistrates and thirty-three subdivisional officers presided over 484 thanas and with the help of only 484 darogahs they looked after 7,23,145 persons over 1,50,000 square miles.[5]

Even after the police reforms of 1861–62 as recommended by the Police Commission (1860), Bengal was served by 50 assistant superintendents in its 38 districts including the Bihar and Assam districts, with no officer for subdivisions on grounds of economy.[6] To implement the recommendations in full, Rs 49 lakh were needed. The amount was slashed to Rs 40 lakh.[7] Financial constraints continued to impede every attempt to strengthen the police system and on the eve of another police reform in 1870, Lieutenant Governor Grey expressed his deep regret in a letter to Lord Mayo (16 October 1869) that 'financial exigencies' demanded 'a sacrifice of efficiency in the civil administration of the country'.[8] As late as 1871, therefore, an insignificant constabulary of 13,000–14,000 men remained scattered over the vast province as 'process-servers' and not as 'a preventive and detective organisation', as a critic of the system pointed out.[9]

The skeleton government was further crippled by the extremely tortuous topography of the Lower Provinces. The land was intersected by large

---

4. *Police Committee Report*, Calcutta, 1838, Appendix A, Minute by F J Halliday
5. *Papers Relating to the System of Police in the Bengal Presidency*, London, 1857, no. xv, pp. 48–75; Halliday's Minute, 30 April 1856 (hereafter, *Halliday Minute*)
6. *Calcutta Review*, xli (1865), 'The Police of Bengal', p. 288
7. C E Buckland, *Bengal under the Lieutenant Governors*, vol. i, Calcutta, 1902, p. 231
8. *Mss. Eur. D. 700*, Letter Book of Grey, 1869–70
9. *Calcutta Review*, vol. lvi (1873), 'The Bengal Police'

rivers like the Padma, the Meghna, and the Brahmaputra and their rami-
fying arteries of unforded small streams and creeks. There were long
stretches of impenetrable jungles and malarial swamps. There were very
few good roads and bridges for vehicular traffic. From the table of routes
through the territories of the Bengal Presidency, compiled by Huttman
of the military office in 1838, a vivid picture of the situation can be
obtained at a glance. The route (no. 101) from Berhampur (Murshidabad)
to Jumalpur (Mymensing) by Bauleah and Bogra, covering a stretch of
183 miles, was intersected by ten rivers including the Ganges, the
Attrai, the Ichhamati and 4 nullahs, and the road near Natore was low,
swampy and unusable except in the dry season. The route (no. 131) from
Chittagong to Sylhet, a stretch of 219 miles, was little more than a footpath
across a dozen rivers and marshes. These routes were just fit for military
traffic.[10] An effective centralised control over the country was ruled out
as a consequence. The districts were like detached units of administration.
Even within the districts, it was difficult to connect remote areas for want
of communication. Faridpur district provides a graphic picture of the
situation in 1837 as revealed in the following table:

Thana	Area	Situation to sadar	Distance
Nawabganj	162 mouzas	northeast across Padma	40 miles or 1 day's journey
Manikganj	157 mouzas	east across Padma	40 miles
Harirampur	180 mouzas	east by south across Padma	12 miles

N.B. A *mouza* has 150 huts and each hut contains roughly 8 people[11]

It has to be remembered that a *thana* consisted of an establishment of
25 people at the most. For Hooghly in 1837, the magistrate reported that
'there is not a single road in the district which a European vehicle could
traverse while the number usable for hackeries in the rains are lamentably
few'.[12] Things did not improve in the 1850s. In 1848, the total metalled

---

10. G H Huttman, *Revised Tables of Routes and Stages through the Territories
     under the Presidency of Bengal*, Calcutta, 1838

11. *Police Committee Report*, Calcutta, 1838, p. 208

12. G Toynbee, *Hooghly*, Calcutta, 1888, p. 106

road mileage in the whole of the Bengal Presidency did not exceed 2,589 miles.[13] Lieutenant W H Greathead in his report on the communication between Calcutta and Dhaka in 1855, throws light on the poor condition of the vital lines of communication from the capital to the heart of erstwhile East Bengal.[14] A S Finlay in his evidence before the Select Committee on Indian Territories in 1852–53 states:

I consider that at present there are no roads in India suitable for commercial purposes of any extent. I am aware that there are, what are called roads; there is one from Calcutta to Delhi; but that is more of a military road than anything else.[15]

The responsibility of building roads devolved on the landlords who made light of this gigantic task and the Public Works Department was not properly organised until 1858 to undertake it effectively.

The government was, doubtless, ill-equipped to bring law and order to the country. In 1838, the Police Committee headed by W W Bird admitted the weakness of the government in much the same language as used by Lord Hastings in his Minute of 2 October 1815, to describe contemporary times. The Committee acknowledged that 'the magistrates are overwhelmed. The Darogahs and their subordinate officers are corrupt, the village watchmen are poor, degraded and often worse than useless and the community at large, oppressed and inconvenienced in various ways, are not only disinclined to afford aid to the police but in most cases had rather submit quietly to be robbed than apply to the police officers for assistance to apprehend the thieves or to recover the stolen property.'[16] F J Halliday, a member of the Committee writing twenty years later as lieutenant governor in his Minute of 30 April 1856, gave no better account of law and order in the country, 'Throughout the length and breadth of the country the strong prey almost universally upon the weak and the power is but too commonly valued only as it can be turned into money.' He confessed that 'the administration of criminal justice was little better than a lottery on which the best chances are with the criminals'.[17] George Campbell in the 1870s called Bengal 'a sleepy hollow' where 'we have in fact asserted

---

13. B. J. C., 9 August 1848, no. 10
14. *Selections from the Records of the Government of India (PWD)*, vol. xix, Report of Greathead, 1855
15. P.P., xxviii (1852–53), Finlay, pp. 19–36
16. *Police Committee Report*, Calcutta, 1838, p. 2
17. *Halliday Minute*, 30 April 1856

our authority less completely than anywhere else in India and where the
people of the remote interior are in a more, so to express it, native
condition'.[18]

The 'native condition' was the village system of watch and ward
organised by the landlords to serve their own interests. But what the
government practised was virtually a dyarchy. It adopted both dispersion
and centralisation simultaneously. It kept 8000 men under the central
command and held the landlords liable for the village watch, manned by
3,00,000 chowkidars. Halliday called it irrational in 1838 'as the chain of
subordination snaps at a point where the true interest of police require
the most complete continuity'. Moreover, the landholders were held
responsible for the detection and apprehension of crime in the *mofussil*
which was altogether incompatible with the condition in which they
'had been legally placed in 1793.[19] D J McNeille, in his report on the
village watch in 1866, acknowledged this duality of the government.
Referring to the omnipotence of the local authority of the landlords, he
pointed out:

> There are but two ways of dealing with this imperium in imperio; one
> is to subvert it, the other is to recognize, confirm and work through it.
> Hitherto we have been paradoxically working in both directions.[20]

The worst feature of this system was that the landlords never failed to
make the government agencies the scapegoat for all their doings and
the government did the same by blaming the landlords for all its lapses.
The police reports are full of such allegations. To quote McNeille again,
the object of the government was 'to keep the landholders' power at a
minimum and their responsibilities at a maximum, a course which, whatever may be thought of its practical effect, involved a confession of
weakness'.[21]

In the end, the government had not only sponsored a parallel government but had also made this parallel government secure because of its own
basic weakness.

18. C E Buckland, *Bengal under the Lieutenant Governors*, vol. i, Calcutta,
    1902, pp. 484, 537

19. *Police Committee Report*, Calcutta, 1838, Appendix A; *Halliday Minute*,
    30 April 1856

20. D J McNeille, *Report on the Village Watch of the Lower Provinces of
    Bengal*, Calcutta, 1866, (hereafter, *Report on the Village Watch*) p. 28

21. *Ibid*, p. 30

The conflict over local authority

A. Village watch

The village watch was the largest and the most localised wing of the British administration. The chowkidars were described as the foundation of the village police in British India by Lord Hastings in 1815.[22] In 1837, Magistrate H C Metcalfe of Rungpore called them the eyes and ears of the magistrate without whom he would be utterly powerless.[23]

The village watches were organised and paid for by the villagers or the zamindar to whose estate they belonged. They were paid by *paikan* or *chakran* service lands where such lands were officially allocated for the purpose. But generally, they were paid a wage of three to five rupees per month. When exclusively paid and instituted by landlords, they were called *gram-saranjami* paiks. They were engaged to facilitate the collection of rent and safeguard the landlords property. In 1793, the service lands were resumed and consolidated in the estates brought under the Permanent Settlement. The government allowed a remission of revenue on these lands and the landlords concerned were expected to retain and maintain the old system of village watch in return. The claim was not made explicit in 1793. It was spelt out in the order of 8 December 1840 by S P Dampier.[24] But the measure destroyed the very system in effect without supplying a government agency in its place. There were estates where no traditional village watch supported by *chakran* grants existed. The watch was either organised by the villagers or by their zamindars on the voluntary contributions of the parties concerned. The principle of remission of revenue had no application there. The zamindars had little to do with the chowkidars when they were appointed and paid by the villagers exclusively. Some *chakran* lands were kept by the government in the name of the paiks, ghatwals and faridars in Hooghly and Birbhum districts. The landlords were asked to supervise their work and fill up the vacancies when the existing incumbent died.[25]

The landlords fully exploited the anomalous situation. They followed their traditional practice. They would keep a village watch clothed and

22. *Halliday Minute*, 30 April 1856
23. *Police Committee Report*, Calcutta, 1838, pp. 310–11
24. B. J. C., 21 February 1843, nos 130–31, Enclosure
25. D J McNeille, *Report on the Village Watch*, pp. 5–27 and Appendix A, p. 39 for number of chowkidars maintained by government, zamindars, villagers and service lands

fed, merely for their personal work. Otherwise, they would allow the
system to fall into disuse. Before 1793, the system of village watch
permitted the landlords to use the chowkidars for their personal work, in
addition to their duty to maintain public law and order. After the Permanent Settlement, no specific law was passed to separate the private function
from the public. As Millet's report in 1842 showed, the goverment had no
right to compel the zamindars to perform public duties under Regulation
22 section 8 of 1793.[26] McNeille most emphatically confirmed this
position in 1866, 'The landholders, as such, are not and never have been
bound to maintain village watchmen.'[27] The whole system was voluntary
and the government tried unjustifiably to make it compulsory for the
landlords. The consequence was obvious. It was a chronic complaint by
the magistrates that chowkidars were employed by the landlords for
collection of rent and oppression of ryots. E A Samuells, officiating
magistrate, Hooghly, in his report of 10 December 1836 on the police of
his district, wrote, 'In nine cases out of ten, he (the *chowkidar*) is to be
found ranged upon the side of the zamindar, engaged in encouraging those
acts of violence which he is expressly employed to prevent—the active
agent of his landlord in the fray and his most unblushing witness in the
court.' As narrated by the commissioner of circuit at Dacca in his report
of 7 July 1837, the abuse had wider application:

> Which of the masters, I would ask, are they likely to serve with most
> alacrity and fidelity: he who exacts of them gratuitous services and
> exemplary obedience or he from whom they daily receive the staff of
> life, to whom they owe their election and whose breath unmakes them
> as his breath hath made?
>
> So if the landholder desires to suppress information of moment to
> the judicial authorities or extend his protection to a proclaimed
> criminal, he will, with a few exceptions, find in the village chowkidars
> ready and obsequious instruments to his plans. That such is a case far
> from infrequent is notorious to all who have been employed for any
> time in the interior.[28]

The practice went on for decades, as can be gathered from police
reports. In his Minute of 30 April 1856, Halliday ascribed the crumbling
state of the *chowkidari* system to usurpation and abuse by landlords. The

---

26. *Halliday Minute*, 30 April 1856
27. D J McNeille, *Report on the Village Watch*, pp. 23–27
28. *Police Committee Report*, Calcutta, 1838, pp. 187, 377

abstract of replies of the magistrates to the circular on the question of 13 November 1854 on which he based his observation, shows that the government had only succeeded in legalising the shocking abuse of the village watch by landlords in the past.[29]

There were two aspects to this abuse. One was the direct employment of the chowkidars for the collection of rent, the oppression of ryots, concealment of crime and for giving false evidence in court. The other was the fact that the payment of the village watch, supposed to be made by the landlords, was also exacted from the villagers. Sometimes, more than the stipulated amount was realised from the ryots on this pretext. The chowkidars who were maintained by *chakran* lands in the estates and were registered with the *darogah* were made special targets of attack by landlords. As they held land within the estate, many abwabs like *mathot* were levied on them as in the case of ordinary ryots. They were also engaged for private purposes. But it was the constant endeavour of the landlord to oust the *chowkidar* from his property and appropriate his land like any other *lakhiraj*.[30] These acts of spoilation had started from 1793 to avoid liabilities of village watches and it gained momentum after Millet's report in 1842, which released the landlords from any such obligation.[31] The Hooghly district provides the best illustration of such resumption of *chakran* lands by the landlords, as it contained the largest area of registered *chakran* among the districts. In 1799, it had 77,197 bighas of *chakran* land to support chowkidars. In 1833, 20,442 bighas had been alienated and 56,755 bighas remained for the purpose. In 1810, the situation was described by the magistrate as follows, 'Resumption had been carried to such an extent that their scanty provision tempts them to join the Dacoits. The landholders (and primarily Durputnidars) persist in resuming the chakran land and where resumption does not take place, the lands formerly held by these subordinate police officers have been changed for lands of an inferior quality.'[32] The story was not different in 1848–50. An inspection made in 1848 revealed that there were 163 chowkidars besides the faridars in that year. In 1850, only 42 chowkidars were left. Of the remaining 121, the lands of 107 had been resumed by landholders.[33] Joykrishna Mukherjee, a major landlord of Hooghly was

---

29. *Halliday Minute*, 30 April 1856, pp. 54–60
30. *Police Committee Report*, Calcutta, 1838, pp. 125, 187
31. *Halliday Minute*, 30 April 1856, pp. 50–51
32. G Toynbee, *Hooghly*, Calcutta, 1888, p. 50 and Appendix L
33. B. J. C., 16 April 1850, no. 149

ordered to be punished in 1855 for ousting one Bhagirath *chowkidar* from his *chakran* on a false pretext of arrears of rent of another tenure, supposedly held by him under the same landlord.[34]

The landlords were, however, interested in the official connection with regard to law and order, if the aspect of supervision and liabilities could be lifted by the government. As the superintendent of police was to find out in 1842, the landlords had a stake in the official dignity attached to the village watch when they were used for public and private purposes. He wrote, '. . . the fault has rested with the zemindars in running up both the duties and this has not been done out of consideration for their Raieuts but for the purpose of keeping up their own influence over the whole body and using the chowkidars in the collection of their rents and summoning in their Raieuts'.[35] In 1859, a magistrate confirmed the above observation when he wrote that in his district (Tirhoot) petty landholders vied with each other over *chowkidari* appointments. The *malik* having 'chowkidars under his influence, thereby gains immense power in the estate, all occurrences are laid bare before the police just in the light he chooses.' Moreover, the evidence of chowkidars carried more weight with the authorities.[36]

The landlords clearly hoped for complete delegation of official authority. As early as 1837, Prosanna Kumar Tagore proposed to the government an absolute takeover of the village watch in his Rangpur estates. He suggested that the existing *chowkidari* system should be abolished and its place taken by the *tahsil* peons and halisanas of the zamindars under the supervision of the local magistrate. He even offered to finance his scheme and stay in his estate for six months for the purpose. But the commissioner of circuit, Bauleah division, J Hawkins strongly disapproved of it and rejected the proposal on the grounds that a local magistrate would be no good at detection and prevention of crime if he was 'dependent only upon the zemindar's servants for information'. Peons were likely to report only as allowed by their master and the magistrate would 'consult the machinations of the zemindar rather than the public good'. Tagore's attempt, therefore, failed.[37] Chhakuram Sinha, a zamindar of Hooghly, in his evidence before the Police Committee, went to the extent of suggesting that 'all local enquiries made by the Darogahs should receive

34. B. J. C., 10 May 1855, nos 182–85
35. B. J. C., 21 February 1843, nos 130–31
36. B. J. C., 21 December 1860, no. 257
37. *Police Committee Report*, pp. 303–10

the counter-signature of the zemindar and his agent and that on all occasions they should act in unison'.[38]

The government, however, incorporated the landlords into the system on its own terms. The landlords subverted the system in practice and lauched an agitation to assert their right to control the chowkidars as their own creatures without reference to the magistrates. This latter strategy was adopted in opposition to S P Dampier's order of 21 August 1849, making it obligatory for the landlords to nominate chowkidars at the wish of the magistrate and maintain them. Joykrishna Mukherjee led the opposition in 1850 as he had a dispute over this order with the deputy magistrate of Jehanabad, Hooghly. He organised a collection of petitions to be made to the government by the landlords of Hooghly, Nadia and Burdwan. Their text was the same, though they were sent separately signed by each landlord, and they challenged the government's right of coercion in the matter. They emphatically pointed out that the chowkidars were zamindari servants and the government had no claim to their service. They reinforced their argument by showing the legal loopholes already admitted by the government and declared that Dampier's action was unwarranted. They even alleged that the government was abusing their police.[39] The government was put on the defensive and it sought to create a regular paid village watch by levying a *chowkidari* tax. A Draft Act to that effect was made public in 1851.

The British Indian Assoication was formed in that year and the Association took up the cause immediately in right earnest. In a strongly worded petition (26 November 1851), it castigated the government's attempt to shift the responsibility of village watch on to the landlords and called the proposed tax arbitrary and illegal. It argued that the government should maintain its police out of land revenue and honour the provisions of the Permanent Settlement. The *coup de grace* came from Chief Justice, Sir Barnes Peacock, who supported their stand in a Minute of 6 March 1854 and Lord Dalhousie made the debate conclusive in the landlords' favour in his Minute of 14 April 1854. He wrote: 'It may be that a scheme involving so sweeping a change as that now recommended will be considered by the government to be premature.'[40] But the bill was again taken up by the Legislative Council in 1856. The British Indian Association petitioned the government on 4 November 1856 against the renewed attempt at *chowkidari* tax and asked the authorities to keep clear of this

---

38. *Ibid*, Minutes of Evidence, Chhakuram Sinha, Q. 663
39. B. J. C., 22 January 1851, nos 147–51
40. D J McNeille, *Report on the Village Watch*, pp. 31–36

institution nominated by the landlords and paid by the villagers. This was backed up by another petition on 24 November 1857. In a petition of 16 February 1857, it withdrew all obligations of the landlords towards discharging police duties. They were called obsolete and the government was advised to have its own police for detective and preventive purposes.[41] The landlords scored the final victory over the government on this issue, in the case of Joykrishna Mukherjee versus Braja Roy and the collector of Burdwan. The case which involved the dismissal of the *chowkidar*, originated in 1855 and was appealed to the Privy Council. In 1863, the Privy Council in its verdict established the authority of the zamindars over all classes of rural police.[42] The Cornwallis Regulation which had in this respect been a dead letter in practice so long was made theoretically so, in 1863. The landlords continued to be the law-givers of the countryside in their own arbitrary and selfish ways.

B. *The District Authorities: The magistrate and the darogah*

The government authority reached down to the *thana* level in a district. A *thana* consisted of several villages and was under the charge of a *thanadar* or *darogah*. A district would have a magistrate and a few of his subordinates at the *sadar* station and a network of thanas or police stations in the interior. The jurisdiction of a *thana* could range from 50 to 300 square miles with a population between 30,000 and 1,60,000. A *thana* like Rajbalhat in the Hooghly district in 1837–38 had an establishment of 1 *darogah*, 1 *mohurir*, 2 jemadars and 20 burkundazes. The cost of the establishment of one *thana* was Rs 140 with the *darogah* on a salary of Rs 25 per month and the burkundazes at Rs 4. In 1838, the cost of establishment of the police force in the entire district stood at Rs 2,302 only.[43] The darogahs were later given a graduated salary from Rs 50 to Rs 100 in three grades. But nothing came in the way of the burkundazes whose pay in most places was, according to one writer, 'below that of the common working coolie'.[44] The whole establishment was grossly underpaid. Even the landlords' clubmen got a monthly salary of rupees seven to ten. The offices were, therefore, looked upon as means to fortune rather than responsible jobs for keeping law and order. The enormous area, the scanty ill-paid

---

41. British Indian Association (BIA) *Petitions*, Calcutta, 1857
42. D J McNeille, *Report on the Village Watch*, p. 85
43. G Toynbee, *Hooghly*, Calcutta, 1888, pp. 38, 168
44. *Calcutta Review*, xli (1865), 'The Police of Bengal', p. 43

staff, their inaccessibility, inefficiency and corruption made the thanas vulnerable to local influence. The darogahs were at the command of the highest bidder. They would allow the most notorious offender to escape for a sufficient bribe. The landlords, being the rich section of the community, could bribe the darogahs successfully to hush up their crimes. This *darogah*–landlord collusion has been recorded in the blackest colours since the time of Lord Hastings. We have the evidence of Dwarakanath Tagore, the leader of the landlord community before the Police Committee in 1838, substantiating such collusion:

> I think that from the Darogah to the lowest peon, the whole of them are a corrupt set of people—a single case could not be got out of their hands without paying money—the wealthy always get advantage over the poor. In quarrels between zemindars and Indigo Planters, large sums are expended to bribe these people . . . If a jemadar or peon is sent to village for any enquiry, there is immediately a tax levied by them from all ryots of the village through the gomastah of the zemindar . . .

He himself paid bribes to darogahs to obtain his ends. Zamindars gave prior authority to their gomastahs to bribe the police. They passed such items in their *mofussil* accounts without enquiry if the case was won. To know that it had been paid, the landlords often sent friends or confidential servants to pay it. The mukhtears got ten per cent on such bribes paid to the police. Apart from direct bribes, they got salaries or presents from zamindars at certain periods of the year and were provided with food while on enquiry.[45] The situation remained unaltered even after the introduction of a better grade of salaries for darogahs. The police report for 1842 describes the police in Jessore thus, 'A more rascally or useless set of police officers are not to be found than in this district. They are all under the influence of the large zemindars and nothing but money will induce them to exert themselves and then the highest pay or the person of most influence carries the day'.[46] As Girish Bose, a *darogah* himself admitted before the Indigo Commission in 1860, the darogahs in Nadia in 10 out of 16 cases took bribes and were purchased by the rich. The burkundazes and jemadars were all corrupt.[47] During the Mutiny, a mass of correspondence between the zamindar and his local agent was seized and 'some of these

---

45. *Police Committee Report*, Calcutta, 1838, Minutes of Evidence, Dwarakanath Tagore, Q. 264–76, Adam, Q. 486 and Appendix A, p. 26
46. *Police Reports for the Lower Provinces of Bengal* (hereafter, *Police Report*), *(1842), second half*, Jessore, p. 58
47. P.P., xliv (1861), R. I. C., Girish Bose, Q. 3471

70 Tensions in Bengal Rural Society

letters too,' as H T Prinsep puts it, 'asked for money to bribe us and other officials'. The zamindar's accounts also showed some payments made under this heading.[48]

The last weapon in the hands of the landlord to subvert the darogahs was to bring a false case against an upright officer for his removal. The darogahs were liable to the displeasure of the magistrate and an off-hand dismissal at the slightest annoyance. We learn from the petition of Ram-kishore Ghose, darogah of Sherpur thana, Mymensing, that he was asked by the joint magistrate to arrest zamindar Nandamohan Choudhury of Sherpur for creating disturbances. He obliged and the zamindar brought a false case against him through one of his ryots alleging oppression, for which he was dismissed by the same joint magistrate.[49] In Nadia, the thanas Santipur, Ranaghat and Ballee never retained a darogah unbribed by the powerful zamindars residing there for any length of time, according to the police report for 1841.[50]

When in the pay of a zamindar, the darogah aided and abetted him in his crime, and refused to move any appeal from the victim of aggression. Such was the case in an affray between the local zamindar and the planters Speede and Rainey, co-partners of the same estate in Jessore. The darogah concerned forcibly prevented them from sowing arrowroot in the disputed land and did not help them even under orders from the magistrate. He leagued with the zamindar's lathials, about 300 strong, who were attacking the factory. The connivance of the darogah was proved and he was dismissed.[51]

The magistrate and his subordinates in the sadar station were far more helpless than the agencies of thanadars and chowkidars on whom they entirely depended for asserting their authority. The latter generally went over to the landlords' side and the magistrate's power remained confined to the sadar station only. The enormous physical difficulties of governing the country were enough to make his superintendence of the charge impossible. The Police Committee in 1838 concluded that 'a very baneful influence on the efficiency of the police and the comfort of its inhabitants is the great extent of country over which the jurisdiction of each magistrate extends'.[52] Samuel Wauchope (1844–73) gives a vivid picutre of his predicament in one of his private letters to England while he was serving

48. *Mss. Eur. C. 97/I-III*, Three Generations in India, Part III, pp. 343–44
49. B. J. C., 16 January, 1840, no. 39
50. *Police Report (1841), second half*, Nadia, p. 80
51. B. J. C., 27 May 1841, nos 11–17
52. *Police Committee Report*, Calcutta, 1838, p. 6

as a young magistrate in Hooghly. In 1844 he took over as magistrate of Hooghly which had a population of nearly three million in an area extending 50 miles from the north to the south and 60 miles from the east to the west. He was the sole magistrate as there were no subdivisions. The uncovenanted deputy magistrate was subservient to the superintendent of police. A judge looked after the cases. He refers to that period as the 'old days of utter lawlessness'.[53] In the early period of the union of the offices of collector and magistrate (1831–39) and again from 1859, the magistrate had also to perform the duties of a collector and collection of revenue superseded all other duties. The responsibilities of law and order were relegated to a secondary position, and business of revenue alone exhausted the energies of the most energetic magistrate and kept him confined to the *sadar* throughout the year. He was also liable to frequent transfer. His position vis-a-vis the local authority of the landlords finds a graphic description in an article in the *Calcutta Review* in 1844:

Landholders in every district of Bengal have established a reign of terror . . . Its foundations are the same, viz. an unlimited command of false witnesses and a tribunal from which is practically banished every check which can distinguish a Court of Law from a butcher's shambles. Against the combined treachery of every agent by whom he is surrounded, what can avail the most angelic character of a solitary English youth of five and twenty, isolated in a vast district as large as the three Ridings of Yorkshire.[54]

J P Wise, a Eurpoean zamindar of Dacca in his evidence before the Colonisation Committee in 1857 described his contemporary situation in identical terms:

Throughout Bengal, there is a complicated system of oppression . . . The young magistrate shifted about from place to place, is no protection; money has its influence and the powerful succeeds. How can it be otherwise? The magistrate when yet an inexperienced youth, is put over a large district with perhaps 5000 towns and a million of people; he is almost a stranger to the language and only two or three years from college; his points of weakness are weighed to a nicety and are worked upon by the most crafty people in the world.[55]

53. Samuel Wauchope Papers, Archives of the Centre of South Asian Studies, Cambridge
54. *Calcutta Review*, vol. i (1844), 'The Rural Population of Bengal', p. 196
55. P.P., vii (1857–58), Part I, J P Wise, Q. 2643

Many of the magistrates began their careers with a heavy loan from the landlords who served as their banians in the city to curry favour. The landlords lent money to the magistrates and judges in the *mofussil* to neutralise their power in their estates.[56] They were also not above corruption. Gross cases of corruption and indebtedness, prejudicial to independent action, were reported against magistrates and commissioners of police like Sturt, Birch, Patton, Ousley, Barry and others. Sturt, collector of Bakarganj was found guilty of embezzlement of Rs 50,000 from the treasury and Barry, deputy magistrate, Serajganj, Pabna, was found using his authority for private purposes like holding *benami* estates. The Calcutta police commissioners who were heavily indebted to merchants like Motilal Seal and Dalhousie wrote thus on discovery of the affair, '. . . the Calcutta Police office is no better than an Augean stable and like it must be washed clear'.[57]

Sometimes services were also purchased by offering land and property. Umeshchandra Roy, zamindar of Santipur, offered some land to Mr Law, the deputy magistrate, and further assisted him in building a house. After Law arrested some of his lathials for creating trouble and deposed against him in a case privately, Roy took umbrage and brought a case against Law for holding land without lease.[58] Where these methods of bribing failed, petitions alleging corruption and misconduct against the magistrates were drawn up in the names of their ryots and agents to persuade the government to secure their transfer or discredit them. Such petitions were brought against Reily, the commissioner of Sunderbans, for a private deal with some grantees to allow them leases at a concessional rate.[59] Iswarchandra Ghosal, the deputy magistrate of Jehanabad, Hooghly, annoyed Joykrishna Mukherjee by his orders to appoint chowkidars at the landlord's expense. The latter then moved a petition against him by one of his agents, accusing him of misconduct including immoral traffic with a brahmani woman.[60]

A common tactic was to harass the officials by false cases and intimidation. Ramratan Roy and Haronath Roy of Narail, Jessore, were tried in

56. *Mss. Eur. C. 97/III*, pp. 60–62
57. *Scottish Record Office GD 45/6/101*, Dalhousie Muniments, Letter to Sir John Littler, 6 July 1849, re Major Birch and Patton and 3 November 1849, re Col. Ousley and Captain Hicks; H Beveridge, *Bakarganj*, London, 1876, p. 339 for Sturt; B. J. C., 24 July 1850, no. 97 for Barry
58. B. J. C., 27 March 1850, no. 142A
59. B. R. C., 10 December 1857, no. 42
60. B. J. C., 22 August 1849, nos 111–14

several cases by the principal *sadar amin*, Lokenath Bose. They tried to win him over by intimidation 'in various ways with a view to conciliate me on their behalf' as he put it himself. Failing this, they brought a case to the *sadar* court stating that Lokenath's father had executed a bond of Rs 9,000 to one Bhagabati Charan Ganguly of Bagbazar twenty-five years ago which was purchased by them and a case of bill of discovery was brought against Lokenath and his brothers. An attorney of the Supreme Court was made to file an affidavit to that effect. Lokenath was disqualified to try their cases and thus bypassed.[61]

Some magistrates could not be corrupted or harassed. They tried to enforce law and order with their small police force and the landlords took the field against them with their formidable army of clubmen. Both sides fired pistols and charged with spears and sticks. Harvey narrowly escaped being manhandled during his encounter with the Chittagong landlords in 1837. The Nakashipara zamindars overpowered the magistrate and his burkundazes on more than one occasion in the 1850s. They kept lathials up to 1000 men and openly defied the police for years. The magistrate confessed that the police were no match for them. Keshabchandra and Ishwarchandra themselves led the team with guns and pistols, threatening to shoot the *darogah* and finally carried away two of their own men from custody, as reported by Jackson during his inspection of Nadia.

Mohan Meah and Gagan Meah, the taluqdars of Bakarganj, were ordered to be arrested for creating disturbances. They fortified their house with a ditch and palisades and resisted the police with 300–400 armed men equipped with guns, spears, bows and arrows. The ordinary police force of a *thana* failed in their attempt. Then, chowkidars and burkundazes of several thanas and the neighbouring zamindars were asked to assist. An army of three darogahs, 300 chowkidars and 30–40 burkundazes finally approached their house. As they opened fire, most of the chowkidars and burkundazes fled. One *darogah* and a *burkundaze* were severely wounded but the Meahs could not be captured. The magistrate of Bakarganj admitted that the police burkundazes with their swords and shields were no match for the trained spearsmen generally employed by the landholders.[62]

61. B. J. C., 23 May 1849, nos 149–50
62. B. C. J. C., 24 February 1837, no. 46; 24 January 1837, no. 55 for Harvey; B. J. C., 12 January 1854, no. 149 and 2 March 1854, no. 5 for Nakashipara zamindars; B. J. C., 16 February 1854, no. 86 for Mohan and Gagan Meahs

The courts

The courts of the magistrate and the judge were located in the *sadar* station. It was extremely difficult for poor peasants to come from the remote interior to the *sadar* station and file a suit. Alexander Ross, judge of *sadar diwani adalat* in his Minute of 22 May 1832 wrote:

> In the most trivial cases, they are compelled to undergo the fatigue of a journey to the station of the magistrate, in many cases exceeding a distance of 100 miles, to submit to the harassment of a daily attendance in the Magistrate's court for weeks together and to suffer all the inconveniences and often distress occasioned by a long absence from their homes and interruption to their occupation.[63]

The situation did not improve in the remote interior even in the 1850s. In 1858, a district like Bakarganj (as big as Wales) had seven civil and criminal courts, manned by a magistrate, an assistant magistrate, three deputy magistrates, three civil court officers, the principal *sadar amin*, the *sadar amin* and the *cazee*. But all of them sat at the headquarters. The sea-shore stations in the south of the district were without any court and the people there had to undertake five days' journey to reach Barisal and get in touch with the collectorate and criminal courts. This again involved 'crossing and re-crossing a great many formidable rivers,' as the inhabitants of the area put it in their petition to the registrar of the *sadar* court in 1860. The consequence was a denial of justice and manslaughter was a common occurrence. Such hardships were common in other districts and resulted in a dislike of the people to resort of the government.[64]

The minimum cost of lodging a plaint was Rs 1 for a case of the value of Rs 16. Private agents like mukhtears had to be paid for separately and the minor officials of the court bribed, to get the file moving. Here is a table showing cost of suit and defence in the *zillah* court:

(a) Cost of Plaintiff sueing for 150 bighas of land
    bearing revenue; value Rs 930
    Institution stamps: Rs 50
    Miscellaneous stamps: Rs 9
    Pay of Peons: Rs 80
    Vakeel's fees: Rs 46
    Witness Maintenance: Rs 9   = Total Rs 194

Contd..

---

63. *Police Committee Report*, Calcutta, 1838, Minute of Ross, p. 6
64. B. J. C., 18 September 1860, no. 184

(b) Cost of defendant in similar break-up		= Total Rs 90
(c) Court of Appeal:	Appellant	= Total Rs 108
	Defendant	= Total Rs 52
(d) Sudder Court:	Appellant	= Total Rs 128
	Respondent	= Total Rs 102

Source: P.P., xii (1831–32), Mackenzie Q. 421

The whole procedure of lodging a plaint – plea, peons and witnesses – was indeed prohibitive for the poor, due to expense, delay, harassment and the formality of a written presentation. Only the rich and the educated could afford such sophisticated, legal luxuries. They could keep a number of vakeels at the *sadar* to represent them and manage their cases. As early as 1789, Shore observed that all the principal zamindars had their vakeels in Calcutta. From the beginning the courts were converted into engines of oppression by the rich landlords. Again in the Minute of 18 June 1789 Shore noted that the people preferred 'short injustice' to 'protracted justice' which accounted for the innumerable false complaints lodged for the sole purpose of defeating and interrupting the measures of the government. 'When the end to be obtained by preferring them is answered,' he observed, 'the complaints disappear'. H Strachey, judge in Midnapore wrote in 1802 deploring the delays, the long procedures and intricacy of the trials. As false witnesses were easely procured by paying very little money, it was easy to fabricate cases. He admitted that 'the natives have attained a sort of legal knowledge as it is called, that is to say, a skill in the arts of collusion, intrigue, perjury and subornation which enables them to perplex and baffle us with infinite facility'. In his opinion, 'a rich man can seldom be convicted of a crime at goal delivery. If committed on the strongest positive testimony before the magistrate, he without difficulty brings twenty witnesses in his trial to swear an alibi or anything else that may suit his case or he can bribe the prosecutor or his material witnesses.' False complaints and conspiracies supported by perjury were common. Strachey regretted the fact that 'British regulations have created a class of informers, sharpers, intriguers, suborners and false witnesses.'[65]

---

65. P.P., vii, *Fifth Report*, Appendix 1 for Shore's Minute of 18 June 1789, pp. 187–190 and Appendix 10 for Strachey; also E G Drake-Brockman, *Notes on the Early Judicial Administration of the District of Midnapore*, Midnapore, 1904, pp. 21–22

The author of '*An Enquiry into the Alleged Proneness to Litigation of the Natives of India*' noted, in 1830, that litigations here as in England, were more common among the upper and middle classes to whom property belonged. The landlords made full use of it to realise their demands. The amount of revenue realised from stamp duty between 1 May 1828 and 30 April 1829 was a staggering Rs 9,40,761 and in view of the expenses involved in a suit, the addiction could be safely ascribed to the rich. The poor could not afford it, as evident from the fact that on the introduction of stamp duty by Cornwallis, 14,000 cases were struck off in a single court.[66] The facility of appeal to higher courts remained a chief weapon in the hands of the landlords as the poor peasants could not afford the expenses of the lower court.[67] The appeal could be taken further to the Supreme Court and the Privy Council abroad if necessary. Some landlords like the raja of Burdwan and Joykrishna Mukherjee did go up to the Privy Council against the government over *lakhiraj* and *chowkidari* questions.

The court was a puppet in the hands of the rich because of their better command of the purse. The threat of taking the matter to the court was enough to bring the weak opponent to his knees. In a straight fight in the court, the landlords could present the case better through their lawyers and witnesses, with all the sophistication needed to ensure a favourable verdict. But they took care to subvert the court in other ways. They kept a good many judges under their influence by offering them heavy loans. We have the evidence of Rammohan Roy in 1831 who explained to the Board of Control the reason for the great extent to which money was lent to judges and other civilians. It was to secure their patronage and benefit from 'their friendly disposition' when the 'natives' had estates within their jurisdictions.[68] Judge Sweetenham of Dacca borrowed money from the Dacca Bank against the security of the Wises, the zamindars of Dacca and the latter paraded their connections before the public to their advantage. Superintendent of Police Dampier reported to the government in 1850 that 'people have no confidence in our courts in cases where Wise is involved'.[69] The most glaring abuse was reported against Session Judge Wyatt in Rungpore. He was accused, by the jail *darogah* in a petition in 1852, of habitually taking bribes, borrowing money from zamindars up to Rs 40,000 and selling verdicts at huge prices. In one case, Rs 25,000

---

66. An Enquiry into the Alleged Proneness to Litigation of the Natives of India, London, 1830, *IOL Tract*, vol. xxxvi, pp. 2–49
67. P.P., v (1831), Mill, Q. 4059–60; also Appendix 39, p. 726
68. P.P., v (1831), p. 728
69. B. J. C., 17 July 1850, no. 28

was taken, of which Rs 15,000 was drawn in advance and Rs 10,000 taken after the verdict. A list of witnesses who supported the allegation included former magistrates and collectors, the magistrate incumbent and leading zamindars P K Tagore and Shambhu Roy.[70]

It was easier to corrupt the principal *sadar* amins. A typical case was reported against *Moulavee* Muhammed Kulleem, principal *sudder* amin of Bakarganj in 1853. In the case of the reversal of the sale of estate, Tuppa Selimabad, in two halves, the auction purchaser Allee Meah, bribed the principal *sadar amin* with a *taluq benami* to have the former proprietor's petition for reversal dismissed by him. On enquiry, the case was amply proved.[71] But the easiest way was to corrupt the amlahs. They were the most vulnerable to bribes because of their low pay of around Rs 30 per month. Pearychand Mitra's articles on the court amlahs in 1854, and the 'Revelations of an Orderly' (1857), give a vivid picture of the rapacity of the amlahs.[72] The Police Report for 1850 describes a case in Nadia in which the *sheristadar*, Meer Munshi, and the recordkeeper of the magistrates' office had to be removed, for tampering with witnesses in collusion with a zamindar, to secure the release of prisoners in a crime of dacoity.[73] In Midnapur about the same time, in a case to set aside sale of 8 annas (or half) of an estate between raja of Mahishadal and government, the government *vakeel* was suspended for his supposed collusion with the plaintiff with whom he had various transactions as a private individual.[74]

Attempts were also made by landlords to pack the courts with their relatives and dependents. The most notorious case was the Cogmari League in the Dinajpur courts. The main culprit was the *sheristadar* of the civil court, Bhubanmohan Neogi, a considerable zamindar on his own showing. It was the sheristadar's intention to surround himself with his own relatives and dependents and these were humorously referred to in the office as the 'Bar to Complaint' and the 'Bar to Justice.' The *sheristadar* had two brothers Rajmohan and Jagomohan Neogi in the same office with himself, a third, Huromohan Neogi, was the *sadar munsiff*, while the magistracy, collectorate and subordinate police offices were

---

70. B. J. C., 24 June 1852, nos 80–82
71. B. J. C., 21 July 1853, no. 172; also B. J. C., 4 September 1856, no. 124 for another case
72. *Calcutta Review*, xxii (1854), The Court Amlahs in Bengal; also P Khan, *The Revelations of an Orderly*, Calcutta, 1857
73. *Police Report 1850*, p. 58
74. H V Bayley, *A History of Midnapore*, Calcutta, 1902, p. 96

filled with men from Cogmari in *zillah* Mymensing, the family residence of the *sheristadar*. The *nazir*, the *mohurir* and the *peshkar* also had estates in the district and all of them built up property by levies from people coming to the courts. Magistrate E Latour, in his letter to the superintendent of police of 17 February 1842, declared that the police and the magistrate's courts were powerless against such conspiracy. People had no confidence in the courts. The magistrates stayed for only two or three years but they were the cause of people's ruin. The *peshkar* was connected with dacoits and they plundered Dinajpur. Bad characters swarmed into their estates for immunity from capture.[75] Similarly in Burdwan, the Chakdighi zamindars, Hari Singh Rai and his brother Kisto Rai exercised, according to Superintendent of Police Dampier (report of 30 January 1844), 'the greatest and most improper influence over the ministerial amlah and the police. No order can be passed, nothing done affecting these two men or their dependents without their receiving instant information of it and I will believe that they hold all the amlahs in their pay.' In the criminal court, the *peshkar* and the *nazir* were ryots of the zamindars. The former's father also served as the priest of the zamindars.[76] In Nadia the Palchowdhurys of Ranaghat had most of the principal amlahs as taluqdars in their estates and it was feared that they 'will not, from fear of their violence or other corrupt reasons, act against their wishes or interests in cases in courts'.[77] In Birbhum also, the *sheristadar* was a big zamindar and connected by marriage with a powerful zamindar. The *peshkar* was his brother. Other officers were his relatives and there was too much family influence in the court of the magistrate.[78]

This kind of corruption was only to be expected in a country where land was the only means of support. As a writer put it in 1857, 'Take almost anyone in the police, the revenue, the salt or the excise . . . it will be found that almost every individual has his undertenure in one or two villages or his thirty bighas or his small but independent talook'.[79]

The landlords made a mockery of the system of justice by further resorting to perjury and forgery. What Strachey wrote in 1802 about perjurers was still true in 1860. In the words of a keen observer:

---

75. B. J. C., 17 July 1843, nos 84–85; also B. J. C., 18 July 1842, nos 54–62 enclosures; also *Police Report 1841, second half*, pp. 36–37
76. B. J. C., 4 March 1844, no. 113
77. *Police Report 1841, first half*, pp. 90–91
78. *Police Report 1842, second half*, p. 64
79. *Calcutta Review*, vol. xxix, July–December (1857) 'Life in the Rice Fields', p. 135

the courts are infested by a swarm of professional witnesses who gain their daily bread by perjury . . . sometimes, they are retained in the regular service of wealthy suborners who, having estates in several zillahs, can, by moving them from one jurisdiction to another, keep them fresh for use.[80]

This was literally true. In a case before Judge Torrens of 24 Parganas, that is, Gurudas Roy of Narail vs Kalicharan Roy (9 July 1846), a certain Madhusudan, involved in false evidence before, in other districts was found out to be a hireling at a trifle. In the case of Kasinath Bandopadhyay vs Huromoni Dasi (21 July 1846) before Torrens, one Rajkrishna Bose was alleged to be in the habit of giving false evidence and forging false deeds.[81] The police report of 1842 describes how Umeshchandra Roy and his brother, Bhagaban Roy, zamindars of Santipur, Nadia, committed subornation against one Dashu Pramanik, to whom the first was heavily indebted and bore a grudge for not making up two cases of illegal imprisonment. The case failed and the perjurer was punished but the instigating zamindar escaped punishment. The report concludes:

In fact, from the Rajah down to the lowest Talookdar with very few honourable exceptions, no zumeendar in Lower Provinces would hesitate at subornation of perjury to procure his own ends. It is one of their modes of attack and defence to which apparently they attach no moral delinquency.[82]

Forgery accompanied perjury. Mohadeb Das, a notorious forger in Midnapur, was heavily punished for his established practice of forging mostly kobuliyats and paddy contracts in the zamindar's interest. The most credible version of the sorry state of affairs comes from the pen of Pearychand Mitra, a young Bengal critic of zamindari abuse:

Some of the zamindars have forgers at their command and on such occasion (false cases) the services of those skilful men are sure to be at high premium. As for witnesses, they are 'multitudinous as the leaves of vallambrosa,' so that one rupee a head is almost a fixed price. The Court Amlahs receive parvanis or annual presents from zemindars; and special fees in such cases are and must be the sure means of ensuring

---

80. *Calcutta Review*, vol. xxxiv, January–July (1860), 'The Law Courts of Bengal Presidency', p. 64.
81. *Decisions of the Zillah Courts*, 24 Parganas, 1846, pp. 46–57
82. *Calcutta Review*, vol. i (1844), 'The Rural Population of Bengal', p. 215

triumph over the opposite party. And, with such an amount of armoury and ammunition, the zemindar will in nine cases out of ten obtain the verdict, despite the sagacity of the judges who must form opinions from what is judicially before them. When the cases are tried on appeal by European Judges, the Amlahs are of course not put to much trouble on account of the zemindar. A few words and the decree is affirmed.[83]

The racket was extended to the *sadar diwani adalat*. Joykrishna Mukherjee of Uttarpara, Hooghly, kept a group of seven vakeels at the *sadar diwani adalat* who indiscriminately admitted special appeals by certificate. One judge alone had to do the work of rejecting these appeals. The result was that in 1848, 1,106 appeals were admitted against 799 rejected. The registrar discovered the racket and dismissed the vakeels on the ground that special appeals should be special and restrictive. *Mofussil* decisions could not be made unnecessarily, and were subject to appeal of the harassed parties who got a decree from the lower court. Joykrishna petitioned the government on 1 August 1849 against the decision, pleading that it snapped the link of the *sadar diwani adalt* with the *mofussil*. But when it was referred to the Landholders' Society, they went against Joykrishna. The vakeels were in his pay and certified any appeal taken to the court.[84] Even the Supreme Court was not immune from this kind of influence. Joychand Palchowdhury of Ranaghat was under summons of arrest from the Supreme Court on a charge of illegal imprisonment of some people in his house. When the bailiff approached him in Calcutta, his followers told him that Joychand could purchase the lives of three men involved in the Supreme Court.[85]

The parallel government or the *imperium in imperio*

There was apparently little government control in this period. The scaffold was badly battered and subverted by the landlords. There were large areas left to be self-governed by them. In his evidence before the Police Committee in 1838, William Adam, the famous author of the report on vernacular education and perhaps the best informed person about the

83. *Calcutta Review*, vol. vi, July–December (1846), 'Zemindar and Ryot',
    p. 344; H. V. Bayley, *Report on the Settlement of the Majnumutha Estate
    in Midnapore (1844)*, Calcutta, 1884 (hereafter, *Report on the Settlement
    of Majnumutha Estate*), pp. 241–42
84. B. J. C., 29 January 1851, nos 30–32
85. B. J. C., 1 April 1844, nos 112–14

happenings in the interior, had the following to say about great zamindars like the raja of Burdwan or the nawab of Murshidabad:

> In point of fact, these men do exercise an 'imperium in imperio' which has in many instances forced itself on my attention and which is, I believe, in many instances paramount in the estimation of the people to the authority of Government. Can you destroy this influence? You cannot. It belongs to their position, their wealth, their property, their caste, their descent etc.[86]

D J McNeille, in course of his enquiry into the village watch, came to know the interior equally intimately and he discovered in 1866 that the same 'imperium in imperio' (he used the same expression) instead of being destroyed, had grown from strength to strength:

> The great radical evil which has hitherto so greatly weakened the arm of the executive in dealing with crime in this country is one much wider in its character than the underpayment of village watchmen. It is the utter inability of the public authorities to secure the co-operation of the people in the administration of the law ... But it is in great part owing to the operation of a power which is established throughout the land with a far firmer root in the minds and habits of the people than the whole authority of Government. This is the power of the landholders and their local agents whose reign, silently acquiesced in, extends to every house, in every village of the country and whose influence is used in support of or in antagonism to the law, just as may appear most advantageous to their interests.[87]

The lathials

The lathials or the clubmen were the police of this parallel government. They were recruited from the disbanded militia of former independent chiefs, Brajabashis or upcountrymen in search of a career in the Lower Provinces, evicted peasants who looked for a living and the *goala* caste reputed for their martial qualities. Almost every landlord kept over one hundred such men. Some zamindars like the Baboos of Nakashipara kept up to a thousand men. But it was not necessary to keep them in readiness all

---

86. *Police Committee Report*, Calcutta, 1838, Minutes of Evidence, Adam, p. 51
87. D J McNeille, *Report on the Village Watch*, Calcutta, 1866, p. 28

the time in such numbers. They could be hired, as many as required, on the eve of a disturbance. They offered their services themselves.[88] Most of the dacoits formed part of the landlord's militia and their masters protected them in every way from being captured. The Palchowdhurys of Ranaghat, Gokul Krishna Ghose of Hooghly, Biswanath Sircar of Bagoora, Prankisto Pal of Latudaha, Nadia, and the zamindars of Nakashipara were notorious for their involvement in dacoity.[89] The confession of a dacoit, Bisto Ghose, to the commissioner for suppression of dacoity reveals that he was employed by the Nakashipara zamindars on a wage of seven to eight rupees and promised protection by including his name in a list showing him in their service. The lathials tried to eke out a living by dacoity, with the knowledge of their patrons. As lathials and dacoits impersonated each other mutually and got ready asylum in the zamindar's *cutcherry*, the commissioner found it impossible to suppress dacoity.[90] According to Commissioner E Jackson, Keshab Baboo of Nakashipara had half of the absconded dacoits in the country in his pay as lathials in 1854.[91] This was especially because the zamindars preferred a 'shukt budmash' or a tough rogue to other men, as Sreemonto Ghose, another dacoit put it in his confession. With five or six such men, they could plunder a whole village which the respectable servants would not undertake to do. The Palchowdhurys of Ranaghat frequently collected large bands of ruffians to gain their ends in land disputes by force and intimidation. They were used in family quarrels like the one between Ishan Baboo and Keshab Baboo of Nakashipara which looked like a civil war.[92]

Sometimes, the fight would be between distant rural zamindars. Thus, one Muhammad Ali, a zamindar of Burdwan invaded the territory of a Hooghly landlord with his lathials and overpowered a *darogah* in the process in 1851.[93] Absenteeism was no bar to such aggression. Radhakanta Dev of Shovabazar, Calcutta, had a quarrel with Baikunthanath

---

88. P.P., iv (1959), Forbes, Q. 2442–53, Underhill, Q. 4773
89. B. J. C., 27 March 1838, no. 106 for Gokul Krishna Ghose; *Police Report 1845*, p. 27 for Biswanath Sircar; *Police Report 1850*, p. 45 and that for *1852*, p. 45 for the Nakashipara and Latudaha zamindars
90. *Report of the Commissioner for Suppression of Dacoity in Bengal*, 1855, no. 53, pp. 55–56
91. *Report of the Commissioner for Suppression of Dacoity in Bengal*, 1854, no. 160, p. 18
92. *Ibid*, for 1856, Appendix A
93. B. J. C., 10 December 1851, no. 106

Munshi of Taki over the control of a market in Serampur, Hooghly. The *munshi* had attacked the raja's farmer who superintended the market for him. Radhakanta, who kept 40–50 lathials in his Shovabazar house, increased the number and sent a large reinforcement to the spot from Calcutta. Two persons were killed in the ensuing violence.[94] Sibnath Ghose, an absentee *taluqdar* who shared an estate with Rainey, a planter in Khulna, carried on a civil war with him for years by ordering his men from Calcutta. The superintendent of police was of the opinion that the absentee landlords could prevent such acts by orders to their agents.[95] Joychand Palchowdhury bought a zamindari in Burdwan in 1841 *benami* and wanted to oust a *patnidar*. A force of 300 men, collected from Hooghly and Naida and armed with swords, lathis, bows, arrows and rockets challenged the *patnidar*. Both sides fired rockets and showered arrows. The fight lasted for three hours and many people were wounded on either side. The *darogah* and his men failed to resist them and were ultimately bought over by the Palchowdhurys.[96]

More than one magistrate confessed in the course of the period that the lathials were far too strong for the effete police of the government. In 1837, W H Elliott, then magistrate of Murshidabad, contrasted the two forces in some detail. A *burkundaz* was paid Rs 4 per month whereas a *sardar* was paid Rs 5 to 7 on a regular basis as well as nazars or tributes from the parties seized. A good *sardar* frequently received Rs 10 in advance for disturbance and up to Rs 100 for his services afterwards. The obstructing *burkundaz* was often got rid of by his own *darogah* who connived with the enemy, whereas the zamindar's men got all sorts of protection from their masters. They were kept hidden in the estate or moved from *zillah* to *zillah* to prevent their arrest. Their families received liberal support. He concluded:

> What a contrast to all this does the life of a police burkundaz afford: and is it to be wondered at that the men who fill this grade cannot stand in the day of trial against the picked men of the other classes who are opposed to them?[97]

The rule of *lathi* was more effective than the rule of law. It lasted throughout the nineteenth century. J C Jack describes how Nilkantha Saha,

---

94. B. J. C., 26 July 1848, nos 86–87; B. J. C., 9 August 1848, no. 104; B. J. C., 16 August 1848, no. 131
95. B. J. C., 5 February 1844, nos 64–65
96. *Police Report 1841, second half*, p. 93
97. *Police Committee Report*, Calcutta, 1838, p. 349

a zamindar of Bakarganj, began in 1844 to build up what he himself described as his 'lathir zamindari' or rule of *lathi* or club. The criminal annals for his estate alone recorded in a period of fifty years more than forty serious riots, in twenty of which lives were lost.[98]

The zamindari system of justice

The majority of the rural people preferred the quick, summary and cheap justice, meted out at their door by the landlords in their arbitrary and partial way, to government institutions. Adam, in his evidence before the Police Committee in 1838, gave an eye-witness account:

> In Murshidabad district, zamindars generally exercise an undefined jurisdiction over their own ryots who submit to their authority to the extent of money-fines and imprisonment for two or three days. The people voluntarily prefer their complaints to this tribunal in the confidence that their representations will be fully understood. I was led to conclude that the authority of the Nawab of Murshidabad or the assumptions of his dependents overlaid and neutralised the authority of the officers of Government.[99]

In 1846, Pearychand Mitra found the zamindars continuing to take cognisance of civil and criminal cases in their zamindaris although prohibited by law. They exercised the powers of judges and magistrates. The ryots submitted to their decisions in consequence of the inefficacy of the judicial institutions and the great expense and trouble in resorting to them.[100] When the landlord's interest was not involved, the indigenous justice was fair and cheap, as it came from a man on the spot who was thoroughly conversant with the customary law of the land and native expectations. Seraj Biswas, a ryot of Nadia, in his evidence before the Indigo Commission, spoke favourably of zamindari justice 'because the zamindar hears the complaints and fines a man according to his means'.[101] As a writer pointed out in the *Calcutta Review* in 1865, 'the zemindar, too, is generally sufficiently politic to give some support to the fabric of his power. He knows within what limits his violence and extortion will be endured and beyond those limits, he does not care to go. In order that he may be allowed

98. J C Jack, *Bakarganj Settlement Report* (*1900–08*), Calcutta, 1915, p. 85

99. *Police Committee Report*, Calcutta, 1838, p. 77

100. *Calcutta Review*, vol. vi (1846) 'Zamindar and Ryot', p. 336

101. R. I. C., Q. 1144

to be unjust where his interests require it, he endeavours to be just where
they are not concerned; so that in much that comes before him, he gives
a shrewd, prompt, cheap and popular decision more delightful and satisfactory to the tenantry.'[102] They expected no fee as judges but extracted
from the pockets of the suitors fines to line their purses. Many of them
resorted to physical punishments like beating with shoes in order to
humiliate. Some of them kept regular jails for the purpose of imprisonment. The Roys of Narail and the Palchowdhurys of Ranaghat were
notorious for their private jails.[103] The practice prevailed down the century. Here is a remarkable extract from the diary of a landlord of Bakarganj
as it fell into the hands of Jack in his tour of the district:

3 February:
> Sent Rahimuddi and Rajkumar Sil to bring in three or four men who
> were fined but the money not yet realised. Tried a case of poisoning
> Jiaruddi by his wife with the help of her lover Arman Ali. The woman
> is not our tenant, so on carefully considering the evidence produced
> before me, the guilt of Arman Ali having been proved, I have fined him
> Rs. 100. This is a serious case of murder . . . The Police failed to detect
> anybody . . . Samaruddi who was fined Rs. 10 by the Mirdha, paid
> Rs. 2 as he was too poor to pay more and he was excused.[104]

The alternative system of justice was complete with courts of appeal for
hearing from the lower courts. In Rajshahi, 'zamindari bichar' or justice
was the highest mark of the landlord's authority. 'In some estates, there
is a regular hierarchy of courts,' observed O'Malley in his gazetteer of the
district, 'an appeal lying from the Naib to the Diwan or Manager and from
the latter to the proprietor himself just like a court of first instance, a judge
and the High Court'.[105]

Conclusion

The ultimate upshot of this subversive activity was that the British system
of justice and police failed to strike a new balance of power in the interior.

---

102. *Calcutta Review*, vol. xl (1865) 'Criminal Administration in Bengal',
      pp. 281–84
103. *Police Report 1850*, p. 52 for the Roys of Narail; B. J. C., 1 April 1844,
      nos 112–14 for the Palchowdhurys
104. J C Jack, *Bakarganj Settlement Report (1900–08)*, Calcutta, 1915, p. 81
105. L S S O'Malley, *Bengal District Gazetteers, Rajshahi*, Calcutta, 1916,
      pp. 124–25

The *lathi raj* remained virtually unassailable. The government failed to replace it by the rule of law. The structure and processes of power in an agrarian society could not be disturbed by the inadequate government agencies. They were, by and large, converted into additional sources of strength for the rural elite. Regulations failed to ensure equality before law. Many revenue and tenancy legislations laguished for lack of enforcement. The limitation clauses of the Permanent Settlement were tampered with. *Khudkasht* ryots became rarer day by day. The *pargana* rate of rent was pushed up by false evidence of dependent ryots. Abwabs were freely collected. The power of distraint was thoroughly abused. Attachment of crop and cattle by the landlords left the peasants without the resource to establish their rights in regular suit. Notices of arrears were given without their knowledge by the amlahs of the collectorate in the pay of the landlords. The courts were used as the agency to collect real or supposed arrears of rent at an enhanced rate as legal harassment was the first thing the ryot wanted to avoid. The *benami* transactions were made under the Sale Law to quash undesirable under-tenures. The government could not ensure a free society to release the energies of the depressed majority, the producers of wealth.[106]

It is probable that the landlord's power to rig the administration appears magnified because of the chronic under-government of the province. But there is no evidence to prove that a relatively strong government in the late nineteenth century made any difference. The imperium was basically a weak government. There was no possibility of a trial of strength to test the staying power of a semi-feudal social structure. A strong government was perhaps not the only thing to call the tune. It was clearly not a problem of law and order nor the failure of a few goal-getting legislations. The whole question of land–man ratio, urban–industrial outlet, size and resources of the small peasant economy, soil and climate were involved. The landlords remained the *de facto* sovereigns as long as these factors did not undermine their position. The government could at best set the machinery of justice in motion and leave the country to its destiny.

---

106. See Chapter 6 for details

Four

Landlords and Planters: The
Uneasy Collaboration (1830–1850)

The challenge of indigo: Men, money and material

Indigo was a native crop but 'from the seventeenth to the twentieth
centuries, indigo was a fugitive among industries, wandering from Gujarat
in western India to the West Indies and then back to Bengal in eastern
India'.[1] It was chosen as one of the East India Company's major investments in cash crops in the eighteenth century. Louis Bonnard (1777) and
Carel Blume (1778) were perhaps the earliest pioneers among European
planters in Bengal whose products could compete with the West Indian
product. Many West Indian slave-driving planters were also encouraged
to apply their experience in Bengal.[2] The commercial residents were in-
structed to promote this valuable cash crop by liberal advances. The plantation system was fairly established at the turn of the nineteenth century.[3]

In 1813, the opening of India to Free Trade meant that the East India
Company had to give up its monopoly in everything except opium and

1. B Kling, *The Blue Mutiny*, Philadelphia, 1966, p. 15
2. D H Buchanan, *The Development of Capitalist Enterprise in India*, New
   York, 1934, pp. 36–38
3. R. I. C., (1860), Eden, Q. 3660; also, *East India Company, Reports and
   Documents Connected with the Proceedings of the East India Company in
   Regard to the Culture and Manufacture of Cotton-wool, Raw Silk and
   Indigo in India*, London, 1836; see the section on indigo

salt. Remittance was made difficult as a result. As Indian raw cotton and cotton piece-goods lost their market with the competition of American raw cotton and Lancashire piece-goods from the second decade onwards, India was left with few items of export. Her bullion could not be taken out to pay dividends to the Company's shareholders. Indigo was the answer. It had a demand in the world market. The following table shows the steady rise of indigo as an export item from Bengal (in round figures):

Indigo from Calcutta to UK (in cwt)

1812–13	49,475	1821–22	62,175
1813–14	50,096	1822–23	75,405
1814–15	68,746	1823–24	53,782
1815–16	76,661	1824–25	73,812
1816–17	58,580	1825–26	1,04,831
1817–18	48,732	1826–27	53,355
1818–19	45,642	1827–28	1,01,584
1819–20	70,932	1828–29	65,631
1820–21	51,066	1829–30	89,026

Source: P.P., x (1831–32), Part II, Appendix 34

The value of indigo exported from Bengal was estimated to be Rs 2½–3 crore in 1829.[4] The dizzy speculation, characteristic of a boom period, led to over-trading and a slump. Many agency houses faced liquidation. Though the Bentinck government chided them for irresponsible business, it allowed them to draw credit from the Bank of Bengal to survive the ordeal. Their conduct was contrasted with that of European capitalists who were hailed as responsible people of resource and enterprise.

The Charter Act (1833) terminated the trading career of the East India Company and authorised the unrestricted entry of European skill, and capital. The commercial residency was finally given up in 1836. India was whisked out of the narrow orbit of remittance trade into the world market. The finished products like cotton piece-goods, mass-produced in England in the age of the Industrial Revolution, had to be sold on reciprocity of

---

4. P.P., viii, (1831–32), General Appendix 5, no. 43, pp. 272–3

other goods. Already, between 1815 and 1824, the British exports to India had gone up from goods worth Rs 1,49,068 to Rs 11,38,167.[5] By 1830, they were being dumped in Indian warehouses without the prospect of ever being sold even at the cost price. The Free Traders' eyes naturally fell on the indigo trade which again started looking up after a short-lived slump. The existing manufacturers were marked out for encouragement and European colonisation was promoted to give it a further boost.[6]

As much of the existing production of indigo was taken up by private traders, the government had to expand its scope still further or find similar cash crops to meet the growing bill of Home-Charges. To solve the remittance problem, it resorted to indirect financing of cash crops like indigo, a process which came to be known as the 'hypothecation system'. By this system, the East India Company at home and in India, served as an exchange bank to trading houses in India. Certain staples were selected which, when consigned for London, would be treated as a source of credit and against which three-fourth of the value of the goods was to be advanced from the treasury in India to the trading parties. This was a tremendous boost to indigo cultivation. Local agency houses were no longer dependent on the private savings of officials and babus for their speculation. In 1837, the value of goods hypothecated for advances in Bengal was £9,20,858 and in 1839–40, it reached its all time high of £11,62,202 (in round figures).[7] The government clearly had a stake in indigo for remittance alone, apart from pressures in England for an expansion of private trade.

By that date, the government had begun its assault on estates by vigorous resumption of invalid tenures. The seal of the Permanent Settlement had been broken and the straitjacket of landlordism breached. The government had even started model farming in *khas* mahals, but the experiment was far from rewarding. It was looking for a new, virile agency of improvement at this take-off stage. This was the time when the merchants and existing planters in Calcutta were pressing for a mandate from the governments of England and India for such an enterprise. The

5. B N Banerjee, ed., *Sambad Patre Sekaler Katha: Selections from Samachar Darpan (1818–30)*, Calcutta, 1344 B.S., vol. i, p. 158, quoting *Samachar Darpan*, 2 September 1826, in vernacular

6. Desh-U-Lubun Ocharik of Calcutta, Letter to the author of 'View of the Present State and Future Prospects of the Free Trade and Colonization of India', London, 1830, *IOL Tract 36*, pp. 32–36; also, P.P., viii (1831–32), General Appendix 5, no. 43, pp. 272–73

7. P.P., x (1852), Appendix 2

prospective settlers and the merchants and planters clamoured for the right to hold property in the interior and summary powers to enforce indigo contracts. The question of European settlement received serious attention in parliament.

The government was prepared to legislate favourably in order to encourage European settlement in the interior. The European planters got the warmest welcome from Bentinck, despite his liberalism and ryotwari proclivities. His Minute of 30 May 1829 sums up the whole situation admirably:

> If all the ancient articles of the manufacturing produce of India are swept away and no new ones created to supply this vacuum on the exports, how will it be possible for commerce to be carried on and how can any remittance on private or public account be made to Europe? If bullion alone is to supply the balance, soon will the time arrive, when under the increased value that scarcity must give to money, it will no longer be possible to realize the revenue at its present nominal amount. It is, therefore, the bounden duty of Government to neglect no means which may call forth the vast productive powers of the country now lying inert from the want of adequate encouragement ... I am assured that much of the agricultural improvement which many of our districts exhibit may be directly traced to the indigo planters therein settled; and that as a general truth it may be stated that every factory is in its degree the centre of a circle of improvement raising the persons employed in it and the inhabitants of the immediate vicinity above the general level.[8]

Metcalfe also made an eloquent advocacy of European settlers' right to hold property in India by pointing out their political utility as sentinels of a precarious empire in the interior. They were hailed as the harbingers of improvement by the press as well. Congratulating the government on giving permission to Europeans to colonise India, the *Friend of India* wrote in 1837:

> There can no longer be any doubt that upon their settlement in India rests whatever hopes may be formed of the future improvement of the soil.[9]

Regulation 5 of 1830 armed the existing planters with summary powers of distraint for enforcement of contract for a spell. They were purged of

8. P.P., viii (1831–32), General Appendix 5, no. 46
9. *The Friend of India*, Editorial on Colonisation, 11 May 1837

the stigma of being interlopers and were admitted to official grace. Regulation 6 of 1837 opened the door for Europeans to come and hold property in their own name outside the factory site.

The planters so enfranchised constituted a major challenge to the rural society. The introduction of cash crop agriculture on a large scale and the money behind it had far-reaching consequences. It may be argued that very few planters brought capital with them from England.[10] The capital was raised locally either by the agency houses and banks or by the government system of hypothecation. It is also true that their skill was visible in the factory and not so much in the field. They hardly indulged in capitalist farming even though they held property by *benami* and the law was lax in the matter. In Nadia in 1830, most of the indigo cultivation was operated by the system of advances.[11] Nevertheless, investments were made in agriculture on a large scale. The value of cash crops was demonstrated beyond doubt. The factories were the forerunners of the modern agro-industry.

The physical presence of so many planters in the interior had a direct impact on the agrarian structure and the local politics. The following table gives a detailed picture of the European planters and their land occupation in the *mofussil* in 1830:

District	Factories	Planters	Assistants	Land occupation (bighas)
Maldah	3	24	7	70,757
Dinajpur	—	3	2	821
Purnea	8	65	12	1,31,436
Pabna	19	99	38	1,69,347
Bagura	4	18	7	14,710
Murshidadad	—	35	16	1,29,966
Birbhum	1	7	—	15,125
Nadia	19	56	18	1,59,517
Tippera	7	7	—	19,200

Contd..

10. P.P., vi (1830), Lord's Committee, Evidence of Ramsay, p. 230, R Davidson, p. 251, Harris, p. 302 and Dunlop, p. 323
11. B. C. J. C., 1 June 1830, quoted in R Saha, *British Administration in Nadia*, Appendix E

District	Factories	Planters	Assistants	Land occupation (bighas)
Dacca Jelalpur	—	74	38	1,22,151
Dacca	—	10	11	34,392
24 Parganas	—	5	2	5,100
Barasat	—	2	2	1,480
Jessore	2	63	30	1,20,633
Midnapore	2	24	1	6,870
Burdwan	—	8	6	22,258
Rangpur	2	24	7	21,405
Rajshahi	5	10	11	68,700
Mymensing	1	35	19	64,945
Murshidadad (Addl.)	—	5	1	29,500

Source: *P.P., viii (1831–32), Appendix 5, no. 60*

The landlords' response

The landlords' past relations with the planters was far from cordial. The native landlord-planters had had to face withering competition from them from the beginning of the nineteenth century. Gopimohan Tagore was one of the leading Indian planters at the turn of the century in Rangpur. He had to face stiff competition from the European planters. The Indians owned sixteen manufacturing plants in the district. The value of indigo manufactured by Indians for export was only Rs 14,000 while that of European manufacture was Rs 6,30,000. As Buchanan-Hamilton observed, the greater part of Indian manufacturers were 'poorer than when they began'.[12] The ordinary landlords bitterly complained of the planters' infiltration into their estates and of the attempts to trap their ryots by giving advances. The alleged arrears had to be worked out by ryots under compulsion decreed by the collector in 1800. This led to a series of complaints and counter-complaints lodged before the collector by landholders and the planters in 1801 criticising each other. The growing market for indigo even induced village headmen to set up vats in their holdings. In 1823, a planter wrote to the collector asking if he could prevent one of

---

12. *Mss. Eur. D. 75*, Buchanan-Hamilton Papers on Rangpur, vol. ii, pp. 56–58; also *Mss. Eur. G. 11*, Book 5, Table 38 pp. 66–67

his own ryots putting up a couple of vats within the range of his own operations.[13] The picture was no different in Dinajpur. The planters utilised the mondals or village headmen as whipping boys to thrust indigo contracts on small farmers. Buchanan-Hamilton noticed that landholders were 'very unwilling that the manufacture should be extended or even continued'. Their chief complaint was that the planters were insolent, violent, meddlesome and they caused difficulties in rent collection as they forced ryots to work out their contracts first.[14]

The indigo boom of 1823–30 led to a spectacular expansion of Indian enterprise in indigo. In Nadia alone, 140 Indian planters were recorded by the resident of Kumakhali in 1824. It brought in its wake, patent conflicts between the Indian landlord-planters and the European planters.[15] Such native enterprise in Dhaka was smothered by European planters using violence. Judge Walters, shocked at the 'open daring violence directed to the destruction of rival factories', wrote in his report:

... where is the instance in this part of the country of the native zamindar who unaided by European partners or influence, has erected indigo factories and successfully carried on the speculation without being in the end obliged to admit his more powerful neighbour to a share in his concern or being himself perhaps cast into jail for standing up in defence of his own rights?[16]

The *Asiatic Journal* in its editorial in 1836 supported this kind of vandalism by European planters to whittle down Indian competition.[17]

When colonisation or the unrestricted settling of Europeans was seriously contemplated by the government in 1829–30, the issue was widely debated in Indian circles. Many landlords were scared by the threat of the expropriation of their patrimonies by European settlers. It was also felt that they would encroach upon estates and snatch at their only means of subsistence. Another contention was that all the lands suitable for the cultivation of indigo were already taken up for the purpose and any further

13. E G Glazier, *Further Notes on Rungpore Records*, Calcutta 1876 (hereafter, *Rungpore*), pp. 26–27 and Appendix 28
14. F Buchanan-Hamilton, *Dinajpore*, Calcutta, 1833, pp. 311–16
15. R Saha, *British Administration in Nadia*, Calcutta, 1973, p. 146
16. P.P., viii (1831–32), General Appendix 5, no. 74, The Court of Directors to Bengal Government, 10 April 1832, para 17 quoting Walters
17. *The Asiatic Journal*, vol. xix (1836), 'Indigo Planters'
18. *Sarbatattwadipika* (a vernacular journal), vol. ii, no. 3, 1236 B. S. (1830–31)

competition would not be welcome.[18] In a petition to the Court of Directors in 1829, this section of landlords spelt out their fears to the government. They dreaded subversion of their authority in the *mofussil* and expressed concern at the prospect of rice being replaced by indigo, causing scarcity.[19]

But this was not the representative mood of landlords as a whole. The following by a correspondent of *Sambad Kaumudi*, a leading vernacular journal, explains the situation in 1831:

> At the time when the petition against colonization was signed, to whatever zamindar's house we could go, the chief topic of conversation was the good or evil to be expected from the English settling in this country and engaging in agriculture. Some said that evil was certainly to be anticipated from it. 'Sir' said they, 'what injustice the indigo planters are doing'. . . The zamindars replied: 'We do not anticipate any evil whatever from their coming. On the contrary, the landlords will receive more rent, more labourers will be required and they will receive higher wages; the land will be improved and we shall see many other improvements. When there is a deficiency of rain, the cultivation will be carried on by raising water by machinery. Knowledge will be promoted in the country villages. Now the people are afraid whenever they see the sahibs but then they will be familiar with them. The poor receiving higher wages, there will be a great diminution of robbery in the country.'[20]

The more influential party of landlords led by Rammohan Roy and Dwarakanath Tagore in Calcutta carried the day by their wholehearted advocacy of the planters' cause. Rammohan, in the Town Hall meeting of 15 December 1829, made a bold defence of the planters' case in support of Free Trade and colonisation:

> . . . As to indigo planters I beg to observe that I have travelled through several districts in Bengal and Behar and I found the natives residing in the neighbourhood of indigo plantations evidently better clothed and better conditioned than those who lived at a distance from such stations. There may be some partial injury done by the indigo planters; but on the whole, they have performed more good to the generality of the natives of this country than any other class of Europeans whether in or out of service.

---

19. D H Buchanan, *The Development of Capitalist Enterprise in India*, New York, 1934, pp. 36–37
20. *Sambad Kaumudi* quoted in *Bengal Hurkaru*, 22 August 1831

In this same meeting, Dwarakanath also voiced a similar optimism:

> . . . I beg to state that I have several zamindaries in various districts and
> that I have found the cultivation of indigo and residence of Europeans
> have considerably benefited the country and the community at large;
> the zamindars becoming wealthy and prosperous, the ryots materially
> improved in their condition and possessing many more comforts
> than the generality of my countrymen where indigo cultivation and
> manufacture is not carried on; the value of land in the vicinity to be
> considerably enhanced and cultivation rapidly progressing. I do not
> make these statements merely from hearsay but from personal obser-
> vation and experience, as I have visited the places referred to repeatedly
> and in consequence, am well acquainted with the character and manner
> of indigo planters. There may be a few exceptions as regards the general
> conduct of indigo planters but they were extremely limited and are
> comparatively speaking of the most trifling importance.[21]

When Rammohan reached England, he projected the same picture of
the planters before the Board of Control.[22] Able support came from the
Indian press. The *Reformer* edited by Prosanna Kumar Tagore, (Dwarakanath's cousin) published the following editorial in favour of the planters:

> . . . India wants nothing but the application of European skill and
> enterprise to render her powerful, prosperous and happy. The re-
> sources and capabilities of India are incalculable and were European
> skill and improvements more generally diffused throughout the
> country, the change would be so great, both in the condition of the
> people and the appearance of the country as to bear no resemblance
> to what it does at present . . . The idea, therefore, that the introduction
> of a few thousand more Europeans into India among eighty million of
> people would be injurious to their interests and detrimental to their
> welfare is perfectly absurd. The reverse would be the case.[23]

It may appear strange to find a substantial group of landlords defending
European planters in the general background of tension and hostility,
especially when the settlers were cancelling out Indian competition in the
field of indigo. The purpose of this chapter is to highlight this spell of
collaboration in an otherwise grim history of confrontation, marred by
frequent violence. It seems to be important to know how these catalytic

---

21. *Report of the Meeting in Support of Colonisation*, Calcutta, 1830, pp. 4–5
22. P. P., v (1831), Appendix 39, p. 722
23. *The Reformer* quoted in *Bengal Hurkaru*, 16 January 1832

agents were received by a rural society and to understand the social processes leading to their assimilation or rejection in it.

By 1830, the indigo boom was followed by a slump and the factories of Indians which had mushroomed over the preceding three years disappeared as suddenly as they had sprouted.[24] The European competition was also an important contributory factor. Whatever the reason, the landlords gave up their hopes of a quick gain in indigo against such formidable competition. The agency houses which were tottering on their feet, were helped in their recovery by the hypothecation system. They thrived on the ruin of Indian factories, backed by official patronage and resources of the agency houses and banks, and the European control of the export market. There was little scope for Indian enterprise to compete with their European rivals.

This was also the beginning of a steep rise in the rental profits of landlords as shown in the first chapter. Their occupation as landlords brought enormous profits ruling out their enterpreneurial effort in any other field. Looking for enhancement of rent, they found excellent paymasters in the planters. The planters were anxious to gain a foothold in the interior at any cost. As very few estates were brought to the hammer for arrears of revenue, they had to apply to the landlords for under-tenures. A period of collaboration was clearly in sight. Even Dwarakanath, who made his mark as a planter at this time, welcomed the European planters, regardless of the competition in indigo in view of increased rents. As it has been observed earlier, the landlords were, in general, optimistic of the planters' role in the improvement of their estates and the profits flowing from it. The expectations were not belied. The indigo trade soon started looking up and was well on its way to peak prosperity from 1834 to 1847, due to a steady rise in America's and Europe's consumption of the dye. In 1842 the indigo trade soared and constituted 46 per cent of Calcutta's exports by value and amounted to £1,84,33,565 in money-value in 1844–45.[25] The indigo investments must have leaped considerably during the period before the Union Bank failed in 1847. The planters counted on landlord collaboration and kept them in good humour by giving out liberal rents and bonuses. Those who wanted to have large unoccupied farms, managed to get them from the zamindar's *khas* possessions.

The landlords got high premia on leases, high rents and loans at a low interest in the next few years. Sometimes, huge arrears of rent were cleared

24. J H E Garrett, *Bengal District Gazetteers*, *Nadia*, Calcutta, 1910, p. 32
25. B Kling, *The Blue Mutiny*, Philadelphia, 1966, p. 21 for 1842 figures; P.P., ix (1847–48), Appendix 2, no. 247, p. 437 for 1844–45 figures

by the planters to obtain a lease. Thus, J C Palchowdhury, zamindar of Ranaghat, Nadia, took premia for patnis and leases at the rate of 3 or 4½ times the annual rent and a year's rent for izaras or short leases. Baboo Ramratan Roy, zamindar of Narail, sold a *jumma* of Rs 7,500 to the Shikarpur concern, Nadia, for Rs 19,000 where collection was only Rs 5000, and exacted Rs 10,000 as *bukeya* or rent in arrears. Dwarakanath Tagore could collect Rs 3000 over *jumma* of a lease annually. The Hizlabat Concern, Pabna, paid him Rs 10,000 for a *jumma* of Rs 7000. The profit firmly committed him to the planters' cause. Last but not least, the Bengal Indigo Company, the largest concern in Nadia, surpassed all such transactions in the amount and variety of perquisites it had to pay to secure its leases. R T Larmour, manager of the company, described the following before the Indigo Commission:

> Rs. 4,433 salami or bonus for a jumma of Rs. 9,000, carrying an annual loss of Rs. 800; salami: Rs. 2,216, presents to Amlahs: Rs. 1,065 and peshki or loan of Rs. 30,000 at 6%, for another jumma of Rs. 4,092; salami: Rs. 1,200, present to Amlahs: Rs. 600 and a loan of Rs. 4,000 at 3%, for a third jumma of Rs. 5,775.[26]

In many estates, the European planters brought wasteland under cultivation. The planters were at this early stage primarily interested in raising the crop and not the rent from the ryots. Dwarakanath testified in 1829 that one of his estates had not yielded sufficient income to pay the revenue demanded on it but on the introduction of indigo, not a *bigha* remained untilled, and he secured some profit too. Several of his relatives earned large incomes likewise.[27] The planters' role in the improvement of estates continued to benefit landlords, if not their ryots. Umesh Chandra Roy, zamindar of Santipur, Nadia, in his evidence before the Indigo Commission in 1860 admitted that in the final analysis, there was no doubt that the state of his zamindari had been improved. The planters had cleared the wastelands, and the *chur* lands on the river, which were fit for nothing, had been successfully cultivated with indigo. Indigo had raised revenues by Rs 300 in some cases.[28]

Finally, the planters had provided the greatest security for the prompt payment of revenues. In general, they were punctual in their payment of

---

26. R. I. C., Q. 166 for Palchowdhury, Q. 2972 for the deal of Ramratan Roy, Q. 1996–7 for Larmour; P.P., vii (1857–58); Q. 3997–8 for Dwarakanath's deal
27. *Report of the Meeting in Support of Colonisation*, pp. 27–30
28. R. I. C., Q. 3899

rent. Sambhunath Mukherjee, a zamindar of Nadia, acknowledged before
the Indigo Commission that the Khalbolia concern paid its rent even before
it was due and that he had been pleased to renew their lease over the past
thirty years.[29] The planters undermined the village moneylenders by
supplying much needed rural credit to the peasants by way of advances at
the rate of Rs 2 per *bigha*. The advances from the factory were literally
snatched away from the ryots by the zamindari amlahs for the realisation
of the zamindar's rental demands. In 1836, the Bansberia concern in
Rajshahi had to be closed down on account of commercial failure. The
result was that the raja of Natore had to pay the revenue in copper pieces
since the closure of the indigo factories had stopped the circulation of
silver. It was like collecting £10,000 in farthings and forwarding the
bulky load to Calcutta, there being no system of local bills of exchange at
the time. Silver flowed in after the factory opened again at the raja's
request.[30] Beaufort, the joint magistrate of Pabna, elaborated the process
in his letter of 26 October 1854 to the commissioner of Rajshahi:

> The ryots are always glad enough to take advances because it gives
> them the means of paying their rents and for the same reason, the
> zamindars do not interfere before the time has arrived for sowing. It is
> well known that the agents of the landholders are at hand to receive the
> rents when the advances are being made and are often present in the
> planters' cutcherry for the purpose.[31]

A further vivid corroboration of the transactions comes from Freeman,
a substantial landlord-planter of the forties, 'The ryots come into our
offices with the collectors of the native zamindars and bring their accounts,
and the money merely passes from our hands into the hands of the
zamindar's collectors and the next day it is taken and paid as government
revenue.'[32]

The planters received such a reception due to the government's assault
on landlord rights by resumption, and the zamindars' need for a political
alliance with a body of Europeans who had a vested interest in the land,

29. R. I. C., Q. 3538
30. *The Landholders and Commercial Association of India: Memorial to
    Sir Charles Wood, Secretary of State for India*, London, 1861, p. 44,
    footnote
31. *Selections from the Records of the Government of Bengal*, vol. xxx,
    Parts I–III, *Papers Relating to Indigo Cultivation in Bengal*, Calcutta, 1860,
    (hereafter, *Papers Relating to Indigo Cultivation*), no. 90
32. P.P., vii (1857–58), Q. 1807

to aid their struggle against the government. As Rammohan Roy explicitly avowed:

> The European settlers being more on a par (*sic*) with the rulers of the country and aware of the rights belonging to the subjects of a liberal government and proper mode of administering justice, would obtain from the local government and from the Legislature in England, the introduction of many necessary improvements in the laws and judicial system, the benefit of which would, of course, extend to the inhabitants generally whose condition would thus be raised. The presence, countenance and support of the European settlers would not only afford to the natives protection against the impositions and oppression of their landlords and other superiors but also against the abuse of power on the part of those in authority.[33]

Such a policy of mutual support was also outlined by a vernacular journal, *Sarbatattwadipika*, in identical terms in 1831.[34] The idea was literally translated into action during the final phase of the struggle against land resumption between 1836 and 1842.

In 1836, Macaulay moved the draft of Act XI making the British-born settlers amenable to the *mofussil* civil courts instead of the Supreme Court at Calcutta. The planters in a body refused to be tried by Indian judges in the *mofussil* courts. The landlords thought of supporting the planters to rally them in their struggle against resumption. The planters were averse to any measure that threatened the security of their tenure. They had already petitioned parliament for the right to acquire land in the interior. Resumption was sure to have an adverse effect on the land market. The two parties with landed interests were united by this common cause against resumption. The landlords gave their support to the planters' cause against the so-called Black Acts of 1837, despite the blatant racial stance of this European opposition. In 1838, 1,400 British residents and 200 Indians participated in the meeting in the Town Hall to protest against the Black Act. Dwarakanath Tagore cemented the bond between the Indian landlords and the planters by his historic speech, already quoted in the chapter on resumption. This was a costly political move. The planters were quick to reciprocate their support of the zamindars on the resumption question. The political alliance was consummated in the

---

33. P.P., viii (1831–32), General Appendix 5, no. 76, p. 341
34. *Sarbatattwadipika*, vol. ii, no. 3, *passim*

Landholders' Society (founded in 1838) which enlisted most of the planters on its rolls.[35]

The other important political gain from the connection was that western ideas of proprietary rights were reinforced, to the advantage of local landlords. The planters brought with them English notions of life, liberty and property and the technique of constitutional agitation for such rights. With the land–labour ratio in their favour in the thirties the landlords pressed for an unfettered proprietary right that would allow them to quash undesirable under-tenures at will. The limitation clauses of the Permanent Settlement with respect to ryot rights would then be inoperative and they would be free to dispose of their estates at their will. The principle was recognised in the settlement of the Sunderban wastelands after 1830.[36] The evidence of Morrell, a Sunderban grantee of the forties before the Indigo Commission in 1860, makes the point clear:

Q. 2382: Do you consider yourself the absolute proprietor of the land?
A. : Yes, as a grantee from the government.[37]

The landlords' proprietary pretension effectively precluded all official interventions into agrarian relations for a long time, as the planters kept up their campaign for redemption of the land tax and the establishment of absolute proprietary rights. From the evidence of J T Mackenzie in 1858 before the Colonisation Committee, it is clear that the planters coordinated their moves with the principal zamindars for an agreed stand on redemption at 25–30 years purchase.[38]

Collaboration at work

Under these circumstances, the planters found collaboration practicable in the interior. One of its earliest instances was the mediation initiated by Rammohan and Dwarakanath in 1826 between Kashinath Roy, a zamindar-cum-planter of Nadia, and E Thompson, the planter of the Bamandi concern. On the security granted by Rammohan and Dwarakanath, Kashi-nath agreed not to commit any further transgressions such as building a

---

35. *Report of a Public Meeting held at the Town Hall, Calcutta on the 24 November 1838*, London, 1839, pp. 27–30; also, *Report of the Meeting in Support of Colonisation*, Calcutta, 1830, pp. 16–19

36. F E Pargiter, *Sunderbans*, Calcutta, 1885, pp. 35–38

37. R. I. C., Morrell, Q. 2382

38. P.P., vii (1857–58), Mackenzie, Q. 3670

rival factory within the vicinity of the concern or making advances to Thompson's ryots—provided all cases instituted by Thompson to harass him, in the lower and higher courts were unconditionally withdrawn.[39] In 1830, George Harris, a planter of Nadia, found taluqdars eager to give leases to Europeans so that he had no difficulty in securing a plantation of 36,000 bighas.[40] W Forlong of Hills, White and Co., one of the two monopolistic indigo concerns in Nadia and Jessore, acknowledged before the Indigo Commission in 1860 that in his long experience as a planter, he had no difficulty in procuring patnis and leases. Once the financial terms were agreed upon the zamindars showed no hesitation in handing over their ryots to the planters. R T Larmour, manager of the Bengal Indigo Company, the other monopolist in the area, said he could count on the consent and cooperation of the zamindars in cultivating indigo even in be-ilaka villages (those not belonging to the planter as landholder) without payment of any further bonus.

Many zamindars spoke of the good relations they shared with the planter. For example, Baboo Srihari Roy, zamindar of Chandipur in Nadia, who was on friendly terms with Forlong, recalled how he had once used his influence for the naib of Lokenathpur Concern to induce the ryots of village Basto to sow the seeds though the terms were not agreed upon by the factory.

The observations of collectors and magistrates record a fair amount of reciprocity between landlords and planters, sometimes for special reasons. James Cockburn, an ex-planter and later a deputy magistrate, found how zamindars tried to enlist the support of an Englishman in their personal feuds over joint estates. In the ijmali or joint estate of the De Choudhurys of Ranaghat, Nadia, three brothers agreed to give a lease to a planter but the fourth brother refused. He was very powerful and hostile to the others. The three brothers thought that by getting the factory on their side, they would get an Englishman to back them against their rival.[41] Something similar happened in Jessore in a slightly different way. Ramratan Roy, zamindar of Narail, was in a constant feud with his cousin, Gurudas Roy. The latter wanted to oust the planter, Chollet, from an izara of a village. Ramratan willingly came forward to help the planter and despatched his lathials or clubmen to his aid in attacking his rival's peons and cutcherry.[42]

39. E Thompson to Magistrate, Nadia, 10 March, 1826, quoted in R Saha, Calcutta, 1973, *British Administration in Nadia*, pp. 151–52
40. P.P., vi (1830), pp. 302–6
41. R. I. C., Cockburn, Q. 440–44
42. *Police Report (1841), first half*, p. 85

Again, Ramratan Roy, who later played a key role in the indigo disturbances, had favoured a planter against Prankisto Pal, zamindar of Latudaha,
Nadia, over a *patni* of some villages. Both Prankisto and Hill had a claim to
the *patni* as there was irregularity in the deal with Ramratan. Under Act IV
of 1840, Prankisto won but quarrels arose and the villages were attached
by the collector in 1846. On 26 December 1846, Ramratan handed in a
petition for sale of the *patni* for arrears of rent. It was sold and purchased
by Ramratan's *mukhtear* and given back to Hill. Prankisto brought a suit
against the parties for collusive transfer and won the *patni* back.[43]

The landlords and the planters joined forces against the recusant ryots
to subdue them. In the Faridpur district, the local zamindar Gopimohan
Dutt jointly led an expedition with Dunlop of Panch Chur factory, with
their combined force of lathials numbering 700–800 men, in an effort to
oust the ferazees from the *chur* and crush their mighty leader, Doodoo
Meah. Doodoo Meah was falsely implicated for rioting and the case was
jointly fabricated by the baboos and Dunlop, as was evident in the verdict
by Judge Dick of the *sadar* court.[44]

The cooperation extended into the very field of competition, that is,
indigo planting. Several indigo concerns were run on a partnership basis.
The best example was provided by Joychand Palchowdhury of Ranaghat,
Nadia. He sold a *patni* for Rs 80,000 which carried an annual loss of
Rs 4000–5000 on the *jumma*, in mitigation of which he bought a share of
4 annas (1/4) or 9 factories of the Katgarrah Concern at an equally high
price. Palchowdhury was to become a central figure during the indigo disturbances. Prosanna Kumar Tagore bought a 7 annas share of the Islampar
Concern in Rangpur (from Ferguson who was running at a loss) along with
the Bagunbari Concern. Later, he purchased the whole concern himself with
one Logan as his partner. Logan mismanaged the concern and Prosanna
Kumar repurchased the whole. The latter gave it up in 1856–57.[45]

The greatest mainfestation of the collaboration was Dwarakanath's
efforts as one of the directors of the Union Bank to sustain the indigo trade
in its crisis in 1846. Dwarakanath allowed extensive loans to the agency
houses and their indigo concerns. It meant the gravest possible risk for the
creditors of the bank. Still, Dwarakanath would argue that the best course
of action was 'to just quietly get out of it with as little loss as possible'.

---

43. B. R. C., 21 January 1851, no. 41
44. *Trial of Doodoo Meah and his Followers*, Calcutta, 1847, pp. 47–181,
    Appendix 95
45. R. I. C., Q. 2907 for Palchowdhury, Q. 3754–5 for P K Tagore

'It must be effected soberly and advisedly,' he wrote to the secretary, Mr Stewart, 'and not by stopping the advances to the injury of the concerns for this would have made bad worse'.[46] The Board of Directors was largely swayed by Dwarakanath and his men. 'They composed Dwarakanath's tail and outvoted everybody else'.[47] Dwarakanath's will shows that he had six factories and this might have prompted his action, but the fact that 90 per cent of the bank's capital was locked up in indigo investments before its collapse in 1847 goes to prove his sincere cooperation. He was the worst hit in the end as Carr, Tagore and Co. went into liquidation almost concurrently with the bank and its entire liability fell on his sons.[48]

The parting of ways

The collaboration between the planters and the landlords was an unstable one. The disadvantages soon outweighed the advantages. Local skirmishes continued to mar the relationship. The police reports for 1838–40 contained such instances of conflict. Even Dwarakanath was involved in a conflict with Woodin over the sowing of indigo in Faridpur.[49] The Riot Act or Act IV of 1840 was passed to tackle disturbances in the interior including those between planters and landlords. But the clashes with the planters were perhaps not too grave as few incidents of the period, 1835–45, find mention in Eden's list of serious crimes (involving planters) submitted to the Indigo Commission. The elements on either side probably took the field to settle their petty disputes. There was no positive rupture yet. The respectable section of landlords and planters did not allow their alliance to be weakened by such incidents. But as the advantages began to wear out, the hostilities surfaced and even the latter group began to drift apart.

The planters led the way. In 1841, the Indigo Planters Association was formed as a separate body side by side with the Landholders' Society to protect the planters' special interests. Its purpose was to eliminate mutual

---

46. *Bengal Hurkaru*, 18 January 1848
47. *Ibid*, 20 December 1847
48. N K Sinha, *Economic History of Bengal*, vol. iii, Calcutta, 1970, pp. 119–20 for Dwarakanath's will; S C Chakrabarty, ed., *Autobiography of Devendranath Tagore*, Calcutta, 1962 (in vernacular), Appendix 14 for details of Carr, Tagore and Co. and its liabilities for Devendranath
49. B. J. C., 25 July 1839, no. 64; *Police Report (1838)*, p. 105 for affray, by Dwarakanath and similar affrays, p. 72; B. J. C., 12 December 1839, no. 17; *Police Report (1839)*, *second half*, pp. 87, 101

conflicts over factory sites and areas of operation. Gradually, the indigo districts were parcelled out among planters who could establish local monopolies over specified areas. The landlords were apprehensive of this formidable combination.[50]

In 1841 and 1845, new Sale Laws were enacted with specific provisions, protecting planters' interests. The Indigo Planters Association pressed the government in a petition in 1841 for a complete security of their under-tenures to safeguard their investments in indigo, silk and sugar. They upheld the cause of resident ryots against landlords, to free their ryots under advance from zamindari influence. In 1843, a complete stocktaking of European landholders was made by a special circular before Act I of 1845 was passed and many were found holding land on temporary leases. The Act, for the first time, gave security to bona fide leases at fair rent for 20 years where the parent estate was dissolved through sale. The landlords' strong objection to the measure went unheeded by the government.[51]

The European settlers also started utilising the press for their own benefits. 'A foreigner' in a letter to the *Bengal Hurkaru* in 1844, described the Landholders' Society as a 'dark, malignant influence'.[52] The Landholders' Society had become virtually moribund by the mid-forties, after the resumption issue had died down. The question had so long held the two parties together in a tie of friendship. After the issue was settled, the tie seemed to snap. At this critical juncture Dwarakanath, the architect of the collaboration, died in 1846. The relationship entered its worst phase when the Union Bank failed in 1847. The planters were no longer in a position to supply rural credit as before. Four concerns in Krishnagar and Jessore used to advance £4,00,000 annually before the fall of the bank. Now their advances fell by half.[53] The landlords' share of the indigo investments suddenly contracted. The bedrock of the landlord–planter relationship too began to crack at this critical time.

---

50. R. I. C., Minute of Lieutenant Governor Grant, 17 December 1860, pp. 70–72
51. B. R. C., 10 August 1841 no. 29 for IPA petition of 10 April 1841. Mr Richards, as Secretary, IPA sent this petition to the government and that makes the official recognition of the organisation in 1841 absolutely clear. Grant roughly gave the date of its inception as 1845 in his Minute of 17 December 1860 and his mistake has been repeated in many books; *ibid*, no. 14 for LHS protest and government stand; B. R. C., 9 January 1843, no. 89 for the list of European settlers
52. *Bengal Hurkaru*, 6 January 1844
53. P.P., vii (1857–58), Mackenzie, Q. 3908

The fall of the Union Bank reduced the financial resources of the planters considerably. The plantation system became rigid and gripping. To recover the alleged balances and to enforce contracts the planters resorted to strong-arm methods, insisting that the ryots give priority to the payment of rent to their zamindars. The landlords took the field with their lathials more frequently than before to subdue their mighty European subjects. Violence became a common occurrence and racial equality before the law, a rallying cry. The young and over-zealous magistrates were criticised for enjoying the hospitality of planters and favouring them in administering justice.[54] The planter's exemption from criminal courts in the *mofussil* became a favourite editorial for Indian journals.[55] The mounting hostility was evident in grave instances like the long-drawn fight between Sibnath Ghose, a *taluqdar*, and Rainey, a planter in *thana* Noabad (Khulna) or the kidnapping and confinement of a *taluqdar* in Dhaka by the planters, Wise and Glass, which was included in Eden's list of serious crimes in 1860.[56] The following graphic review of the situation in 1847 by Seton-Karr gave the subject wide publicity:

> Not one but a hundred instances can be given of fair stand-up fights where two, three or half a dozen lives were lost with a proportionate return of the wounded of battles where the hired up-country Brajabashi fought with a determination which would have done honour to the Company's ranks in any campaign; of hair-breadth escapes where the planter waylaid by a band of lattials only saved himself by the fleetness of his good steed; of armed hosts attacking our factories and levelling them with the ground: of whole bazars plundered by one party with a retaliation as effective from the other: of boats stopped and either rifled of their freight or made to pay toll with a regularity as admirable as the Government revenue; of successful manoeuvering where the planter, able to master only some two or three hundred clubs, carried his point in the teeth of eight hundred or a thousand of the enemy.[57]

At this hour of crisis, when law and order seemed to collapse in the countryside, J E D Bethune, law member of the council, brought four bills

---

54. *Sambad Probhakar*, 2 August 1848
55. *Sambad Purnochandroday*, 7 August 1852
56. B. J. C., 17 April 1843, nos 87–107; also B. J. C., 5 February 1844, nos 64–65 and 4 March 1844 nos 111–113 for Sibnath Ghose vs Rainey; R. I. C., Appendix 21 for Eden's list
57. *Calcutta Review*, vol. vii (1847), 'Indigo in Lower Bengal', p. 192

to make the British-born subjects amenable to the Company's criminal courts in the *mofussil*. The four bills called the Black Acts by the European community, raised a storm of controversy when they were made public in 1849. The Europeans opposed it furiously and launched tremendous campaigns in India and in England to defeat the measure. They held public meetings and sent petitions to the government, claiming exemption on the grounds of the venality of native courts and their susceptibility to pressure from the zamindars.[58] The local gentry was equally agitated over the issue and they organised similar meetings to counter the attack. Ramgopal Ghose made a trenchant criticism on behalf of landlords, of the double standards of justice and the men who supported it, in his pamphlet, 'Some Remarks on the So-called Black Acts'. He wrote:

> Is it fair and just that the native zamindar may be dragged into court, fined and imprisoned for neglecting to perform those duties which the white men belonging to the race of the governing body shall leave undone and laugh at the impotence of the Magistrate and at his inability to deal out even-handed justice while he lives protected by class privileges.[59]

The planters' plea that few cases involving them were brought to the Supreme Court was explained by another spokesman as the consequence of an unequal fight. And their clamour for exemption as a birthright was criticised as having no precedent in Canada or Mauritius.[60]

In this campaign for and against the proposed Act, the planters proved to be the stronger party in the end as the issue was referred to the home government. The planters had a more powerful lobby there. This was the time when the Free Traders were pressing parliament to end the charter of the East India Company or ask the Company to undertake measures for security of property and judicial reform in the *mofussil*.[61] The pressure on the Court of Directors can be gauged from what President Hobhouse wrote to Bethune confidentially in 1850 regarding the Black Acts:

> . . . the feeling here against your Black Acts was so strong that I thought you ought to be acquainted with the whole truth in regard to your proposed legislation and now that I find that the Governor General

---

58. B. J. C., 26 March 1851, no. 2
59. R Ghose, *Some Remarks on the So-called Black Acts*, Calcutta, 1851, p. 24
60. *Bengal Hurkaru*, 12 January 1850
61. P.P., xxvii (1852–53), Appendix 7, pp. 509–10

partakes in that feeling, I trust you will resign your offspring to their
fate with the resignation of a philosopher.

He wrote to the governor-general at the same time;

I think it would be far better to do nothing than to do anything after the
fashion proposed by your legislative Councillor. He is a clever man but
he is far from a safe man.[62]

It was not surprising that the whole issue was shelved for the time being
and then left to be considered by a Royal Law Commission. The landlords
felt cornered by the European community of business monopolists draw-
ing support from both Calcutta and London. In 1851, they also formed
their own organisation, the British Indian Association, with no European
membership. The political breach, as we shall see in the next chapter,
widened in the 1850s, leading up to the indigo uprising of 1860.

As we have seen, the period of collaboration was not a picture of perfect
harmony followed by that of complete disharmony. It was interspersed by
spells of friendship and hostility. Neither is it true that two distinct phases
of collaboration and confrontation succeeded each other, the following
chapter deals primarily with confrontation. They, in fact, overlapped. The
hostilities around 1830 were like a sharp undercurrent to the tide of
collaboration in the period 1835–45. Again, even before collaboration had
spent itself, new grounds of hostility ate into the period of harmony. For
purposes of analysis, the keynote of each period has been given its due
emphasis.

The chief significance of the period under discussion was that the
planters had successfully infiltrated into the interior. They had, however,
achieved it by collaboration with landlords. The landlords had a lot to gain
from such a connection. They increased their rental profits. The coming
of the planters as landlords prevented the government from attacking
landlord rights, as contemplated by Harrington's draft regulation for
protection of the ryots' right. The landlord–planter alliance chiefly helped
to make resumption harmless for the landholders.

But once the planters were entrenched in the *mofussil*, they began
behaving like catalysts. They got the government to pass Act XII of 1841
and Act I of 1845 which secured their under-tenures considerably and
entrenched upon landlords' rights. The official favour shown to the
planters as rural entrepreneurs made a great difference and the landlords

---

62. *Home Miscellaneous Series*, vol. dccclix, Hobhouse Papers, Letter of
    24 June 1850 to Bethune and of 7 September 1850 to the governor-general

soon sensed the danger of a politically and economically influential rival
in the *mofussil*. The planters formed their own political association and
resolved their intra-party quarrels to establish virtual seigneuries in the
indigo districts. By judicious hospitality, they won over magistrates to
their side and posed a serious challenge to the landlords' local authority.
Their firm link with the Free Traders at home was demonstrated during
the agitation over the Black Acts. The political threat of the planters'
presence in the *mofussil* was foreboding for the landlords.

The economic challenge was no less serious. They emerged as a new
element in the agrarian economy and brought about new equations in
agrarian relations. J H Reily recalled an instance from his experience as
collector in Jessore, between 1838 and 1846 which makes it clear. Ramratan Roy of Narail purchased the village Khajura and tried to enhance
the rent. The ryots in a body handed over their *jumma* to the local planter,
John Tweedie, the proprietor of Hazarapur factory. When Ramratan
instituted about 300 summary suits in a single day against the ryots,
Tweedie deposited the amount of the claim—a large sum.[63]

Sometimes, the planters offered a bonus and factory appointments to
village headmen, to thrust indigo contracts on the ryots under their influence. Such direct dealings undermined zamindari superiority and affected
agrarian relations.[64] Some of the enterprising planters like W G Rose,
Dombal, Sage and the Bengal Indigo Company started *nij* cultivation or
capitalist farming from an early period. Such attempts, however, failed to
influence the existing mode of production. They even failed to secure
peasants as hired labour. The planters had to import tribal labour from a
distance to keep the factories and plantations going. Few landlords took
after these model farms. Even the enthusiasm of these handful of entrepreneurs was dissipated by the economic crisis, leading to the collapse of
the Union Bank in 1847. They either reduced their *nij* cultivation or gave
it up altogether.[65]

The indigo investment brought money to the actual cultivator. But most
of it was juggled out of their pockets into the coffers of the landlords. The
landlords, the village headmen and the factory assistants were the only

63. R. I. C., Reily, Q. 2548
64. R. I. C., Reily, Q. 2559, Forlong, Q. 2921; also, *Papers Relating to Indigo
    Cultivation*, Calcutta, 1860, pp. 136–45 for Biswases, Jotedars of Pora-
    gatcha, Dariapur, Meherpur, Nadia and servants of J White of Bansberia
    factory
65. B. J. C., 30 March 1841, no. 48 for W G Rose; also R. I. C., Rose, Q. 325–48,
    R P Sage, Q. 544–63, Larmour, Q. 1970

people to benefit from indigo transactions. Even where such interceptions did not take place, the investment hardly rewarded the cultivation of indigo by the actual cultivators. For example, a sum of Rs 50,000 as advance to the primary producers might appear as a large investment in the rural sector; it really meant Rs 2 per *bigha* for each ryot in its spread effect, which was a small wage for the employment of his land, labour and capital, sometimes at the cost of his subsistence crop that is, rice.[66] Still, the advances acted as buffers against any further landlord exaction and pauperisation of the peasantry before the spectacular rise of agricultural prices in the fifties. But after 1847, the investments dwindled and both landlords and planters began to scramble for the peasants' surplus. As the fortune of indigo trade showed signs of decline, the planters, as catalysts of agrarian change, backfired.

The general effect of the planters' penetration into the *mofussil* was, however, not inconsiderable. They had quickened the process of commercialisation, raised the value of land by bringing waste and *chur* lands under cultivation and created an unprecedented demand in the land market. They were undoubtedly responsible for further monetisation of the rural economy and its linkage to the export trade. The importance of cash crops in the world market was impressed upon the countryside more than ever before. The river-borne country trade was destined to assume large dimensions in the near future.

---

66. R. I. C., Eden, Q. 3658, Reily, Q. 2591, Rev Long, Q. 1650

Five

Landlords and Planters: The Growing Confrontation (1850–1860)

The economic confrontation

During the earlier period between 1830 and 1850, the planters had played a very significant role through their pioneering attempts at capitalist farming. They brought capital to the interior, set up expensive factories and by their dogged pursuit of indigo as a cash crop, proved to the countryside, to landlords and to rich peasants alike, that higher agricultural profits could be made from raising valuable crops rather than from rent. They held out the promise of an agricultural breakthrough. They set up a model of farming before the community wherever they carried out *nij* cultivation or self-cultivation.[1] But they primarily raised indigo by ryoti cultivation. Cash advances were made to the planter-landlord's own ryots or *be-ilaka* ryots belonging to other estates, at the rate of Rs 2 per *bigha*. Sometimes, the seeds were also supplied by them. These were the planter's only contributions. The actual cultivator grew the indigo plant in his small holding with his crude implements and brought the produce in bundles to the factory for sale at 8–12 bundles a rupee. But the advances and the price

---

1. R. I. C., Durup de Dombal, Q. 729–36; B. J. C., 30 March 1841, no. 48 for W G Rose of Ramnagar factory, Murshidabad, which was started in the closing years of the eighteenth century with 14,000 bighas of *nij* cultivation. In 1841, it still had half of it under *nijabad*.

of the seed were deducted from the sale proceeds. No innovations were made to improve the cultivation of the indigo crop. The planter's skill lay in manufacturing high quality dye from the plant.

The agricultural operation was so simple and traditional that quite a few landlords were drawn to the trade and had plantations and factories of their own. Dwarakanath Tagore, Prosanna Kumar Tagore, Ramratan Roy, Haronath Roy, Joykrishna Mukherjee and the Palchowdhurys of Ranaghat were the leading zamindars in this direction. As noticed in the first chapter, Ramratan Roy of Narail, Jessore, and Joykrishna Mukherjee of Uttarpara, Hooghly, were the most business-like of them and they successfully combined landlordism with business. The petty resident landlords and other inferior tenure holders were the more enthusiastic lot who took up cash crop farming in earnest. Districts like Nadia, Jessore and Murshidabad were dotted with small factories and plantations owned by local landlords. In 1830 though, Indian enterprise was still perfunctory, since the planters were politically and economically much stronger. But by the 1850s, the landlords in the trade meant business and could not be smothered easily. They raised not only indigo but also sugarcane, date, mulberry and tobacco in response to market demands. Those who had been only lending money discovered that, with the opening of the railways in 1854, foodgrains had an expanding market and switched over to grain dealing. Rice became a major cash crop even where the situation did not permit it. They turned their moneylending and territorial influence to good account. The planters were suddenly confronted with a group of economic rivals from among the so-called traditional landlords. It seemed that there was going to be a direct confrontation over indigo, date and sugarcane. The growing competition between Indian and European planters led to attempted destruction of rival factories. In 1854, Ramratan Roy complained to the government that Messrs McLagan and Mears of the Sinduri and Bijoli Concerns had increased their territory by invading his zamindari and forcibly sowing indigo. In one instance, their men had made a most unprovoked attack on his indigo factory at Solecopah, destroyed his growing crops and broken his factory vats. They were alleged to have connived in 13 similar cases under the protection of the magistrate. The Indian planter-landlords were no longer in a mood to give leases to the European settlers. Srigopal Palchowdhury, zamindar-planter of Ranaghat, Nadia, had five factories and a plantation of 1,800 bighas of *nij* and 2,500 bighas of ryoti cultivation worked by his own ryots. His attitude to the European planters in 1860 may be gauged from the following:

Q. Have you given leases or patnis of lands willingly to factories?
A. No. I have not given leases willingly for I wish indigo to be grown. I can grow it on lands in my possession.[2]

Worse still, was the struggle to dictate crops to primary producers. Grain dealing, moneylending landlords would lend paddy and cash for a return of paddy on their terms. The planters would advance money to the same ryots for a return of indigo. But grains were more profitable than indigo in the 1850s, due to price fluctuations in favour of rice. The rise in rice prices between 1855 and 1860 can be gathered from the comparative table below:

Price of rice per *maund*

	1855	1860
Jessore:		
Coarse Rice:	Rs 1	Rs 1-14 as.
Husked Rice:	10 as.	Rs 1-4 as.
Krishnagar:		
Coarse Rice:	Rs 1-5-9	Rs 2-0-9
Husked Rice:	Rs 0-10-6	Rs 1-4-6
Hooghly:		
Coarse Rice:	Rs 1-2-0	Rs 2-6-0
Husked Rice:	Rs 1-0-0	Rs 2-2-0

Source: R.I.C., Appendix 3

Prankisto Pal, zaminder of Latudaha, Nadia, openly admitted that indigo clashed with paddy and affected money- and paddy-lending.

---

2. See Chapter 1; also R. I. C., Sambhunath Mukherjee; Q. 3530–32; had a plantation of 2,500–3,000 bighas in his estate of Birnagar, Hanskhali, Nadia, operating for the last 17 years; S G Palchowdhury; Q. 3547–52; having 1,700–1,800 bighas *nij* and 2,500 bighas of ryoti cultivation and 5 factories worked by his own ryots; J C Palchowdhury; Q. 142–44; having 5000 bighas *nij* and 11,000 bighas ryoti and 32 factories to his credit; Prankisto Pal; Q. 3558; purchased two factories in 1860; R. I. C.; 2 March 1854, nos 240–42 for Ramratan Roy vs. McLagan and Mears

Indigo preceded rice and then it was too late to sow and gather rice. A host of landlords, big and small, sought to prevent ryots from sowing indigo by levying fines. Joykrishna observed more pointedly that the rise in rice prices would inevitably prompt the *mahajan* to resist indigo cultivation at the expense of rice by his debtor-ryot. Both landlord-mahajans and their debtor-ryots wanted to grow rice and turn as much land as possible to the crop that was more remunerative.[3]

Economic rivalry extended to moneylending as a profession. The best example is provided by the struggle between John White of Bansberia factory and the Biswases of Poragatcha, in Hanskhali, Nadia. The Biswases, the local jotedars and mahajans, had a floating capital of about a lakh of rupees in money- and paddy-lending. John White proposed to buy their stock of grain and secure a monopoly in the grain trade in the area. But disputes arose over the terms of settlement and the Biswases were allegedly plundered of their stock by White.[4]

Last but not least, was the struggle over landholding as such. The planters had gained hold of much of the cultivated areas in the indigo districts in Nadia and Jessore, both as estate-holders, *patni* and other tenure holders. In Nadia, European planters held 65 estates paying an aggregate revenue of Rs 67,145, and 21 patnis paying Rs 2,26,695 to superior landlords, besides numerous other under-tenures. In Jessore, they held 66 estates paying an aggregate revenue of Rs 25,536 to superior holders, beside other under-tenures. At even 1 rupee per *bigha*, the estates and patnis in Nadia constituted 3 lakh bighas, and 1 lakh bighas in Jessore in 1860. It was estimated that in Nadia, two-thirds of the cultivated area had gone into the planters' hands by 1860. In Jessore too, the greater portion of such lands belonged to European settlers. In fact, a veritable scramble for possession of patnis went on in the fifties as the value of land soared, and as Forlong, a leading planter of Nadia put it, the native landlords were jealous at the transfer of major tenures in Krishnagar into the hands of planters and were seething with a feeling of opposition.[5]

---

3. R. I. C., Prankisto Pal; Q. 3562; Joykrishna Mukherjee; Q. 3824; Srihari Roy; Q. 3477–9; for the ryot's reaction, Mir Ramzan Ali; Q. 3234; Badan Choudhury; Q. 3225–6; Nuffi Dass; Q. 1014

4. *Papers Relating to Indigo cultivation*, Cockerell, magistrate, Nadia to commissioner, Nadia, 24 August 1859, Calcutta, 1860, pp. 144–45

5. R. I. C., Appendix 1 for Nadia and Jessore figures for 1860; also *The Englishman*, 24 January 1860, letter of Forlong; W W Hunter, *SAB*, vol. ii, *Jessore*, 1875, p. 251; R. I. C., Forlong; Q. 2912–3 for landlord's jealousy

The polarisation of economic interest was sharpened by the fact that the planters, as a class, had ceased to be useful in the countryside. Their investments had virtually fallen to nil since the failure of the Union Bank in 1847. The system of hypothecation had created an artificial demand of the crop for remittance purposes without reference to market forces. It had resulted in over-trading. As a contemporary observer put it, '39,000 chests, the fruits of surplus of 20 years, encumbering the marts of Europe, stand like evil sentinels to paralyse the value of each new importation'. The fall of the Union Bank was a natural corollary to such a desperate situation of the indigo trade, in which 90 per cent of its capital was locked up. A large number of factories had to be closed immediately. The planters began seriously thinking of switching over from *nij* to ryoti cultivation and giving up extension altogether. Even a giant concern like Hills, White and Co. could not recover from the shock and was still running on borrowed capital in 1860, on which a large interest had to be paid.[6] The indigo trade steadily went downhill in the 1850s, as can be gathered from the table below.

Export figures for two major indigo district (in maunds)

Year	Krishnagar	Jessore
1849–50	13,702	16,818
1850–51	18,718	15,955
1851–52	15,528	9,572
1852–53	10,276	9,654
1853–54	11,377	7,811
1854–55	11,650	12,305
1855–56	10,362	6,585
1856–57	10,205	10,227
1857–58	13,084	10,353
1858–59	8,023	8,635

Source: R.I.C., Appendix 17

Faced by a declining profit margin, the planters resorted to landlordism and began to squeeze rent. Indigo was reduced to a forced cultivation.

---

6. *Bengal Hurkaru*, 9 August 1847, 26 January 1847, 6 October 1847; R. I. C., Forlong; Q. 3171 for Hills, White and Co's debts

The evidence of indigo ryots, missionaries and magistrates before the Indigo Commission showed that no money advance had been made to the ryots for a long period before the revolt of 1860. Cultivation was carried on by them to clear their alleged arrears in the factory books. They had to pay higher rents, abwabs and interests on arrears to the planter-landlords. By Larmour's own showing, out of 23,200 ryots of the Bengal Indigo Company, only 2,448 received an excess in 1858–59. To the landlords, it meant a sharp reduction in the circulation of money in the *mofussil* and a positive difficulty in rent realisation.[7]

The slump in the indigo trade was fought by cutting the cost of production to maintain the same margin of profit. But price control and cheaper indigo did not provide a solution. The planters had to be reconciled to a lower margin of profit. Instead, the planters decided to economise on expenditure by changing over from *nij* cultivation to ryoti or cultivation of indigo by ryots under their advances. The *nij* cultivation approximated to capitalist farming as the planter organised the entire production by personally undertaking to supply all inputs—land, labour, capital, and supervision. Durup de Dombal, R P Sage and R T Larmour, in their evidence before the Indigo Commission, admitted that *nij* was either being reduced or given up and ryoti increased instead. They found *nij* cultivation very expensive. To keep a stock of bullocks, take leases at high premia and pay high wages to induce unwilling ryots or tribal people to work, a large capital was necessary. It was easier to manipulate the settled ryots by advances of money or territorial influence and to get the crop at a minimal cost. But the indigo trade reached such a precarious stage that the planters, as a last resort, reduced their own *ilaka* cultivation or operations within their own estates and made it up by *be-ilaka* cultivation or trespassing into the estates of other landlords. Its chief advantage was that it saved the planter the cost of securing leases at a high premium. The planter would try to control the ryots of other estates by bringing them under his advances without holding the estate himself. The landlords were made impotent in their own estates by such encroachments. This was humiliation at its worst and

---

7. R. I. C., Appendix 9 for Larmour's statement; Nuffi Dass; Q. 1014–33; Gunni Daffadar; Q. 1051–56; Ahad Mondal; Q. 1089; Seraj Biswas; Q. 1144; Fakir Muhammad; Q. 1365; Chandranath Sircar; Q. 692, alleging that Larmour wanted enhancement of rent at 4 annas in the rupee, Madanmohan Bose; Q. 710 and 719: Larmour demanded Rs 2-8 annas per *bigha*. Reily; Q. 2607, in former days, planters acquired zamindary rights to summon ryots for indigo and not to increase rent. Now they do both. Larmour; Q. 1968–70: settling ryots enhances the value of talooks

difficult for them to bear. The planters must have appeared to them as an unmitigated nuisance.[8] The occupation of land by planters in Nadia and Jessore in 1860 was as follows (3 bighas = 1 acre approximately):

Krishnagar	nij	ryoti	ilaka		be-ilaka	
Khalbolia Concern	5,000	14,000	3,722 ryots		1,230 ryots	
Callipole Concern	200	6,300	having both			
Bansberia Concern	4,200	14,000	94 villages		77 villages	
Mohesgunge Concern	9,000	3,000	1,300 bighas		1,700 bighas	
Shikarpur Concern	6,900	20,000	having both			
Lokenathpur Concern	2,000	8,000	-do-			
Nischindipur Concern	4,000	26,000	129 villages		53	
Nandanpur Concern	7,691	2,831	13 villages		51	
Katchikatta Concern	2,825	16,375	unspeci-		4,500–	
Jessore			fied		4,600 bighas	
Sinduri Concern	4,762	35,486	not available			
Nusibshahi Concern	4,500	15,500	having both			
Baboocally Concern	2,000	5,000	-do-			
Sericole Concern	3,000	8,000	-do-			
Jingargatcha Concern						
Formerly	150	7,850	72 villages		99 villages	
Now	25	5,000				

Source: R.I.C., Appendix, Part 1, no. 1

Furthermore, the best lands, mainly highlands, fit for rice cultivation, were sown with indigo by force. This led to depreciation of land values and rent. Indigo had a very low return on such lands, especially in view of the rise in prices of rice and the ryots were against giving up rice for indigo. They deserted to avoid coercion and the landlord found it difficult to realise his rent.[9]

8. R. I. C., Larmour; Q. 1939–72; R P Sage; Q. 542–63; Dombal; Q. 740–43
9. R. I. C., Haronath Roy; Q. 3839; Bijoygobinda Choudhury; Q. 1590; Kalidas Bose; Q. 2450; J H Reily; Q. 2579; Rev. Schurr; Q. 865; Abadi Mondal; Q. 1074

All these subterfuges to maintain profit made the planters look like illegitimate beneficiaries of official favour with no entrepreneurial role in the economy to justify their privilege. There can be no better conclusion to this section than the following editorial from the *Hindoo Patriot* (15 May 1856), the mouthpiece of the landlords in the 1850s:

What is the Indigo Planter? He is certainly not a capitalist; for he usually works with borrowed capital. He is seldom a land-owner. He is not exactly a farmer; for he generally purchases his raw materials from the tillers of the soil. He can hardly claim to be a manufacturer, — so simple is the process which converts the plant into the cake.

The political confrontation

The planters had, in the previous decades, found it possible to secure estates, patnis and other sub-tenures under the landlords at a heavy price for a certain period. Times were harder in the 1850s. The planters had little capital and even sub-tenures were seldom available for sale. As the value of land soared, the landlords themselves began to purchase whatever tenure was offered for sale. The leases of jotes or ryoti holdings were all that could be had. But all under-tenures were subject to liquidation on the sale of the parent estate under the existing Sale Law and the zamindars frequently made use of it to get rid of undesirable under-tenures.

Since 1841, the planters had succeeded in securing protection of factory sites and gardens and bona fide leases at a fair rent for twenty years (vide Act XII of 1841 and Act I of 1845) by their agitation. No further steps were taken by the government to protect under-tenures because 'the zamindars might think,' as J T Mackenize, the Jessore planter, put it before the Colonisation Committee in 1857–58, 'that by and by we intended to do away with the Perpetual Settlement altogether'.[10]

The question could be shelved for some time as the planters were able to get their way with the overlords by judicious payment of premia and loans. But indigo investments had been reduced to half in Nadia after the fall of the Union Bank in 1847. By 1850, it appears to have ceased altogether. The economic confrontation had started. Confrontations were more frequent. The security of under-tenures became once again a matter of survival for the planters, as landlords would not spare them any more.

10. P.P., vii (1857–58), Part II; Q. 3666

It was acknowledged in official circles that the petition of J T Mackenzie of Jingargatcha Concern in Jessore, for protection of his under-
tenures and leases in December 1849, really moved the government
towards a serious consideration of the question. It was backed up by the
well-known firm, Messrs Gladstone, Wyllie and Co. in their petition of
29 October 1851. The petition generated the most animated debate among
officials and a consensus was reached in favour of a legislation for security
of under-tenures. Governor-General Lord Dalhousie set his seal of approval in his Minute of 22 October 1852 in which he declared:

I regard it as of the highest value for giving that security to the property
of the ordinary cultivator or of the man of enterprise and capital without
which it is hopeless to expect any substantial improvement in Bengal
or any material increase of its resource . . .[11]

The issue merged into the wider question of the renewal of the Charter
Act of the East India Company and therefore, the scene of agitation was
shifted to England. A petition was sent by the European community in
Bengal setting out their demand for better government and greater security
of property to the House of Commons on the eve of the Charter Act debate.
Several indigo planters, including J P Wise and K Brodie, personally
represented their case before the Select Committee. All the East India
Trading Companies from Liverpool, Blackburn and Manchester who had
branches in Calcutta, sent their agents to speak for them and present
petitions urging security of under-tenures.[12]

The effects of putting pressure on the government was noticed in
connection with the Black Act agitation of 1850 and admitted by
President Hobhouse of the Board of Control. The East India Company
had either to do what it was told or wind up. The Company chose the
latter course and survived for a few more years. Following the Charter
Act (1853), Bengal was placed under a lieutenant governor in 1854 and
F J Halliday, the first incumbent, took up the cause of the planters with

11. B. R. C., 28 October 1852, nos 2–15, no. 14 contains the petition of
Mackenzie and the forwarding note by Beadon, secretary to the government acknowledges that the question raised by Mackenzie led to the
re-opening of the 'general question of upholding of under-tenures which
was discussed at length in 1840–41'; for Gladstone, Wyllie and Co's
petition, no. 12 and Dalhousie's Note, no. 15
12. P.P., xxvii (1852–53), Appendix 7, pp. 509–10; Appendix 2 for the petitions of the East India Trading Companies

extraordinary zeal. The Indigo Planters Association, in a regular correspondence in 1855, kept up the pressure on the government and the
outcome was the Draft Sale Law of 22 December 1855 which protected
all tenures immediately under the estates. A substantial planter-zamindar,
Freeman, admitted before the Colonisation Committee in 1857, that he
handed over the Draft Act to Grant for implementation. But the Draft Law
could not be made into an act as the protection of under-tenures was made
subject to enquiry into their assets and registration. The Indigo Planters
Association, in a petition, rejected this provision, as their leases were
obtained by various means which would not bear scrutiny.[13]

Halliday was in favour of the universal security of under-tenures
without enquiry and registration in his Minute of 2 September 1856 and
the question was put in the form of a circular for reconsideration in the
official circle. H R Ricketts, a member of the Board of Revenue, advocated
protection of a lease till the capital invested in it had been realised making
a special reference to Mackenzie's case. A more characteristic opinion
came from J H Young, the officiating commissioner of Burdwan. In
supporting Halliday, his special argument was that the planter would
'never trouble his head about the zamindar or his affairs—never be
obliged as it is often the case now I am inclined to think—to advance money
to the zamindar in order to prevent him from carrying out a threat of
default'.[14]

The zamindar's case was ably put by at least one officer, E Samuells
the commissioner of Cuttack, who condemned the government's pre-
occupation with under-tenures and called it confiscation of landlord rights.
He made it clear that agricultural development was equated with indigo
in official circles and as planters were primarily under-tenure holders,
these were made a special case for protection. The landlord's incapacity
as an agent of improvement was thought unfounded by him and it was
pointed out that the planter's advances were made more often to ryots of
be-ilaka areas and not belonging to his under-tenures.

The landlords watched the whole process sullenly. If under-tenures
were protected as a matter of right, the planters would have the same
control over the ryots as they would have from acquiring an estate. The
landlords could be bypassed and the planters could carry on their trade
without reference to them. The proposed Sale Law was, therefore, strongly
condemned by them as an attempt to unsettle the Permanent Settlement

13. P.P., vii (1857–58), Appendix 2 and 7 for Draft Law, Halliday's Note and
    IPA petition. Freeman, Q. 1498–99, 1655, Theobald, Q. 846–96
14. B. R. C., 9 October 1856, no. 6 (Ricketts), no. 11 (Young), no. 30 (Halliday)

and liquidate landlord rights to promote those of the planter. The issue was left undecided due to the Mutiny.[15]

What worried the landlords was not so much the confrontation from the planters as the official patronage rallied to their cause in such a pronounced degree. They realised that they had fallen from official favour and the planters had taken their place. It would no longer be possible to contain them if they remained entrenched in the interior, backed by the ruling authority.

Their suspicion was confirmed in the forthcoming agitation over their equality before law. The old question of the European settlers' amenability to criminal courts in the *mofussil* was renewed by the Law Commission in England at this time and the question was referred to the Legislative Council in India for an enactment, abolishing the exemption of settlers from such criminal procedures. When a bill was proposed to that effect, the settlers mobilised their opposition against it as they had done in the past. They organised a mammoth meeting at the Town Hall in February 1857, justifying their exemption from 'native' criminal courts. They drew up a petition to parliament and sent William Theobald, the secretary of the Indigo Planters Association, to personally represent their case before the authorities in England.[16]

The British Indian Association organised another crowded meeting at the same place a week later and men like Kishorichand Mitra, Rajendralal Mitra, Joykrishna Mukherjee and Ishwarchandra Chunder most solemnly refuted the charge of 'native' incompetence as judges and deplored the double standards of justice, one for Indians and the other for Europeans. Ishwarchandra Chunder placed the issue in its changed context. He observed:

The Indigo planter of a prior day was altogether a man on sufferance; he demeaned himself accordingly; was content to reap the harvest of his own labour without molesting or interfering with the rights or interests of his native neighbours. What at the present time and infinitely beyond all comparison over any other subject fills the mofussil courts with business but the intemperate proceedings of the Indigo Planter ? . . . and it is to be feared that as long as they cannot be prosecuted in the Mofussil Courts, the planters will continue in their

---

15. P.P., vii (1857–58), Appendix 7, p. 390 for Samuells' Note, 24 April 1956, Appendix 7, nos 3 and 7 for zamindars' petitions
16. P.P., vii (1857–58), Theobald, Q. 846–54 stating his mission, Q. 934 reading the petition

career of heedlessness, being aware that they may then go on with perfect impunity.

It was also realised by landlords that for the planter, 'it was the convulsive efforts of an expiring man,' as Digambar Mitra put it in his speech. The planters were going to make the most of it and the landlords had to abolish their legislative protection to remove their threat. A petition was sent to parliament on their behalf protesting against legal disparities.[17]

They were sorely disappointed when the issue was indefinitely postponed by the authorities. The question was not settled until 1861. This was the second consecutive defeat suffered by the landlords seeking official favour vis-a-vis planters and to them, one of far-reaching consequence.

The year of the Mutiny was 1857. The precariousness of the empire was a lurking fear of the government since the days of Metcalfe and he had especially promoted European settlement in India with a view to developing a solid base for the British Raj in the interior. The empire had been shaken to its foundations by the Mutiny. In search of allies and support, the government only found the small army of 2,400 European and 29,000 Indian soldiers who could be relied upon. There were no other European troops till Dinajpur, which was 380 miles away from the capital.[18] A few landlords offered their help but they were not to be trusted as a class in view of what was happening in the northwest provinces. The planters were the only persons to whom the government could safely turn in this hour of crisis. They, doubtless, admirably served the purpose of civil defence in the interior. Six of them, Larmour, Forlong and Burrell in Nadia, and Deverell, Jackson and Watson in Murshidabad were made honorary magistrates, to start with, by Halliday on 1 August 1857 to the exclusion of the Indian landlords. The vanity of the rural elite was pricked beyond measure.[19]

The missionaries and their paper, the *Friend of India* had earlier made such proposals. But the *Hindoo Patriot*, the newspaper of the landlords, had strongly objected to it as the planters were traders with no abiding interest in the land and liable to promote individual interest.[20] They had so far tolerated double standards of justice in the *mofussil*. They had put up with the indignity of appearing personally in the witness box. They had

---

17. *Great Non-Exemption Meeting*, 6 April 1857, Calcutta, 1857, pp. 27–36 for the speech of Ishwarchandra Chunder, pp. 37–41 for Digambar Mitra and p. 85 for the petition

18. C E Buckland, *Bengal under the Lieutenant Governors*, vol. i, p. 6

19. R. I. C., Appendix 25; also B. J. C., 17 April 1856, nos 18–19 and 5 November 1857, nos 229–31

20. *Hindoo Patriot*, 31 May 1856

watched grimly their European lessee given a seat by the magistrate while they were kept standing at summons.[21] But this was 'the unkindest cut of all'. The British Indian Association in its petition of 24 August 1857 strongly protested against this grossly preferential treatment of the planters. The landlords longed secretly for this honour. It was more than an empty title like 'Raja Bahadur'. It signified power. The government had so long expected them to organise the village watch, appoint chowkidars, prevent dacoity, and supply provisions to the soldiers on their march though the estates, on pain of fine and recognisance. Even a *chowkidari* tax was going to be levied on them about the same time.[22] But when the hour came, the honour and authority was bestowed on their bitterest rivals. The planters made full use of the power and lorded it over the countryside, over rajas and ryots alike, in the same arrogant hauteur.[23] Up to the Affray Law of 1854, the two parties were treated more or less equally by the government, but this singular honour tilted the balance in the planters' favour. For the first time, the landlords became seriously apprehensive of a rural authority in the *mofussil*, potentially far more overpowering than they had thought before.

The Mutiny ended in the victory of the British power over the proto-nationalist forces and in a vindication of the British Raj. Indian resistance to alien rule which had been brewing over the dangerous decades before the outbreak, exhausted itself in the Mutiny. In Bengal, the government was no longer in a very conciliatory attitude towards landlords. The old policy of minimum government and maximum dependence on the rural elite gave way to the direct and vigorous rule of the bureaucracy in Bengal.

Meanwhile in England, the cause of the planters was receiving serious attention in parliament. The Select Committee on Colonisation and Settlement in India especially sat in 1857–58 to hear the evidence of nume-rous planters and officials who strongly advocated laws in their favour.

---

21. BIA, *Petitions,* relative to the Draft of Act to Amend the Law of Evidence in the Civil Courts of the Bengal Presidency, Calcutta, 1852, protesting against personal appearance of respectable persons in the witness box; R. I. C., Srigopal Palchowdhury, Q. 3551 narrating the humiliation of such appearance
22. R. I. C., Appendix 25, Chapter 3 for various petty judicial duties assigned to zamindars; also BIA *Petitions*, 4 November 1856 and 24 August 1857 opposing Chowkidari Bill and proposed Chowkidari Tax
23. R. I. C., Srihari Roy, Q. 3472, Larmour threatened to put him down if he did not oblige him in a dispute over a lease, Benimadhab Mitra, Q. 682, Rev J Lincke, Q. 898

William Theobald, the secretary of the Indigo Planters Association, and J T Mackenzie, McNair, Freeman and Wise among others, emphasised the need for the security of sub-tenures and for the reform of justice and the police before making the planters amenable to the administration, justice and police. Many planters held jotes and small ryoti holdings under ryots. Planters like R P Sage needed the protection of occupancy rights of *nij* cultivation on jotes. Later, he was to testify before the Indigo Commission in 1860, 'Without the right of occupancy, we can do nothing in the way of nijabad.' Freeman and Mackenzie especially pleaded for occupancy rights even for *be-ilaka* ryots to enable them to carry out their indigo contracts without landlord interference.[24]

The landlords had no representative there to plead their cause. They carried out their campaign against the planters at home through their journals, the *Indian Field* and the *Hindoo Patriot*. The official sponsorship of the settlers appeared very explicit to them. Even Halliday was directly accused of favouritism and suspected of having a stake in the Bengal Indigo Company. The *Indian Field* expressed its surprise at the regular transfers of magistrates who incurred the displeasure of the planters in Nadia. Even in the *Bengal Hurkaru*, it was reported that an official, enraged at the poor returns of his investment, rummaged through the account books of a concern.[25] That there was some truth in all these allegations was clear from the admission of R D Mangles before the Colonisation Committee, that many officials in his time, including himself, had been mortgagees of indigo concerns and that he himself used to get 10 per cent on his investment. Theobald also admitted before the same committee that before 1837 such had been the order of the day and that men in service kept a strict watch on the factories for a safe return of their profits from them. As for Mackenzie, the Jessore planter, he was a holder of the East India stock up to date.[26]

The other theme of attack was the collusion between the planters and the magistrates. Magistrate Herschel of Nadia, pointed out, before the Indigo Commission, that this allegation had grown louder since the planters were made honorary magistrates.[27] This was partly true as the

24. P.P., vii (1857–58), Theobald, Q. 891–93, Freeman, Q. 1484–1502, 1709, McNair, Q. 2028, 2037, 2500, Mackenzie, Q. 3161–3666, 3741, Appendix 1

25. *Hindoo Patriot*, 5 May 1859; *The Indian Field*, 10 December 1859, and 7 August 1858; *Bengal Hurkaru*, 23 November 1858

26. P.P., vii (1857–58), Theobald, Q. 927, Mackenzie, Q. 3586; P.P., iv (1859), Mangles, Q. 1321–24, 1330–32

27. R. I. C., Herschel, Q. 2815–18

Indian Field already noted eariier that Halliday's action 'irritated the people of Bengal to an extent compared with which the greased cartridge of Hindustan is a trifle'. The *Hindoo Patriot* wrote in bitter sarcasm:

> To be on good terms with the Magistrate is a great thing. To be known so is greater and the greatest is to create an impression that he has a pecuniary interest in the concern. Goodfellowishness of the planter, offer of a grilled *Moorgee* and a quart of beer is grudged to no traveller that puts up at factory.

In another editorial, it alleged that 'it is a notorious fact that no small portion of these cases are decided at the breakfast or dinner table where the planter needs (*sic*) not be represented by a legal agent'.[28]

But the grievance existed before 1857. The *Sambad Probhakar*, a vernacular journal, reported such a collusion between Mackenzie, the Jessore planter, and the magistrate of Jessore, as early as 1854.[29] Dunbar, on his deputation to Jessore to find out the truth of such charges, discovered the indignities of frequent summons suffered by Ramratan Roy of Narail in the hands of Magistrate Toogood. Many landlords spoke of their despair of getting justice before the Indigo Commission. It was complained that the magistrates were in the constant society of the planters and they often held *cutcherry* in the factories of the planters for arbitration in their disputes with the local landlords. The magisterial partiality was officially admitted in the conflict between Watson and Co and Shibsundari Dasi for Chur Ramnagar in Murshidabad.[30]

But the landlords' agitation apparently had no effect on the Colonisation Committee abroad or the government in India. The committee reported in favour of further colonisation urging the government of India to extend every kind of facility to the settlers. A few testimonies against the planters were explained away as exceptions.[31]

At home, the government passed Act X of 1859 which provided security to all under-tenures including the occupancy jotes and brought

---

28. *The Indian Field,* 27 November 1858; *Hindoo Patriot,* 26 August 1858 and 9 September 1858
29. *Sambad Probhakar* (Bengali daily), 2 Ashar 1255 B.S. (14 June 1848)
30. B. J. C., 2 March 1854, nos 240–42 for petition of Ramratan Roy and Dunbar's findings; *Papers Relating to Indigo Cultivation,* Calcutta, 1860, pp. 189–94 for Watson and Co vs. Shibsundari Dasi; R. I. C., Latafat Hossain, Q. 1743, 1755, Bijoygobinda Choudhury, Q. 1583, Sambhunath Mukherjee, Q. 3540, Umesh Roy, Q. 3898 for other instances
31. P.P., v (1859), Session II, p. 276

the long struggle over security of under-tenures to an end, very much in the way the planters would have it, but for a handful of zamindar-planters in Nadia. The details of the Act will be discussed in the next chapter. It is relevant here to note that the measure was the outcome of the planters' sustained pressure on the government since 1830, though at the final stage the cause was caught up in the wider issues of all-round agricultural development.[32] The planters secured their independence from their over-lords as their lessees. Even *nij* cultivation in occupancy jotes could go on without landlord interference. They were able to enter into direct dealings with ryots of *be-ilaka* estates who gained occupancy rights and were no longer in the danger of arbitrary eviction by their zamindars.

The landlords were made captive in their own estates by the planters. In their petition in 1854 to Halliday, the Nadia zamindars had complained that 'every Indigo Planter within the jurisdiction is a little king exercising arbitrary power'. This was much truer in 1859. In 1854, they had thought of two ways to terminate such influence—to make the planters amenable to justice or to exclude them from the land. By 1859, it was clear that the first method had failed. The second was not tried out of fear. They seriously thought of the second alternative in the changed context of a new bureau-cratic attitude with the coming of Grant as lieutenant governor in 1859.[33]

From 1853, agricultural development gained a wider connotation among the Free Traders at home and some officials in India. In 1853, the House of Commons ordered a return of the prospects of cash crops in India and it was revealed that jute, sugar, silk and safflower were gaining over indigo. In the Missionary Petition of 1855, this was especially brought home.[34] Even tobacco and foodgrains, were proving more profitable and commanding an extended market both at home and abroad. These cash crops were grown by ryots under Indian advances without forced contract and dictation of the crop. They were produced in large quantities in perfect response to the market. Officials like Judge G Yule of Rangpur, and A Sconce, of the *sadar diwani adalat* had drawn attention to it in 1855–57. This explains the mood of the Grant administration. The activities of magistrates like Eden and Mangles in Nadia were marked by strict neutrality and enforcement of the rule of law, irrespective of colour. The landlords were emboldened by such proceedings.[35]

---

32. See Chapter 6 for details
33. B. J. C., 26 October 1854, nos 119–20
34. M Wylie, *The Commerce, Resources and Prospects of India*, London, 1857, pp. 47–50, for Parliamentary Return and pp. 65–70 for Missionary Petition
35. *Papers Relating to Indigo Cultivation*, G Yule, officiating judge, Rangpur, to

The revolt

The situation was clearly inflammable. The spark was provided by Eden's *rubakari* or the circular of 20 February 1859 declaring that the cultivation of indigo would be optional to ryots and his letter of 17 August to Hemchandra Kar, the deputy magistrate of Kalaroa, directing him to defend the law if there was an attempt to force indigo on unwilling ryots, leading to disturbances. This was followed immediately by Grant's tour of the indigo districts and sympathetic hearing of the ryots' case as they lined up along his entire route. The trouble, however, started in Baraset, where Eden's order was first made known.[36]

The events of the uprising have been dealt with exhaustively in various published works and need not be repeated here. But the leadership, character and the aftermath of the revolt have been subjected to far less critical analysis than they deserve. This can be taken up as something more relevant to the overall theme of the study.

There are good reasons to suppose that the landlords were solely responsible for engineering the indigo uprising to knock out their bitterest enemies once and for all. It does not appear to have been the spontaneous, national opposition of all sections of society – the ryots, village headmen, the grain dealing moneylending landlords, both petty and big, and the urban middle-class – united by common sufferings and sympathies against a common enemy.[37]

From the first weekly official report on the state of indigo riots in Nadia ending 3 March 1860 to the sixth ending 6 April, the landlords were reported to be the leaders or instigators by the magistrates. Mention is made of Shyamchandra Palchowdhury of Ranaghat, Habibul Hossain, another zamindar, Ramratan Moulik, *patnidar* of Joyrampur, Brindaban Sircar, zamindar of Shivnibas, Ramratan Moitra of Meherpur, Mohesh Chatterjee, himself a petty zamindar, and *Dewan* Ramratan Roy of Narail as the prominent leaders. Ramratan Moulik was reported to have adopted the title, *Neel Bangsha Binashak*, or 'the destroyer of the colony of planters'. Ramratan Roy was found leading a militia of 1,200 men against the Belubaria factory in Pabna. Deputy Magistrate Lingham, narrowly escaped death from the attack and Ramratan's *gomasta* was taken prisoner. If one takes into account the staggering number of confrontations

        government, 20 January 1855; B. R. C., 2 July 1857, no. 34 for A Sconce
        to government 16 April 1857
   36. R. I. C., Eden, Q. 3626–30
   37. B Kling, *The Blue Mutiny*, Philadelphia, 1966, Conclusion

between landlords and planters that had taken place in the short span of five years preceding the revolt, it leaves very little doubt as to the leadership.[38]

Sisirkumar Ghose, a small zamindar of Magura and the Jessore correspondent of the *Hindoo Patriot* on the indigo question, begins his story of patriotism in Bengal by saying that he is going to disclose the long held secret of the origin of this apparently incredible combination of apathetic ryots, and ascribes the leadership and organisation of the whole uprising to Digambar and Bishnucharan Biswas, small zamindars and moneylenders of the village Chowgatcha in Nadia. They were ex-dewans of J White's Bansberia factory, where they made a fortune and left to set up as landlord-moneylenders. Their economic confrontation with White had been noticed earlier. It forced them into the lead when the situation was rife for a revolt. They prevented their ryots from sowing indigo and promised to protect them. 'They sent envoys to other villages to induce ryots to join in the combination and engaged the services of renowned *lattials* (clubmen) whom they brought from the east that is, Barisal. All the villages declined to join them except one, and to that village they sent spearsmen for its protection.' All preparations were made within 8–10 miles of the *sadar* station of Nadia. They provided the peasants with funds for legal expenses. The ally ryots bargained for money like mercenaries as the planters sought to win them over by bribes. They paid them the amount required to neutralise the bribe. The planters obtained decrees against many ryots. The Biswases paid the money. Villages started joining them. In two years, the whole of Bengal was in flames. Factories were tottering to their fall. By then the baboos had spent Rs 17,000 and gone bankrupt.[39]

The account is reliable on evidence from eye-witnesses for both the ryots' initial apathy and the landlords' efforts to rally them to their cause. The sum spent by them for it until they were ruined appears too much to be true, unless drawn from some other source. It has to be remembered that Ramratan Roy of Narail in 1854 had offered to pay the expenses of a commission for an impartial enquiry into the truth of the indigo problem. The Biswases had probably drawn from such sources. It may even be argued that the big landlords sponsored the small landlords and preferred to remain behind the scene. The Biswases took refuge with the Palchowdhurys of Ranaghat after they were bankrupt, along with

38. *Papers Relating to Indigo Cultivation*, Calcutta, 1860, pp. 219–223, 228–60, 300–15; R. I. C., Appendix 12
39. S Ghose, *Indian Sketches*, Calcutta, 1898, pp. 102–7

Ramratan Moulik, the other minor landlord and leader of the revolt from Joyrampur.[40]

The massive evidence from the planters themselves and some magistrates before the Indigo Commission, corroborate the following points. Mahesh Chatterjee, Brindaban Sircar, the Palchowdhurys, the Joyrampur Mouliks, and Prankisto Pal were mentioned as the chief conspirators instigating ryots, financing the organisation, fighting the ryots' law-suits and paying up decrees against them. In general, it was believed that the landlords as a class were principally involved in organising the movement. The British Indian Association was accused of sending reporters and lawyers to the indigo districts to stir up revolt. The effect of the pamphlet, 'Oppression of the Planters', printed at the *Hindoo Patriot* press and circulated widely, was held significant by one planter.[41]

The contention is fortified by what Lieutenant Governor Grant wrote to Secretary of State, Sir Charles Wood, on the outbreak of the revolt on 23 April 1860:

> I have no doubt that many rich natives and many educated natives, anxious to pay off scores with the 'Anglo-Saxon', have been watching the approaching crisis and have been doing their best to make it as fatal to the planter as possible . . .[42]

---

40. B. J. C., 2 March 1854, no. 240; B. J. C., 29 March 1860, no. 259; *Bharatbarsha* (Bengali monthly), 1326 B.S., (January–February 1920), Article on indigo in Nadia

41. R. I. C., Dombal, Q. 752 believed that the revolt was stirred up by paid agents of zamindars in Jessore and Nadia. Larmour, Q. 1983, 2172–84 accused Brindaban Sircar of Shivnibas for paying up damages for breach of contract by his indigo ryots and calling his ryots and agents from Calcutta to his *cutcherry* for conspiracy. Herschel, magistrate, Nadia, Q. 2821–34 believed that mukhtears were sent by the BIA on Rs 100 per month and zamindars to be generally involved in the revolt, especially Mohesh Chatterjee. Forlong, Q. 2921–24, 2960 accused Mohesh Chatterjee and BIA for sending a *mukhtear*, Narayan Mukherjee and Q. 2962, narrated how a Muhammedan ryot confided to him upon oath that they had been misled and a league organised against the factory. Hugh Sibbald, Q. 3301, referred to the impact of the circulation of the pamphlet for two years. A T McLean, Q. 3071, A Hills, Q. 3111, Mears, Q. 3340, Tweedie, Q. 3408, G R Clarke, Q. 3428 for other instances. The last two blamed Joyrampur taluqdars

42. *Mss. Eur. F. 78/79*; Sir Charles Wood Collection, Grant to Wood, 23 April 1860

Needless to say, the rich and educated Indians who comprised the British Indian Association, combined landed interest with education in an eminent degree.

The role of Harish Mukherjee, editor of the *Hindoo Patriot*, in this movement appears to be very interesting from the evidence. He had sent lawyers for the aid of the ryots to the indigo districts. The ryots had gathered in his Calcutta residence for advice, and he had written out their petitions to the government and penned the most scorching editorials against the planters to rouse public opinion. This activity has been simply explained by his concern for the needy, oppressed ryots and an individual effort by writers on the revolt. But in his personal letter to Forlong, a leading planter of Nadia, produced before the Indigo Commission by the latter, he declared himself the party spokesman of the British Indian Association. The letter is worth quoting:

. . . no English gentleman in Bengal stands higher in the estimation of his native fellow subjects than yourself. In private society when the system of indigo planting in Lower Bengal forms the topic of conversation and the conduct of planters is, as is generally the case, condemned, Mr. James Forlong is almost always excepted by name and so even in public discussions in which our countrymen take any part . . . you cannot blame us if we measure your conduct and criticise it by a higher standard than we think of testing the conduct of our own countrymen. It is this principally which combined with (I confess) party purposes that will account for the severity of the articles in the Hindoo Patriot on Indigo planting.

I have mentioned party purposes. You will yourself, I am sure, recognise a sign of future improvement in the capacity manifested of late by some of our countrymen though very few of them and their disposition to mix in politics. One cannot interfere, however, in political matters without being more or less a partisan; and I feel sure you will agree with me that it is far better to be a partisan than to be the cold apathetic being Bengalis so often are.

Source: Baboo Harish Chandra Mukherjee to J. Forlong, 12 March 1859 in Papers Relating to Indigo Cultivation in Bengal, p. 163

Men like Harish Mukherjee and Kristodas Pal illustrated the theory of circulation of elites. The zamindars needed men of calibre to write for them. Both died in zamindari harness.[43]

---

43. B B Majumdar, *History of Indian Social and Political Ideas*, Calcutta, 1967, p. 123

Thus it is clear that the landlords had the greatest stake in the revolt and the greatest responsibility for its occurrence. But all that they wanted out of this revolt was a commission of enquiry to find out the truth of the bankruptcy of European management of indigo trade in Bengal. They were confident that they would be able to persuade the government to withdraw its patronage from the planters and corner them. This was the old demand of Ramratan Roy, and Grant, in his private letter to Sir Charles Wood of 20 July 1860, reported how eagerly the landlords wanted it, even at the risk of inciting a combination of ryots and compromising their position thereby.[44] Herschel, magistrate of Nadia, had seen a circular from the rebels urging the ryots not to stop petitioning till the commission came.[45] When it was acceded to by the government, the movement understandably died down as swiftly as it had sprung to action. Even the two zamindars, Shyamchandra Palchowdhury and Habibul Hossain, were quick to make it up with the planters and allow ryots to sow for the season.[46]

That the headmen of the village did not organise the revolt by themselves needs little elaboration after all that has been said before. The account of Sisir Ghose shows how the ryots bargained for money for their support to the Biswases and how all but one village declined to join. The evidence of head ryots like Nuffi Mondal before the Indigo Commission proves that they were happy with the sowing of indigo as they derived a profit from it.[47] It was the distinct opinion of Beaufort, magistrate of Jessore and Pabna, that the ryot, if left to himself, would rarely evade the contract and that it was the influence of the hostile zamindar that made them refractory. 'When a sudden stoppage took place in cultivation which had been carried on regularly before,' said Beaufort in his evidence, 'I referred it to the influence of the zemindars. I believe there can be no doubt of the fact that the ryots formerly took advance willingly.'[48]

We have it on the evidence of planters, magistrates and a native zamindar, that the headmen of the village were the chief instruments to persuade their flock to cultivate indigo. In most cases, they made a fortune out of advances made for indigo and made the peasants under them sow

---

44. *Mss. Eur. F. 78/79*, Grant to Wood, 20 July 1860, of, R. I. C., Long, Q. 1646
45. R. I. C., Herschel Q. 2830; Cf. B. J. C, 2 March 1854, no. 240, Ramratan's keen desire to have a Commission of Enquiry. He was prepared to finance it
46. R. I. C., Herschel, Q. 2834
47. R. I. C., Nuffi Mondal, Q. 3269–74
48. R. I. C., Beaufort, Q. 195; also, Q. 193, 'It was difficult to know the real feeling of the ryot when brought into Court. He then speaks just as he is told.' Reily, Q. 2564, zamindars taking agreements from ryots not to sow

without remuneration. They appropriated the surplus and by their dishon-
est brokerage erected *pucca* houses for themselves.[49] The evidence of
Eden is the most revealing in this respect:

> The only men who ever go to the factories willingly for advances are
> those who go openly with the intention of defrauding either the planter
> or the ryot. These are the middlemen, generally prosperous ryots who
> have a number of jotedars under them. When in want of money for a
> law suit or any other purpose, they go to the planter who gives a large
> advance, but this man never sows a cottah of indigo himself; he makes
> all his jotedars sow five cottahs or a bigha and thus produces the
> requisite quantity of plant, sends it all to the factory in his own name
> and takes the price himself and never pays a farthing to the jotedar who
> has actually grown the plant.

*Source: Papers Relating to Indigo Cultivation in Bengal. Eden, joint magistrate
of Baraset, to commissioner of Nadia, 19 June 1858, pp. 220–21*

In his evidence before the Indigo Commission, Eden explained how
Larmour of the Baraset Concern succeeded in having a large portion of
their cultivation sown on the eve of the revolt. It was because Larmour
'gained over many of the influential ryots whom he had previously
denounced as turbulent persons by making them dewans, naibs and
gomastas of the factories'.[50] Besides, they were small men with small
resources and the planters could break their backs easily, as could be
gathered from the evidence of quite a few small jotedars who were ruined
by their opposition to the planters.[51]

It is evident that the peasants were too divided to be massively organised for a revolt of this nature. Their superiors organised them because
of their own selfish interests and not out of sympathy for them. The
Palchowdhurys were as exacting as any of their European counterparts
as planters. J C Palchowdhury on his own admission had made little or
trifling advances for a long time before the outbreak and paid a negligible

---

49. R. I. C., W G Rose, Q. 409, Cockburn, Q. 493, R P Sage, Q. 581, 591, and
    Ameer Mullick, Q. 1034–44, a *gantidar* of Nadia having under-ryots to
    sow indigo, two new houses built recently. Haronath Roy, Q. 3834,
    zamindar of Narail, Jessore, explained his indigo operations through
    jotedars, holding 70/80 bighas. They took advance for each of their
    dependents who would sow 5–10 bighas with indigo
50. R. I. C., Eden, Q. 3631 for Baraset Concern's strategy
51. R. I. C., Benimadhab Mitra, Q. 679–90, Chandranath Sircar, Q. 692–700,
    Madanmohan Bose, Q. 710–26, Ameer Mullick, Q. 1034–44

amount for the indigo raised by his ryots. Sambhunath Mukherjee, another zamindar-planter, paid wages equally non-remunerative to his ryots. Both admitted that the ryot derived no advantages whatever from indigo and he planted it only to please them.[52] Others like Prankisto Pal and the Biswases, were usurious moneylenders and grain dealers who kept their ryots under slavery. The Rev Schurr in his evidence confirmed that Prankisto Pal was a zamindar who 'in his talook villages sweeps into his own golas the full crops and fixes his own price'. The Biswases were jotedars and ex-dewans of White's Bansberia factory, where they made a fortune obviously at the expense of their under-ryots. They left the factory and turned to money- and paddy-lending in which they set up a monopoly in the district. It was a dispute over this business with John White that brought them to the forefront of the revolt. Srihari Roy, zamindar of Chandipur, Nadia, and *mahajan*, was annoyed with Mr Roberts of the Khalbolia Concern as he tried to protect one of his indigo ryots, Selim Biswas, from a decree of Rs 300 won by Roy.[53] Ashley Eden, in a letter to the commissioner of Nadia, on 16 August 1860, mentioned the case of the ryots of Balinda, an estate of Prannath Chowdhury in Barasat, who agreed to pay an additional cess of Rs 5000 annually to escape being handed over to the planters. They regularly paid it till they heard that indigo sowing was optional in 1859 and stopped payment. Chowdhury at once applied force to squeeze the ryots.[54]

These reports leave little doubt about the lack of rapport between the landlords and their ryots vis-a-vis the planters. The landlords were only exploiting a need-based relationship, backed by a tradition of attachment to the superior holder and a sense of prostration before their power. Forlong draws a vivid picture of the nature of this need-based relationship and rapport:

At present from the high price of everything, the necessaries of life are procured with difficulty by the mass of the people and small talookdar or a mahajun who supplies the ryots with food, sometimes compels them to act against the planter whose crop interferes with others they

---

52. R. I. C., J C Palchowdhury, Q. 145–88, Sambhunath Mukherjee, Q. 3532–37

53. R. I. C., Prankisto Pal, Q. 3562, Rev Schurr, Q. 826, Srihari Roy, Q. 3477–81; *Papers Relating to Indigo Cultivation*, Calcutta, 1860, pp. 144–45 for Biswases. These men have been hailed as patriots and national heroes in S Ghosh, *Indian Sketches*, Calcutta, 1898 and in N Sinha, ed. *Who's Who in Freedom Movement in Bengal*, Calcutta, 1968

54. R. I. C., Appendix 22

wish the ryot to grow at a rate certainly to the ryot not more remunerative than indigo . . . in every case where opposition to the planter
arises, it is to be traced to the middlemen or mahajun who is in the habit
of supplying the ryot with food at rates almost incredibly usurious and
who, under the pretence of releasing the ryot from subjection to the
planter, has only the wish to place him more under his own.

Source: Papers Relating to Indigo Cultivation in Bengal, pp. 158–59

Durup de Dombal, a Jessore planter, had the following to say in answer
to a question by the Indigo Commission:

Q. If indigo cultivation had been a profitable thing to the ryot, do you
   think that these disturbances could have arisen?
A. Yes, if as I say, they are urged on by influential parties, particularly
   the native landholders who can make the ryot do anything they like.

Source: R.I.C., Q. 768

The Indigo Commission found the indigo cultivation unremunerative
and oppressive and recommended that it should be made optional to ryots
to sow and that the administration should be tightened to prevent forced
cultivation. The government allowed one year's cover under Act XI of
1860 for the fulfilment of existing contracts, after which official support
was withdrawn. The indigo cultivation under European enterprise dwindled sharply in Bengal after this. Their factories were vastly reduced in
number and many were sold out to their rivals—the Indian landlords, who
worked them with profit.[55] The planters made an exodus to Bihar, where
they hoped to survive on *nij* cultivation and greater submissiveness of the
people.[56] The migration of indigo from Bengal to other provinces after the
revolt can be estimated from the following table (in terms of production
per *maund*).

The few who outlived the crisis in Bengal, were mainly big landlords
who switched over to landlordism primarily and concentrated on rent.
These planters, led by Hills, brought the largest number of rent suits under
the Rent Act of 1859.[57] Their organisation also changed its name from

55. B B Choudhury, *Agrarian Relations and Agrarian Economy in Bengal
    (1858–85)*, unpublished thesis, Oxford, 1968, pp. 239–40
56. G Mishra, 'Indigo Plantation and Agrarian Relations in Champaran during
    the nineteenth century', *IESHR*, December 1966, vol. iii, no. 4, for the
    Bihar stituation
57. B. J. C., February 1862, no. 41

Province	1857–58	1877–78
Doab	9,360	1,44,285
Benares	10,000	17,556
Bengal	50,330	16,502
Bihar	18,822	34,857

Source: W M Reid, The Culture and Manufacture of Indigo, Calcutta, 1887, p. 85

Indigo Planters Association to Landholders and Commercial Association. They were, in short, effectively assimilated in the traditional framework of the rural society. In the earlier period, it was easier for the landlords to contain them, as they were not too powerful and worked mainly in collaboration with the landlords. But in this decade, it cost a revolt to achieve the same.

Conclusion

The planters did not attempt capitalist farming by organising the whole process of production. They did not even use their own land on a large-scale nor did they employ their own labour. They wanted to manipulate the existing agrarian framework by nominal advances and remained at its mercy. When they outlived their utility and became a nuisance to the parties constituting that framework, they were expelled by them. Their attempt at agrarian change was half-hearted and could not bring about a substantial material improvement in which the primary producer could have a share. That would have rallied them to their side against the landlords. As that did not happen, the indigenous patrons and clients joined hands to expel the foreign element by what is known as the Blue Mutiny.

Six

Resistance to Rent Control: The Genesis of Act X of 1859 and its Aftermath

Rent control before the Rent Act

The chief concern of the government with regard to the Permanent Settlement was security of revenue. The landlords were the cheapest, safest and the most convenient agency at hand for the purpose, as the government had neither an effective bureaucracy nor adequate experience to address itself to the grassroots. It found their practical position in society highly useful and made no theoretical mistake in giving them due recognition.

The Settlement allowed a profit of 10 per cent on the collection for the agency but as it contained rebates for abolition of *sayer* or toll duties levied by landlords and maintenance of embankments, the profit came to 20 per cent in reality. The punctuality enforced by the Sunset Law for payment of revenue and the low margin of profit allowed to start with, were responsible for the loose nature of the limitation clauses in the Permanent Settlement. The landlords were told not to violate the rights of hereditary ryots as they were supposed to enjoy a permanent tenure at fixed rates. The rent of other classes of ryots were to conform to the *pargana* rate or the average rate of a *pargana* having several villages. The abwabs or surcharges were abolished after having them adjusted in the final demand before the final settlement. The landlords were asked to exchange kobu-liyats and pattas with their ryots. These were documents to establish each

other's rights. All these provisions were rendered virtually ineffectual by
the abolition of the offices of patwaris and qanungos, the only depositories
of village records in the *mofussil* and officered by men thoroughly
conversant with local customs. The law was directed to the landlords only,
with requests to obey a code of conduct towards peasants. The rights of ryots
were not codified or defined.

Still, in the initial years of adjustment to the exactitude of the new
system, quite a few zamindars went to jail for default in payment of
revenue. The security of revenue was at stake. The government decided to
arm the landlords with summary powers to summon ryots and attach their
crop and property in case of arrears of rent by Act VII of 1799 and Act V
of 1812. From the second decade of the nineteenth century, the situation
stabilised considerably. In the fully assessed estates, the summary powers
were used to the utmost to make them as profitable as the lightly assessed
estates. In 1794, Colebrooke had noticed rich peasants behaving like small
capitalists, as they advanced seed and grain to their under-tenants and
sharecroppers. In 1819, he regretted that the Permanent Settlement had
resulted in the sacrifice of this yeomanry by merging all tenant rights in
one category of ryots and leaving them at the mercy of the zamindars.[1]

The regional experience of the collectors confirmed the general picture.
F Barnett, the acting collector of Rajshahi, wrote on 16 August 1811 that
the rights of ryots were never determined nor understood by them. The
'zamindar pretends to consider his ryot a tenant-at-will, tenders a pottah
at an exorbitant rate; the ryot who considers himself a species of Mukar-
raridars conceives that he is entitled to hold his lands at a fixed rent and
therefore refuses the pottah; the zemindar distrains and the ryot is ruined'.
The practice was more ruthless at the level of a petty landlord like a
jotedar. William Armstrong the collector of Nadia, writing in 1811,
described how a village farmer or a *jotedar* forced a sharecropper to agree
to two-thirds share of the crop in favour of the farmer, from the rented
land of which three-fourths was under water. Still, the share of Rs 80 was
taken and the standing crop, plough and cattle, were seized. The matter
was reported to the collector, who advised him to pay the money and then
file a suit. As he had no money and did not hope to get a loan due to the
jotedar's hostility, the collector gave it to him and the sharecropper got
his release. No other step was taken as the latter feared 'that the farmer
would influence a Goenda to label him as a Badmash and put him in jail
to rot there or by a Diwani case fictitiously put him to arrears and sell away

---

1. H T Colebrooke, *Remarks*, Calcutta, 1806, p. 64; also, P.P., viii (1831–32),
   report quoting Colebrooke

his property'. Thomas Sisson, the joint magistrate of Rungpore, wrote for his district on 2 April 1815:

> To conclude that the penalties of the law are sufficient to restrain one removed by a distance of possibly seventy coss from the eye of the judge, who is left to the unshackled control of the whole internal economy of his estate and who is immediately supported in his oppressions by the irresistible phalanx of Police Darogah, Moonsiff, Putwarree and Puramanick, Distress and Sale Laws and long purse, is, I fear, taking too liberal a view of the subject.

He narrated how a double set of accounts was maintained and a fabricated rental, from which all entries of illegal cesses were carefully excluded, was produced to the judge, in proof of the falsehood of any complaint of exaction.[2]

In the case of lightly assessed estates being reclaimed, the bargaining power of the ryots was a lot better. But the landlords adopted two major ways of neutralising that advantage. One method was to win over the mondals and paramanicks, the village headmen, by offering concessional rent and special privileges and then using them as whipping boys to exact a high rent from their less fortunate villagers. As Colebrooke noted in 1974, 'a few leading raiyats gained by indulgence, led the multitude'.[3] Sisson confirmed the practice in 1815 for Rangpur. There, a landlord, Bhairab Baboo, before farming the *pargana* Dimla, bribed the paramanicks with a thousand rupees worth of broadcloth, to get leave to subject their inferiors to exaction and plunder. 'The Puramanicks and Mandals', he observed, 'are by far the most villainous of all concerned in these oppressions, for the Ryots are presumed to elect these officers out of their own body for no other purpose than to have one to act, as circumstances may require, as their protector. They often defray, out of the common purse, the expenses of this man, who is all along playing a double game and actively employed in subverting, at the moment he is thought to be promoting, the rights of his electors.'[4]

The other method was to levy abwabs of protean variety to make up

---

2. *Selection of Papers from the Records of the East India House Relating to Revenue, Police, Civil and Criminal Justice under the Company's Government in India*, London, 1820, hereafter, *Selection from the Records of East India House*, vol. i, pp. 375–400
3. H T Colebrooke, *Remarks*, Calcutta, 1806, p. 57
4. *Selection from the Records of the East India House*, London, 1820, vol. i, pp. 391–95

for the low rent offered to the original settlers as reclamation proceeded and pressure on land increased. Many of the original Rangpur reclaimers and resident ryots held land at a low rent and in excess of what they were entitled to hold. The landlord claimed his share of the agricultural profit by levying abwabs. There was a tacit understanding between the two parties and a compromise was reached on the share-out. Abwabs, therefore, formed an integral part of rent from an early period. While the actual rent seemed to be frozen for a long time, the abwabs took its place and helped in appropriating the surplus of peasants.[5] Things remained unchanged as the government laboured under financial stringency and feared bankruptcy if the landlords were not allowed a free hand to deal with their ryots to enable them to pay revenue punctually.

But remittance, more than revenue, became the need of the day after 1813, when the country was thrown open to Free Trade. The Free Traders were interested in cash crops and increased productivity. Though Cornwallis in 1790 thought that the real value of the land to Britain depended upon 'the continuance of its ability to furnish a large annual investment to Europe', the idea was not given a fair trial, as revenue remained the main concern until the problem of remittance and Free Trade became serious in the late 1820s.[6] The success of the ryotwari system in Madras undermined the Permanent Zamindari Settlement in official circles at home under the influence of the Munro School, as can be gathered from the Fifth Report. The stationary income of the government made it jealous of the huge unearned income of the landlords. At the same time, the need for agricultural development also prompted the government to protect the primary producers and restrain the rent-receivers from maximisation of rent. All these considerations had their decisive influence on Harrington's Minute and Draft of Regulation on the Rights of Ryots in Bengal in 1826, which can be regarded as the first major expression of official intention to intervene in agrarian relations in favour of the ryots. The bill acknowledged 'the omission of clear and definite rules in the Regulations of 1793 and subsequent years, for declaring the rights and tenures of the ryots whose rents were, in many instances, left to be adjusted by pargana or other supposed local rates, no longer in existence or ascertainable'. The want of due enforcement of the provisions like exchange of pattas and

---

5. E G Glazier, *Rungpore*, pp. 45–46 and Appendix 32; *Mss. Eur. D. 75*, Buchanan-Hamilton Papers on Rangpur, pp. 108–9, 115

6. *Extracts from Regulations and Correspondence Relative to Permanent Settlement*, Calcutta, 1884, p. 80; *Report of the Rent Law Commission*, Calcutta, 1880, Appendix

kobuliyats, abolition of the qanungo's office, abuse of summary powers of distraint by zamindars and the insufficiency of the courts of judicature to provide redress were listed as the other factors. He cited the instance of Burdwan where, between 1800 and 1810, the rate of rent had doubled and every peasant was shackled with debt and harassed with the payment of rent which appeared excessive in terms of his net profit. He admitted that a general enhancement of rent all over Bengal had taken place which proved that there had been a setting aside of the rights of ryots by compulsion or otherwise unlawful methods. In his proposed regulation, he provided for the permanent occupancy rights of *khudkasht* resident ryots in their village of residence and made summary powers of distraint amenable to regular and summary suits. The establishment of a fixed *nerikbundy* or a table of rent was made binding on the zamindars. The office of *patwari* was recommended to be re-established.[7] It is doubtful whether mere legislation could affect the rate of rent but still the omission was officially admitted.

But the Draft was not made into a law. The government seemed finally to believe in *laissez-faire* and thought that fixation of rent, to be paid by ryots to the landlord, was as ridiculous as fixing the price of food or wages of labour.[8] The government still could not do without landlords. After all, they secured the revenue and ruled the countryside on its behalf. The landlords were vindicated in their exclusive claim to agricultural profits, arising out of permanent limitation of the revenue demand. What explains this anti-climax and rejection of a regulation which anticipated the future Act X of 1859? Colebrooke had long ago traced bad husbandry to lack of capital in the hands of peasantry, caused by exactions of landlords, and collectors like Sissin of Rungpore had, in 1815, ridiculed the idea that the 'higher the industry of the tenant be taxed, the more he will exert himself and by consequence, the better will be his condition'. He had further asked: 'Will these theorists venture so far as to contend that improvement thrives best under the state of things by which the labour tills in utter ignorance of the proportion which rapacity will allow him to reap?' The Court of Directors had since then, by repeated despatches, asked the local government to replace the zamindari settlement by ryotwari in estates made *khas* at sales for arrears of revenue.[9]

---

7. J H Harrington, *Minute and Draft of Regulation on the Rights of Ryots in Bengal*, Calcutta, 1827, pp. 1–23, 41–60

8. B. R. C., 29 January 1833, no. 3

9. H T Colebrooke, *Remarks*, Calcutta, 1806, p. 48; *Selection from the Records of the East India House*, London, 1820, p. 391 for Sisson

Yet, the historic moment for the ryot's deliverance eluded him, because the planter at this very time became the official favourite as the agent of improvement. The ryot was no longer lionised as the agent for productivity and agricultural development. The planter became the personification of development and, as he was a landlord, the privileges of that class were kept intact. Alexander Ross, who brought about the rejection of Harrington's Draft Regulation by his arguments in favour of *laissez-faire*, suggested at that time that the relation between landlords and tenants should be determined by demand and supply of labour and the lot of the peasants could be improved if the demand of labour was raised by encouraging European settlement.[10] This hint was taken up in 1829–30 by Bentinck and Metcalfe in their minutes, proposing an open door to European settlers. No further official attempts at rent control were made till the planters had virtually outlived their utility and caused the indigo disturbances of 1860. The landlords were joined by an increasing number of planters after 1836 in a scramble for agricultural profits at the expense of the small peasant economy. The occasional legislations like Act XII of 1841 and Act I of 1845 and the Draft Sale Law of 1855 were attempts to aid the planters against the superior landholders, in their disputes over landlord right to squeeze the peasants. The *istemrari* and *mukarrari* rights of ryots were declared non-voidable on sale of the parent estate without the amendments of Harrington, more as a cant than genuine motive. In the campaign of the planters for protection of under-tenures, the ryots' suffering was used as shibboleths against zamindars to gain the planters' ends. The planter had the resources to turn the vague and undefined language of law into their rights but the majority of ryots remained where they were in 1793.

The policy of *laissez-faire* and polarisation of agricultural profits

The landlords secured another long lease of their privileges under the threat of being compromised, thanks to the collaboration of the planters. They were not seriously disturbed till the passing of Act X of 1859. They made full use of the lull in rent control to consolidate their gains. The gains flowed from reclamation and the pressure of the growing population on land and the landlords manipulated regulations and custom to augment their rental profits. Let us take a quick look at the developments since the

10. B. R. C., 29 January 1833, no. 3

famine of 1770, to find out what the Permanent Settlement left for the landlords to reap in the nineteenth century.

A. *Land–man ratio*

The famine of 1770 and 1785 had resulted in large-scale depopulation but the country seemed to have recouped itself in less than 25 years. The landlords had encouraged settlement of ryots by giving them *khudkasht* or resident status at a low rent together with a homestead. With their aid, hamlets were set up and villages organised and if Colebrooke is to be relied upon, the population in 1794 was 'fully adequate to the cultivation of all land that is now waste' and numerous enough for existing tillage and manufacture.[11] The reply of the judges to Wellesley's interrogation in 1802 confirmed the trend of growing population in several districts. The Midnapur population report showed that it had reached the figure at which it had stood before the famine. It was roughly 1½ million. A very fast growth of population by both birth and immigration and increasing cultivation were visible everywhere in the district. In Burdwan, a similar increase of population was obvious from the fact of the extension of cultivation and establishment of new villages. The population was approximately 2 million. In the 24 Parganas, the wasteland brought under cultivation showed a considerable improvement in population and cultivation. The population was more than two million including that of Calcutta.[12] In 1808 Buchanan-Hamilton reported a huge population of 27,35,000 and 30,00,000 in Rangpur and Dinajpur respectively, both having sharecroppers and agricultural labourers in them.[13] The rough estimate of the population of the Bengal Presidency, excluding Assam and Orissa, in the famine period was 10 million, according to Grant's analysis in 1786. In 1802, it was 30 million, according to Colebrooke. The Fifth Report gave it as 27 million in 1812. Adam reported it to be 36 million in 1835. In 1857, it was 40 or 41 million, according to Marshman. The census of 1872 gives the figure of 42 million for the Presidency and 37 million roughly for Bengal proper only.[14]

But the land–man ratio on the basis of the estimated population could be fallacious as rivers, forests, swamps and arid zones were also included

11. H T Colebrooke, *Remarks*, Calcutta, 1806, p. 27

12. P.P., vii (1812), Appendix 10

13. *Mss. Eur. D. 75*, Buchanan-Hamilton Papers on Rangpur, vol. ii, pp. 2–6; F Buchanan-Hamilton, *Dinajpore*, Calcutta, 1833, p. 67

14. *Bengal Administration Reports (1872–73)*, pp. 95–118

in such surveys. It is safer to go by areas under cultivation or considered cultivable at a little expense. According to W N Lees, 30 million acres were under cultivation in 1793 and the figure came to 70 million acres in 1857, implying that 40 million acres were reclaimed over the period of 64 years.[15] This gives a fair idea of the pressure of population on land and the basis for measuring it in relation to estimates of population mentioned above. It appears that the land–man ratio remained almost stationary even after a period of brisk land reclamation. But the density of population to the square mile calculated in the settled areas gives, perhaps, the most reliable calculation of all. The existence of free land in a primarily agrarian economy does not mean that it was free for colonisation by a surplus population from the crowded areas as a matter of course. The landlords tended to hoard land to raise the value of the settled area of cultivation. The surplus population may not have had the capital for colonisation. The attachment of peasants to their ancestral home was sometimes so great that only an extremely desirable prospect could draw them out.

Colebrooke, on the basis of an estimate of the Purnea district, gives the estimate of population density in Bengal as 203 persons to a square mile in 1874. In Bengal proper in 1872, the average density was 389 persons to the square mile. Still, it does not give the true picture as the position varied considerably from district to district. Hooghly district in 1872 had 1000 to the square mile on an average. Burdwan, Birbhum, Nadia, Jessore, Murshidabad, Rajshahi and Tippera had 500 to 600 people to the square mile.[16] What did the pressure of population mean in real terms? R D Mangles stated in 1853 that Indian poverty was due to the fact that more people were engaged in the land than was required to produce enough food for them.[17] Marshman, in 1858, went further to analyse the situation. In his evidence before the Colonisation Committee he observed:

It is of no use to enact laws for the protection of the ryots; a zemindar laughs at them; he knows that nine-tenths of the population or more than nine-tenths depended entirely upon the culture of the soil for the means of subsistence and he knows that if one ryot refuses to accept land on the exorbitant terms he asks, there are ten who will be ready to step into his place; that of course neutralises all the laws that have been passed for the benefit of the ryot. But if the tables were turned and the surplus population were carried into those countries where they are

15. W N Lees, *Land and Labour of India*, London, 1867, p. 196
16. *Bengal Administration Reports (1872–73)*, p. 119
17. P.P., xxviii (1852–53), Mangles, Q. 6196

required, the zemindar would be immediately obliged to conciliate the
ryot and that would produce a greater improvement in his condition
than all the laws could make.[18]

A specific example can be given from the following report on the Nadia
estate under the Court of Wards in 1875–76:

> Almost in every village, there is more demand for land for cultivation
> by the ryots than can be supplied. The ryots from the other zemindari
> also now and then come to settle in our zemindari but no land being
> available for them for cultivation, they go away disappointed. Lands
> which were never cultivated before, are now being taken up for
> cultivation. There would have been a still greater difficulty to meet the
> demand of the ryots for lands, were it not for the death of many ryots
> by the epidemic . . . The demand for arable land has become so urgent
> that the ryots of many villages are ready to take jummas of the lands
> of more than ordinary rates of rents.[19]

The situation became desperate in Rangpur in 1876 when it reached a
density of 619 people to the square mile. Some local pleaders, in a letter
to the collector, reported that the ryots were bidding for land at no profit
or margin. It was a matter of subsistence or starvation for them.[20]

It is evident from what Mangles and Marshman said in the 1850s, that
the pressure of population on land was made worse by the absence of
industrial and urban outlet for the rural surplus. Whatever M D Morris
argues about the compensatory replacement of textile manufacturers by
weavers using imported thread, eye-witnesses like Taylor in 1840 and
Dunbar in 1844 wrote how the old craftsmen of Dhaka fell on agriculture
as a more profitable pursuit than weaving. Since 1788, de-industrialisation
had, according to them, contributed to overcrowding in agriculture.[21]

In 1858, therefore, nine-tenths of the population depended on agriculture for a living. Between 1793–1892, only 2,54,000 persons were

---

18. P.P., vii (1857–58), Part I, Marshman, Q. 9769
19. C. O. W. R. (1875–76), p. 15
20. *The Report of the Rent Law Commission*, Calcutta, 1880, pp. 21–23
21. M D Morris, 'Towards a Re-interpretation of Nineteenth Century Indian
    Economic History', *IESHR*, March 1968, vol. v, no. 1, pp. 1–18 and
    Toru Matsui, reply, p. 20; J Taylor, A Sketch of the *Topography and
    Statistics of Dacca*, Calcutta, 1840, (hereafter, *Dacca*), pp. 305–6;
    Mss. Eur. F. 78/44, Charles Wood Collection, Trade of Dacca, abstract
    from a letter by Dunbar, officiating commissioner of Dacca to Board of
    Revenue, 2 May 1844

involved in industrial production under the factory acts in India. The marginal figure for Bengal need not be guessed.[22] Urbanisation only affected 3 per cent of the people, even in the second half of the nineteenth century, as revealed by the census reports. In 1872, Calcutta, with a population of 4,47,601, was the primary city having an entirely rural hinterland. Dhaka had only 69,000 people and Jessore town had 8,152 out of a total population of over two million in the district. Moreover, towns other than Calcutta only housed people who were almost solely dependent on agriculture.[23]

It should be noted here that the data utilised so far are not wholly satisfactory. No reliable official census was undertaken before 1872. Earlier attempts were mostly guesses and their reliability depended on the ability of the observers. Even Buchanan-Hamilton's population figures for Rangpur and Dinajpur were challenged later by Glazier and Sherwill respectively. But the data, doubtless, give a rough idea of the pressure of population on land, spanning a period of over a century. During this long period, the population curve did not rise uniformly. There were famines and sickness. Malaria swept out the population in Dinajpur and Rangpur between Buchanan-Hamilton's and Sherwill's surveys (1808–1863). But the losses were made up by Santhal migration and emigration from the neighbouring district and a rise in local population in time. The rising population had taken up all arable lands, reclaimed tracts from the waste and brought lands of inferior quality under the plough. But the process did not create a large working force of landless labourers. Indigo factories having *nij* cultivation and the Public Works Department in the 1850s had to import Santhal coolies, or boonas as they were called, for the supply of labour. Obviously their terms were not sufficient to dislodge even sharecroppers from their apparent serfdom.

B. Enhancement of rent

How did the landlords exploit the situation? They profited immensely from the extensive cultivation and reclamation of the wasteland in the lightly assessed estates, brought about by the sheer pressure of population on land and enterprise of the yeomanry. Most of Midnapur and Bakarganj districts were reclaimed from jungle in this way. In the districts where reclamation was carried to the optimum point and in the already settled

---

22. Quoted in B Chandra, 'Re-interpretation of Nineteenth Century Indian Economic History', *IESHR*, March, vol. v, no. 1, p. 61

23. *Bengal Administration Reports (1872–73)*, pp. 115–16

districts, they went for a straightforward enhancement of rent. The lands were classified into various grades according to their fertility and produce. *Bastu* or homestead lands and lands growing cash crops like indigo, sugarcane, tobacco and bamboo invariably paid a very high rent. A table of rent rates complied from the reports of collectors between 1793 and 1870 for Hooghly illustrates the point (rent per *bigha* or one-third of an acre):

Year	Sali or arable plain			Soona or high land			Sugarcane
	Class I	Class II	Class III	Class I	Class II	Class III	Land
	Rs	Rs	Rs	Rs	Rs	Rs	
1793	3	2-4	1-8	3	2-4	1-8	Not available
1837	2 to 2-4	1-12 to 2	1-4 to 1-8	3	2-8 to 2-12	2 to 2-8	2–4 Rs
1850	7-8	6	4-8	7-8	6	4-8	N. A.
1870	12	9	6	12-18	9	6-12	12–24 Rs

Source: O'Malley and Chakrabarty, Bengal District Gazetteers, Hooghly, Calcutta, 1921, p. 167

The rent had apparently quadrupled since 1837. The tendency to consider the rate of rent of rice lands only, obscures the fact that lands bearing cash crops always paid a much higher rent and offset the low rent for the former. In the table above, sugarcane land showed a six-fold increase at its peak in 1870. The rates obtainable from zamindari papers are not reliable as Pearymohan Mukherjee, a member of the Rent Law Commission (1880) and a leading Hooghly zamindar, quoted the rates for the *sali* variety in his estate at Rs 4, 3 and 2 per *bigha* for the first, second and third classes of land before the Commission in 1880.[24] The deputy collector of Lalgolah, Murshidabad, made a local enquiry in *thana* Rampurhat in 1872 and found that there was an *asal* or original rent on the estate paid by none. The non-cultivating brahmins paid at double this rate, mandals or village headmen paid at 2½ times and the general body

---

24. *Report of the Rent Law Commission*, Calcutta, 1880, p. 42

of cultivators at 3½ times.[25] In Nadia, rent for rice land had risen by more than 100 per cent between 1793 and 1872. It is interesting to note that homestead and betel leaf growing lands paid an average rent of Rs 1-4-0 and Rs 4 per *bigha* while rice land paid only 9 annas in 1793. For a holding with all categories of rent, which was usually the case, rent should be much higher than supposed. By 1872, homestead and tobacco lands bore more than double the rent of 1793 on those lands.[26]

It has to be remembered that money was extremely scarce throughout our period of study. Cornwallis noted its depressing effect on ryots in 1787. The collector of Hooghly in 1843 wrote to the accountant general that the lower classes used only copper coins and the circulation ranged between Rs 5000 and Rs 10,000 but never exceeded the latter sum.[27] Rev Schurr pointed out in 1860 that the acute want of money was the reason for ryots' acceptance of indigo advances.[28]

The scarcity was reflected in agricultural prices. The price per *maund* of rice in Jessore between 1801 and 1873 gives a good idea of the purchasing power of money:

Price of ordinary rice per *maund* in rupees and annas

1801	About 4 as.
1843	8–9 as.
1853	12 as.
1863	Rs 1–8 as.
1873	Rs 1–4 as.

Source: R S Sen, Report on Jhenidah, Magura, Bagirhat and Sunderban Sub-divisions in Jessore, Calcutta, 1874, pp. 64–65

For Mymensing, the price of rice per *maund* was Rs 1 in 1818 and Rs 1-6-0 in 1840.[29] For Hooghly, it was as follows (price in seers per rupee):

---

25. W W Hunter, *SAB, Murshidabad*, London, 1875–76, p. 127
26. J H E Garrett, *Bengal District Gazetteers, Nadia*, Calcutta, 1910, pp. 82–83
27. *Public Record Office 30/11/150*, Cornwallis Papers, Cornwallis to Dundas, 14 August 1787; G Toynbee, *Hooghly*, Calcutta, 1888, pp. 99–100
28. R. I. C., Rev Schurr, Q. 778
29. F A Sachse, *Bengal District Gazetteers, Mymensing*, Calcutta, 1917, p. 67

| 1793–1813 | (average of 21 years) | 40 seers or 1 *maund* |
| 1861–1865 | (average of 5 years) | 21 seers or a little over ½ *maund* [30] |

For Birbhum, it was Rs 1-0-9 per maund in 1788 and Rs 1-4-5 in 1872 [31]

From these figures, it can be very broadly concluded that the price of ordinary rice in Bengal for the central period of study stayed at 12 annas per *maund* on an average. Considering that a conversion of currency from *sicca* to the Company's rupee at 100 old rupees equal to Company's Rs 106-10-8 in 1838, the average should be even less. The price (at its peak) had doubled within this period. In 1809 the diet allowance in the courts of Hooghly for indigent prosecutors and witnesses was only 1 anna daily per head.[32] In 1839, 32 prisoners could be fed for 1 rupee a day in Mymensing. In the twentieth century, the same cost only Rs 8.[33]

It is clear, therefore, that the notion that the price of rice rose at a higher rate than rent in the period 1793–1872, is largely a myth. Moreover, the averages partially hide the truth. As communication was extremely difficult and the villages were virtually insulated, there was no chain of internal markets or urban outlets for the surplus produce. In many areas, an abundance of harvest resulted in a glut in the local market and arrears of rent as a consequence. The peasant had to surrender his whole crop to earn a rupee and that made it impossible for him to pay rent to his landlord in cash. We have the following evidence of Rammohan Roy in support:

Q. 43: Have the cultivators any means of accumulating capital under the present system?

A.   : Certainly not. Very often, when grain is abundant, and therefore cheap, they are obliged . . . to sell their whole produce to satisfy the demands of their landlords and to subsist themselves by their own labour. In scarce and dear years, they may be able to retain some portion of the crop to form a part of their subsistence but by no means enough for the whole. In short, such is the melancholy condition of the agricultural labourers that it always given me greatest pain to allude to it.

---

30. L S S O'Malley and M Chakrabarty, *Bengal District Gazetteers, Hooghly*, Calcutta, 1912, p. 161
31. L S S O'Malley, *Bengal District Gazetteers, Birbhum*, Calcutta, 1910, p. 66
32. G Toynbee, *Hooghly*, Calcutta, 1888, p. 94
33. F A Sachse, *Bengal District Gazetteers, Mymensing*, Calcutta, 1917, p. 67
34. P. P., v (1831), Appendix 39, pp. 719–21

Taylor testifies to the same problem for Dhaka.[35] Moreover many debtor-ryots had to sell their crop at a dictated price to their mahajans. In Midnapur, rate determination with reference to crop prices was given up by H V Bayley during his survey (1844–52) as 'no real selling prices could be obtained for each individual ryot's case' because of the existence of forced sale.[36] The export figures of so-called surplus districts could well be the crop surrendered by the peasant, in perverse response to the market.

C. Abwabs or surcharges

Abwabs have been explained as occasional tributes from ryots to their landlords by scholars and considered as a negligible element in the ultimate incidence of rent on the ryot. But there are reasons to regard it as a regular form of rent. Abwabs were historically linked with rent from pre-British days and the nawabs made it a mechanism for enhancing the original rent roll prepared by Todar Mal in Akbar's times. While the original rent remained virtually frozen, abwabs more than made up the static income from rent. For Bakarganj between 1728–63, J C Jack calculated it to be 7 lakh in *abwab*, over 8 lakh in revenue on an average. The government did not make any survey and settlement to justify a scientific rent. So, abwabs were handy for an arbitrary enhancement. As most of the land in the interior was in the hands of the reclaimers enjoying a fixed, low rent, any share in their agricultural profits had to be claimed by abwabs. The landlords followed the same practice both before and after 1793, as they made no survey or measurement either and promoted reclamation by offering low rent to the pioneers.[37] As we have noticed already, the lightly assessed estates in Rangpur and Dinajpur with reclaim-able waste were the strongholds of abwabs in the nineteenth century. Besides many zamindars had made a deal with their ryots to claim low rent rates and make it up in abwabs so as to reduce the face value of their assets for a light assessment at the Permanent Settlement in 1793. Rangpur was such an area.

The auction purchasers had no way of knowing the appropriations by ryots. They never undertook a detailed survey, except an occasional

---

35. J Taylor, *Dacca*, Calcutta, 1840, p. 296

36. H V Bayley, *A History of Midnapore*, Calcutta, 1902, p. 44

37. J C Jack, *Bakarganj Settlement Report*, Calcutta, 1915, pp. 79–80, 92; also, G Toynbee, *Hooghly*, Calcutta, 1888, p. 62 for long established abwabs in settled areas

measurement of the holdings of recusant ryots. J C Jack did not exaggerate when he wrote that his settlement office in Bakarganj in 1900–1908 looked like a lost property office where landlords crowded in to trace their holdings for the first time in their lives.[38] The landlords of the Bhogchar and Chanchra estates in Jessore were reported about the same time to be ignorant about the lands for which rent was paid but aware of parties paying it.[39] There was no other way for the landlords to get their dues than taxing the peasants per head. The number of peasants or *proja* as they were called, mattered to them more than acres. The abwabs, therefore, constituted a significant sum for a ryot along with his actual rent. The ryots paid it voluntarily not so much due to a feudal hangover as a make-shift arrangement for a share out of agricultural profits. Coercion was employed when there was a tug of war over the distribution. The more powerful and oppressive the landlord, the larger his share of the agricultural surplus. The importance of abwabs as rent was not fully understood until the Campbell administration tried to suppress it in 1872. McNeille, in his memorandum on the Revenue Administration in 1873, was the first to show an insight into the mechanism of abwabs. 'It being tacitly understood', he wrote, 'that abwabs paid, rent-roll will not be interfered with. If Government intervenes, the compact will break up and litigation will ensue. A most serious struggle would follow, the most calamitous under British rule so far. Via media should be to repress excesses while winking at others.'[40] The forebodings were well founded. The Pabna Uprising of 1873–74 was the direct outcome of Campbell's measure. In *pargana* Yusufshahi, where the trouble first originated, the actual rental had not been raised for a long time but zamindars were, as the Bengal Administration Report (1872–73) put it, 'in the habit of realising heavy cesses of various sorts which had gone on for so long that it was scarcely clear what portion of their collections was rent and what illegal cesses'. It was a tacit understanding between landlords and tenants to share agricultural profits in a low rent area in this way. Enhanced rent took the shape of cesses on the basis of mutual understanding. The action taken by the government in 1872 led the landlords to play the safer game of including the cesses within the rent and this instigated the ryots to oppose the move to the utmost.[41]

---

38. J C Jack, *Bakarganj Settlement Report*, Calcutta, 1915, p. 43

39. M A Momen, *Jessore Settlement Report*, Calcutta, 1925, p. 155

40. D J McNeille, *Memorandum on the Revenue Administration of the Lower Provinces of Bengal*, Calcutta, 1873, pp. 142–44

41. *Bengal Administration Reports (1872–73)*, p. 24

What was the nature and amount of the abwabs? In Rangpur, the earliest inventory made in Saruppur estate in 1790 showed abwabs being one-eighth of the rental. The classic description of abwabs was given by Thomas Sisson, collector of Rangpur in 1815:

> Not a child can be born, not a head religiously shaved, not a son married, not a daughter given in marriage – not even one of the tyrannical fraternity dies – without an immediate visitation of calamity upon the ryot.

What Glazier, collector in 1876 found was not a whit different from the above account.[42] In his survey of the Majnumutha estate in Midnapur in 1844, Bayley discovered 61 varieties of cesses and abwabs. Two groups were in vogue. The customary or *russomoti* variety and the miscellaneous ones. Among the latter group, on the single item of marriage, there was a marriage tax of 2–4 shillings on both parties, 2 shillings on widow marriage, 9 shillings for marriage of a dependent or slave, 2 shillings for carrying an umbrella in marriage ceremonies, 2 shillings for feasts, 2 shillings for marrying into another's zamindari. The total *russomoti* collection of the Majnumutha estate amounted in 1815 to £430-18s-3d (at 2 shillings = 1 Rs). Raja Anandalal Roy of Majnumutha estate objected to the abolition of the *paramanik* cess in his estate, then taken *khas* by the government, and openly declared that ancestral custom should supersede regulations.[43] The Maldah Settlement Report (1928–35) quotes the amount of *abwab* in old Maldah as one-third of the total rent and the same for the twentieth century, that is, not less than the government's land revenue of the whole district.[44] The Jessore Settlement Report deplores the practices, continuing unabated since the Permanent Settlement, despite government regulations abolishing them in 1872. The cesses varied between two to four annas in the rupee for a big list of items like marriage, festivals and so on. 'Abwabs are realised with an iron hand,' the report goes on, 'and are considered to be the first charge on the tenant even in preference to rent.'[45] In Dhaka at the time of the Settlement (1910–17), the abwabs amounted to 25 to 33 per cent on rent. It was handed down

42 E G Glazier, *Rungpore*, p. 45; *Mss. Eur. F. 86/165*, Temple Collection, Substantive Law for Determination of Rent, Answers to Circular, Glazier, 16 August 1876, paras on Rangpur abwabs

43. W W Hunter, *SAB, Midnapore*, pp. 110–11; H V Bayley, *Report on the Settlement of the Majnumutha Estate*, pp. 89–95; also, H V Bayley, *A History of Midnapore*, Calcutta, 1902, pp. 47–51

44. M V Carter, *Malda Settlement Report*, Calcutta, 1938, pp. 80–81

45. M A Momen, *Jessore Settlement Report*, Calcutta, 1925, p. 124

from pre-British days and the custom died hard. In a letter to the Board
of Revenue, the collector reported in 1821, 'Rents were increased and
abwabs continued and to the present day, the landlords of Dacca have
developed this precedent (i.e. consolidation of abwab in rent as in 1793)
and augmented their rents by the inclusion of abwabs; not unnaturally a
fresh abwab is immediately imposed. It is not the amount of the abwab
but the lever that is created for the enhancement of rents that consitutes
the evil of the system in Dacca.' Nothing better illustrates the mechanism
and purpose of abwabs than the word 'lever' here.[46] Speaking of the
effect of prohibiton of abwabs in Bakarganj, J C Jack writes:

> It is a prohibition which the Bakarganj landlord had consistently and
> flagrantly disobeyed. A conservative estimate would place the total
> amount collected as abwab in Bakarganj at not less than the entire Gov-
> ernment land revenue and one-quarter of the entire rental of the district.

In individual estates, he noticed abwabs amounting to half of the rent in
one case and more than the rent collected in another. According to Jack,
the abwabs multiplied from the middle of the nineteenth century. The
worst part of the business was that whatever ryots paid as rent was shown
against the abwabs and rent was kept in arrears and receipts refused.[47]

D. Measurement

In districts like Jessore and Midnapur, the rent was traditionally kept low
and virtually frozen as a concession to the reclaimers. But the tactics of
measurement were largely employed to enhance rent at the fixed rate.
Various nals or poles of shorter size than the standard one were used for
as many cubits in measurement to claim the existence of more bighas in
a holding than had been recorded and so to double or treble rental at the
existing rate. In Jessore, the pole used for measurement had 441 square
inches in a square cubit for thanas Jhenidah, Solekopah, Harinakunda and
Magura and 567 square inches for Mahmudpur and Shalikha, while the
standard measure was 324 square inches. In other words, length of an acre
in bighas varied by about a *bigha* from place to place.[48] The same practice
was reported in Midnapur in the Settlement Report (1912).[49]

46. F D Ascoli, *Dacca Settlement Report*, Calcutta, 1917, pp. 43–44
47. J C Jack, *Bakarganj Settlement Report*, Calcutta, 1915, pp. 79–83
48. R S Sen, *Report on Jhenidah*, Calcutta, 1874, p. 78
49. B Sanyal, *Midnapore Settlement Report, Minor Settlement Operations*, Calcutta, 1914, Appendix VII

In Khajura village within Narail estate of Ramratan Roy in Jessore, the rental was doubled and trebled by him in 1856 by assessing excess lands found in the possession of ryots by such measurement. In the Ramnagar estate, a rent roll was prepared by such measurement in 1808. M Funicane, who was sent in 1883 on special duty to Jessore, to enquire into the condition of the lower classes, examined the *cutcherry* papers and found that 'this so-called measurement was in fact an expedient for enhancing the rents'. A second measurement was carried out in 1883. The papers of the Chanchra Raj *cutcherry* examined by Funicane in 1883 showed such measurements made in 1882 of the holdings of two ryots, Jamir Mollah and Dhanesh Mondal. They allegedly held five and seven bighas in excess and were made to pay rent for this excess land.[50] The ryots frequently held more land than they paid rent for, in the reclaimed areas. Measurement by rope or pole was the only means for the landlords to detect them. But once employed, it was carried to excess. Colebrooke mentioned in 1794 how landlords forced their ryots 'to consent to the doubling of their rates upon a stipulation for a fair measurement'.[51] Measurement was so abused in the period 1830–1860 that Act VIII of 1869 section 96 had to be passed to protect ryots against it.

E. *Eviction*

The second strategy to override the rights of *khudkasht* ryots of long standing was to oust them outright and make a fresh rent roll with them or the newcomers. In his survey between 1838 and 1844, H V Bayley noticed a rapid diminution in the number of *thani* or *khudkasht* ryots and the consequent increase in the number of *pahi* or *paikasht* ryots. In *pargana* Balijura, there were 712 *thani* and 548 *pahi* ryots before 1833. After 1833, 455 thanis were left and the number of pahis swelled to 897. In *pargana* Kismut Pataspore, the number of thanis before 1833 was 620. It later reduced to only 267. In *pargana* Doro Dumnan there were 4,195 thanis and 1,953 pahis formerly. At the time of the Settlement, there were 3,014 thanis left and the pahis had become a crowd of 5,613 people. In 1790, Midnapur had two-thirds of its territory in jungle and the thanis were given *jungleburee* leases at quit rent for reclamation. With the pressure of population on land and progress of reclamation, the pioneers at a quit rent were apparently dismissed or converted into *pahi* ryots at an enchanced

---

50. M A Momen, *Jessore Settlement Report*, Calcutta, 1925, Appendix W
51. H T Colebrooke, *Remarks*, Calcutta, 1806, p. 57

rent.[52] In Jessore, the Narail zamindars resumed many gantis in 1840 after buying two new estates (numbers 178 and 179) and made a fresh settlement at an enhancement of 2 annas in the rupee.[53] The *zillah* court decisions provide many more examples of illegal ouster and enhancement. In Rangpur the conduct of Rani Swarnamoyi of Baharbund in ousting Jhulan Bibee, a *jotedar*, for arrears of rent and replacing her by one Ataullah Sirdar was held illegal by Judge Bell in the case Ataullah Sirdar vs Jhulan Bibee (number 11 of 1853). In Dinajpur, the case Phool Muhammad Jotedar vs Doorgakant and other zamindars (number 59 of 1852) shows how the original rent of the *jotedar* of Rs 32-3 annas for 33 bighas and 6 cottahs of land was enhanced to Rs 75 plus Rs 18 as *kabul beshi* or voluntary agreement, after the zamindar had succeeded in getting a distraint order in collusion with the *cazee* and attaching his crop and cattle.[54]

These instances are taken from cases where the ryots had won. But it is perhaps needless to say that there were numerous cases in which the ryots had silently surrendered or suffered from the decisions of a falsely instituted case. It was a time honoured practice of the landlords to bribe or win over the village headmen and leading ryots by indulgence or rent rebates and make them swear to the high rent as the *pargana* rate. Colebrooke mentions this in 1794. Funicane, in his tour of the Jessore district in 1883, found the practice of giving *hajjot* or rebate to mondals and mollahs in the Chanchra Raj estate ranging from 20 to 40 per cent on the *jumma* and confirmed what R S Sen reported to be the practice in Jessore in 1874.[55] In the Dhaka division, the situation was described in 1872–73 as follows:

When a village had gone on strike, the landlord singles out a few of the leading men and bribes them to his side with a false measurement with a null of length greater than that used in the village or he throws in a few bighas of land into his pottah under the denomination of 'keyfeut' or 'hajut' or 'oozoree' or some other fancy name. These men then go to court ready to swear anything against the men on strike and in a day or two, some of them find their houses burnt down about their ears.[56]

52. H V Bayley, *Report on the Settlement of Majnumutha Estate*, Calcutta, 1884, pp. 272–300
53. M A Momen, *Jessore Settlement Report*, Calcutta, 1925, p. 118
54. *Decisions of Zillah Courts*, Calcutta, 1853, pp. 29, 45–46; *ibid* (1851), p. 20, case no. 142 of 1850 for another case
55. M A Momen, *Jessore Settlement Report*, Calcutta, 1925, Appendix W
56. *Bengal Administration Reports (1872–73)*, pp. 35–36

Raja Kishorilal Goswami of Serampur, having estates spread over several districts, admitted that the reduction of rent or *hajjot* was allowed to prodhans or village headmen according to 'their status in the village or for services their families have done to the landlord's family,' as he put it with characteristic understatement.[57]

The final resort, of course, was the Sale Law. By bringing the estate to sale for arrears all the undesirable under-tenures were thrown out and then the estate was repurchased *benami* by the landlord. It required large capital and tremendous local influence to be the seller and buyer of one's own estate. As noticed in the first chapter, the practice was as old as the law itself. It explains why Raja Barodakantha Roy of Jessore was found to be a notorious *benamidar* in his Bakarganj estates.[58] The impact of the sale of the parent estate on the ryots can be gathered from the following vivid account by Henry Ricketts in 1850 which contributed to the framing of Act X of 1859:

> I can imagine no condition more pitiable than that of the inhabitants of a zemindari transferred by sale for arrears . . . All the tenures of all classes are open to revision . . . We can talk of it and write of it with indifference, but to the tenants of an estate, a sale is as the spring of a wild beast into the fold, as the bursting of a shell in the square. It is the disturbance of all they had supposed stable. The consequence must be a recasting of their lot in life with the odds greatly against them.[59]

Thus, the landlords had successfully exploited the growth of population to their supreme advantage. It had helped large-scale reclamation of the waste and brought immense profits to the landlords of the lightly assessed estates in 1793. The pressure of population on settled areas had deprived the ryots of all bargaining power against their landlords. Armed with summary powers and the purse to command the inadequate system of justice, the latter could virtually dictate terms to the ryots. A few undefined clauses in the Permanent Settlement to protect *khudkasht* ryots had been whittled down. The landlords had appropriated much of the peasant's surplus by enhancing rents upto double or more of the *pargana* rate and by countless cesses. The rise of price was not enough to offset these exactions. There had apparently been a virtual polarisation of profits. In

---

57. P Mukherjee, *Opinions of Mofussil Landholders on the Bengal Tenancy Bill*, Calcutta, 1883, (hereafter, *Opinions*), p. 62

58. H Beveridge, *Bakarganj*, London, 1876, pp. 155–56

59. B. R. C., 28 October 1852, no. 3, Enclosures, Minute of Ricketts, 10 May 1850

1830–31 Holt Mackenzie estimated, on the basis of the Court of Wards records for all the districts, a profit of 100 per cent on the *jumma* for landlords. At the same time, we have this glaring contrast of rural poverty from Rammohan Roy:

> To those who ever made a tour of these provinces, either on public duty or from motives of curiosity, it is well known that within a circle of a hundred miles in any part of the country, there are to be found very few, if any, besides proprietors of land, that have the least pretension to wealth or independence or even the common comforts of life . . . The benefits which the proprietors enjoy is principally owing to two circumstances: first, the extended cultivation of waste lands which formerly yielded no rent; secondly, subsequent increase of rents, much beyond those rates paid by cultivators at the time of the Perpetual Settlement, in defiance of the rights of khudkasht ryots . . .

Source: P.P., v (1831), Appendix 39, pp. 724–24

In 1841, W G Rose reported the situation in identical terms: 'It is a notorious fact that the ryots of Bengal are worse off now, that is, poorer than they were fifty years ago and getting poorer and poorer every day. . . hardly a single village in Bengal is able to pay its rents.'[60] K Brodie, a planter with wide experience in Mymensing and Jessore, gives an appalling picture of rural poverty a decade later in 1853. He found the ryot 'always in debt and always in need' and only one or two of them possessed even a bedstead. A few pieces of earthenware and two pieces of cloth a year were all they had. Few possessed brass vessels and children moved about naked.[61]

Income tax was levied for the first time in 1860 in Bengal and, in 1862–63, the number of people with the qualifying income of Rs 500 per annum was only 64,677 in a population of roughly 40 million.[62] If we take the evidence of Digambar Mitra, assistant secretary of the British Indian Association and a landlord himself, given at the monthly meeting of 26 July 1861, the zamindari profit was admittedly 100 per cent on the *jumma* on the grossly assessed estate and 50 per cent on estates of Hooghly, Burdwan and 24 Parganas. They were undoubtedly the handful of men who qualified to pay income tax.

---

60. B. J. C., 30 March 1841, no. 48
61. P. P., xxviii (1852–53), Evidence of Brodie, Q. 7438, 7473, 7486–97
62. P N Banerjee, *A History of Indian Taxation*, London, 1930, pp. 78, 93

We have so far discussed only zamindari rates of rent and profits for which data are available. If the rental profits of the intermediaries are taken into account, the polarisation of agricultural profits in favour of landlords becomes apparent. We can form some idea of the final amount paid by the primary producer with reference to Nadia, Rangpur and Midnapur. The intermediaries collected from the under-tenants double the amount they paid to their overlords.[63] Obviously, capital formation at the grassroots level was ruled out.

The immediate background of Act X of 1859

The problems of distribution of agricultural profits and capital formation at the level of primary producers did not concern officials as they believed in the entrepreneurial efforts of the planters and their supposed ability to transplant capitalist farming in a small peasant economy. The measures to protect garden and factory sites and bona fide leases at fair rent for 20 years (Act XII of 1841 and Act I of 1845) and *patni* and other immediate tenures (Draft Sale Law of 1855) were all designed to protect the planters' interests as explained in Chapters 4 and 5. As the planters came to occupy ryoti jotes in larger numbers in the 1850s and changed from *nij* to ryoti cultivation, the protection of ryot's occupancy became paramount for them and it has been noticed in the preceding chapter that they have paved the way for Act X of 1859. But this was not quite the whole story. The Rent Act had other implications of greater significance. Though the planters had shifted the official attention from the primary producers for well over two decades and monopolised it, circumstances began to favour the ryots and brought them to the forefront of official consideration again. Even in 1847–48, when the indigo planters were still basking in the sunshine of official favour, the Select Committee on Sugar and Coffee Plantations observed that indigo cultivation had passed its peak of prosperity. Cotton had a distant future in view of the supply of American cotton, and sugar, coffee, tobacco and safflower had a better prospect than indigo. These articles had to be promoted if the remittance and export–import trade were to be kept going.[64] The annual turnout of indigo for export in the 1850s went down steadily from 18,718 maunds in

---

63. J H E Garrett, *Bengal District Gazetteers*, *Nadia*, Calcutta, 1910, p. 83; E G Glazier, *Rungpore*, p. 43; *Report of the Rent Law Commission*, Calcutta, 1880, pp. 7–9 for Midnapore
64. P. P., xxiii (1847–48), Part III, Appendix I to Eighth Report

1850–51 to 8,023 maunds in 1858–59 for Krishnagar and from 15,964 maunds to 8,633 maunds for Jessore over the same period.[65] There was an official remittance of 3 million pounds and a private one of 1½ million to be despatched in goods in 1853 and the staggering sum of 4½ million was described as 'a great incubus upon the India trade' by C E Trevelyan in his evidence before the House of Lords in 1852–53.[66]

The Free Traders, in their numerous petitions, expressed their dissatisfaction with the limited extent of commerce with India and the little progress made in the development of varied resources. The problem of raising cash crops and agricultural development as a whole were linked up with the sale of Lancashire cotton piece-goods, Sheffield cutleries and Bristol salt. They demanded measures to improve market and communication, the growth of cash crops and the physical condition of the subjects of the empire. The Liverpool petition demanded that 'such laws be passed as may effectively protect the cultivator from oppression on the part of the collectors of taxes, zamindars and others and enable them to recover from the proprietors of the land compensations for unexhausted improvements'.

The whole argument of Free Traders after 1830 was for a system of trade in which India received the manufactures of England in exchange for her raw materials. In 1853, the House of Commons ordered an enquiry into the state and prospect of cash crops in India, following demands from Free Traders. The fact that cash crops like sugar, jute, coffee and tobacco had a greater prospect than indigo were revealed to the government. To Free Traders, by and large, the phrase 'cash crop' was not synonymous with indigo and the indigo planters were not the only group who needed J Jeffreys assistance. The representative of the Liverpool East India and China Association even suggested a government initiative in the matter by way of *tuccavi* advances to the yeomanry.[67] It was gradually realised that both the promotion of cash crops and the market for manufactured goods in India depended on the material condition of the majority of the people. The Manchester petition pointed out with concern how the progress of people in industry and wealth had been retarded and people had been altogether left in a state of misery, disgraceful to their rulers.[68] Capital formation at their level and the improvement of their purchasing power were all that mattered. The question was raised

65. R. I. C., Appendix 17
66. P. P., xxxii (1852–53), Q. 6640
67. P. P., xxxii (1852–53), Appendix D for the Petitions; P. P., xxviii (1852–53), Jeffreys, Q. 7700–10
68. P. P., xxvii (1852–53), Appendix 7

during the Select Committee enquiry in 1831–32 but the decision to support the planters had annulled it. Ellenborough had observed in 1830, 'To make the people of that country consumers of the manufactures of England, we must first make them rich. That object is remote indeed, but we must endeavour to attain it.'[69] It was brought up again on the eve of the Charter Act debate of 1853. A searching enquiry was made into the cause of Indian poverty and Rev Keane, Mangles and Brodie testified that overcrowding on the land, *mahajani* and zamindari exaction, government taxation and drain of wealth were the factors behind it. The need for the protection of ryot's rights, and a fair return upon their investments to allow capital formation, and improvement of their physical and cultural condition by a better system of justice and education would provide the answers to the question of trade prospects. It was divulged by Gladstone, representative of Manchester Gillanders and Co., that the value of cotton of lower value for export to Bengal had risen from £4,01,000 to £22,27,000 in 1852 by adapting them to the needs of the lower classes.[70] Sisirkumar Ghose, the spokesman of the landed middle class, was later to ridicule the official concern for Indian poverty and the measures to develop agricultural resources by giving agricultural scholarship in an attempt to restore purchasing power to the masses and secure a market for British-made goods at the dictate of Manchester.[71]

The debate in official circles over protection of under-tenures and leases was triggered off by the petition of Mackenzie, the planter of Jessore, for protection of his date plantations in 1849. Henry Ricketts, in his notes of 10 and 17 May 1850, defended his scheme of registration of leases and tenancy rights not only of planters but also of tenants protected under the Permanent Settlement. Sconce, at that time collector of Chittagong and later instrumental in bringing about the Rent Act, was the first to make a clear distinction between actual cultivators and jotedars in the broad category of under-tenants and to strongly condemn the exploitation of the former class by the latter. In the Minute of 19 February 1850, he made a special plea for the protection of *khudkasht* interests. 'Our law speaks of khoodkasht ryots as if they held under a succession which like Jacob's ladder reached up to the clouds,' he went on, 'whereas in truth

69. J W Kaye, *The Life and Correspondence of Charles Metcalfe*, London, 1854, p. 178
70. P. P., xxxii (1852–53), Keane, Q. 7779–7809; P. P., xxviii (1852–53), Mangles, Q. 6196, footnote 6289, Brodie, Q. 7448–91, 7506, 7638 and Gladstone, Q. 8049
71. S Ghose, *Indian Sketches*, Calcutta, 1898, pp. 108–9

now as at any past time, a khoodkasht right is susceptible of being created.'
This single passage was to explode the old idea of pre-Permanent
Settlement moorings as the basis of *khudkasht* rights and open up the
possibilities of creation of occupancy rights for a shorter incumbency. He
also spelt out the implications of the phrase 'fair rent' which remained a
key phrase for a share out of agricultural profits between the landlord and
the tenant. He suggested its fixed rate on the basis of a return of the
collections of the last five years. In other words, he was in favour of a
fixed *pargana* rate or a customary rate. Trevor, the legal remembrancer,
argued in favour of government intervention to protect 'the most important
community, the ryots', but raised the point that in a share of agricultural
profits due to rise of prices, the landlord had a definite claim for profitable
use made of his land.[72] Welby Jackson, a judge of the *sadar diwani adalat*,
in a Minute of 27 August 1852 opposing the landlord's summary powers
of ejection, described the resident ryots as 'the most valuable and by far
the largest portion of the peasantry' and 'the yeomen of the country' and
regretted that they had to prove their rights from beyond the time of the
Permanent Settlement. In 1854, in his report on a tour of inspection, he
went a step further to support the cause of the yeomanry in Bengal.
'Cultivation has been greatly extended wherever the state of the country
admitted of its extension,' he wrote, '. . . but the extension of cultivation
which has brought new tracts under tillage has not been effected by means
of any outlay on the part of the zemindars; they have allowed the peasantry
to bring the lands under the plough and have participated with the
peasantry in the profit derived from them'. 'It is to them, the men of
enterprize and action,' Jackson pointed out, 'that the estate must look for
further progress in the same direction.'[73] The petition of the missionaries
to the Legislative Council of India (1855) had a decisive influence on the
official deliberations of the period. It drew pointed attention to the fact
that the landlords were growing in wealth and power while the tenants
were sinking into penury and dependence in the *mofussil*. They maintained
that the extension of cultivation was brought about by the pressure of
population and its profits were monopolised by the zamindars. They
hindered capital formation in the tenantry. Taking Rs 2 a *bigha* as the
average rent, they calculated that a ryot earned about Rs 5 on a *bigha* and

---

72. B. R. C., 28 October 1852, no. 3 for Ricketts, no. 6 for Sconce and no. 11
for Trevor
73. B. R. C., 20 January, 1853, no. 10; *Selection from the Records of the
Government of Bengal*, vol. xvi; W B Jackson, *Report of a Tour of
Inspection*, Calcutta, 1854, (hereafter, *Report of a Tour*) pp. 12–14

after paying Rs 2 as rent, had only Rs 3 to subsist on. As the average holding was of 12 bighas, the annual income of a ryot was Rs 36 or Rs 3 per month, leaving aside payment of debt and cesses. Their condition was precarious.[74]

Its impact on the Legislative Council could be gathered from the fact that E Currie, the future framer of the Rent Act and member for Bengal, made serious opposition to the protection of under-tenures only as leading to improvement of the country during the debate over Grant's Draft Law of 1855. His objection was that it did not touch the level of ryots.[75] In 1856, the deliberation took a positive turn towards protection of resident ryots from a tendency to protect intermediaries like the planters. Collector C G Bellie of Hooghly, while applauding Rickett's scheme of registration, remarked that a registration fee of 5 per cent on the *jumma* meant that only those paying at least Rs 100 in annual *jumma* were intended. He pleaded for the inclusion of the lowest ryot for registration. The collector of Tippera raised the same objection of a prohibitive fee for registration which excluded most of the peasants in the country. F C Fowle, collector of Jessore, emphasised the role of the ryots in a country's economy. He wrote:

If a ryoti system prevails, it would be more apparent that on the ryot depends the commerce and manufacture and his welfare means the welfare of the country.

He wanted all subleases to be banned as the system of subletting left the ryot 'the beggared victim of a merciless mahajan'. It was his decided opinion that the country had not improved at all for the past half-century. The same rude materials were in use to assist husbandry and the ryots were denied the fruit of their labour.

These opinions even influenced Halliday, the lieutenant governor, who was known for his pro-planter bias, to declare in his Minute of 2 September 1856 that the Permanent Settlement had sacrificed the actual cultivators. Whenever an estate would forfeit to the government, it should be re-settled with the actual proprietors to redress the wrong done at the Permanent Settlement.[76]

---

74. P. P., vii (1857–58), Part II, Appendix 6
75. *Proceedings of the Legislative Council of India*, January–December 1856, vol. ii, Calcutta, 1856, p. 327
76. B. R. C., 9 October 1856, Enclosures, no. 12 for Bellie, no. 20 for Fowle, no. 30 for Halliday's Minute

Along with the question of occupancy, the rate of rent figured prominently in the discussion. The commissioner of Bhagalpur, in a note of 30 December 1856, thought that the registration of under-tenures did not go far enough. 'I wish to see some provisions restricting the rights of present proprietors' he argued, 'to increase at will or by a suit in the civil courts, the rent of tenures held with or without documents at a fixed jumma for a certain number of years, say 12, before the attempt to increase was made.'[77] But the Minute that contributed most to the framing of the Rent Act was from A Sconce, the judge of the *sadar diwani adalat* in 1857:

... when we are invoked to develop agriculture, let it never be forgotten that it is from the ryot, from the man who ploughs and sows and not the Talookdar that the development is to come. It is time to part with the notion that the agriculturists cannot distiguish between profitable and unprofitable crops and that they will not adopt the former in preference to the latter. . . The most erroneous of all notions is to describe or limit the development of agricultural resources by the payment of advances or to measure, for example, the advantage of advances by the manufacture and export of indigo. If upon that we build agricultural development, we build upon deception and delusion. Who that has seen, has not admired the careful, almost triturated cultivation of tobacco and wheat-fields in the higher lands of Rice Countries? Who grows the safflower, who produces the immense crops that supply our greatest markets with jute and oil seeds? From such facts are the objects of agricultural improvement most truly present to us and the means by which it may be attained most correctly indicated. Our greatest and never-sleeping purpose it seems to me should be to secure our agricultural population, the utmost benefit of their labour and to disencumber them always within the bounds of reason and law, from an intruding succession of middle tenures.

His presumption was, therefore, that a residence for 12 years should give occupancy rights to the *khudkasht* ryot and his rent should not be enhanced if it was fair, that is, equal to the *pargana* rate. He hated the idea that 'season by season like a ripe fruit, the Ryot should be pecked at till the stone should be bared'. As a *jotedar*, by vertical mobility, tended to become an intermediary having under-ryots, the government should not encourage subletting.[78] Sconce followed it up by another Minute on the Bill to amend the law relating to the recovery of rent, which was renamed

77. B. R. C., 30 April 1857, no. 4 for commissioner of Bhagalpur
78. B. R. C., 2 July 1857, no. 34

the Rent Act in 1859. For the ambiguous 'resident ryot,' he would have prescriptive occupancy ryots holding for at least 12 years at uniform rate, as the category for special consideration. But on the question of fixing rents, he gave his opinion in favour of fixed rents. This provoked Judge Raikes, of the *sadar diwani adalat*, into justifying competition rent. He referred to Sconce's measure as one which went to the other extreme of aggrandising the ryot at the expense of the zamindar. H C Metcalfe, judge of Tippera, supported Raikes. He thought that the fixing of a *pargana* rate was unfair to the zamindar. They and other men of capital would find it positively discouraging to undertake any work of improvement. The prospect of raising cash crops would be remote if its benefits solely went to the cultivator.[79]

In the Legislative Council the question of the distribution of agricultural profits was hotly debated between Ricketts and Currie. Ricketts wanted it to be determined by the collector at two-fifths of the crop value as rent. Currie insisted on *pargana* rates as 'wiser and more prevalent' and felt that the rate, suggested by Ricketts was too high. Peacock argued against the determination of rent by collectors and would leave it only to the courts. Currie emphasized the role of the bureaucracy in the matter, in view of its great significance in the situation of the northwest provinces and threatened to withdraw the bill if the point was not conceded. The seriousness of the government intention to intervene into agrarian relations can be measured from this debate.[80] The period of debate was over. It remained for Currie to take into consideration the salient points of the debate and give final shape to the Rent Act of 1859.

The question of protecting the ryots against enhancement of rent and ejection was precipitated by another development in the government monopoly of opium cultivation, primarily in Bihar. The government used to make advances through the khatadars or village headmen to the actual cultivators for growing poppy. The crop was virtually dictated and the price kept low. The landlord's authority was badly undermined by such a procedure. Still the landlords were powerful enough to evict ryots and raise their rents to the highest possible level and appropriate the profits of the crop. The low price could be maintained as long as a compromise could be made with landlords to keep down the rent of opium lands. But in the 1850s, the policy of compromise broke down as the landlords went on

---

79. B. R. C., 26 May 1859, no. 2 for Sconce, no. 4 for Raikes, no. 12 for Metcalfe
80. *Proceedings of the Legislative Council of India*, January–December 1959, vol. v, Calcutta, 1859, pp. 221–32

levying higher rents up to Rs 6 a *bigha* for such lands. The government found it difficult to keep the price or advances down. The opium commissioners made repeated appeals for a legislation to cancel out landlord interference and enhancement of rent. The opium monopoly was the only compensatory allowance for the government after the perpetual settlement of revenue. A measure like the Rent Act could not be delayed after this.[81]

The Act gave occupancy right to all ryots holding land for at least 12 years without break in an estate. The definition of ryot included all who were recorded as ryots in the zamindar's rent roll and there was no provision against subletting. Thus very substantial middlemen, like the Rangpur jotedars, with four layers of under-tenants and paying rent of upto half a lakh, were recorded as ryot. Many small jotedars with *korfa* ryots under them, like the gantidars of Nadia and Jessore, were also termed ryots. Under-tenants like korfas and koljamas, who were the actual cultivators, were kept out of its scope. The classification of ryots into occupancy and non-occupancy groups by itself excluded a vast majority of tenants-at-will, many of whom were actual cultivators. From the high registration fee proposed by Ricketts in 1856, it was clear that the government had had the substantial ryots or jotedars in mind. The Rent Act recognised them and fortified their position where they already existed and created them as a special category, whereas in reality, they were shoulder to shoulder with the non-occupancy ryots, enjoying the same rights and paying virtually the same rent. In practice, a new class of ryots was created and the so-called occupancy ryots behaved like middlemen, subletting their holding and parasitically exploiting their under-ryots. It was unlikely under these circumstances that the mode of production and the size of holding would be affected in any way. The mass of actual cultivators were not going to benefit from it. As Glazier, collector of Rangpur, put it, 'the protection of only occupancy ryots would leave more than half of the tenantry unprotected. This would protect ryots who grow up into a harder set of small landlords and leave the others at their mercy to the condition of serfs.'[82] Nevertheless, legal protection was given to the small class of rural capitalists who, in a large measure, organised rural

---

81. R. I. C., Appendix, Part II, Opium, nos 1 and 2, pp. 350–73; also B Choudhury, *The Growth of Commercial Agriculture in Bengal*, Calcutta, 1965, vol. i, pp. 57–70

82. *Mss. Eur. F. 86/165*, Temple Collection, Answers to Circular, E V Westmacott, collector, Dinajpur, H R Reily, manager, Chanchal Estate, Maldah, Glazier, collector, Rangpur; R D Hume, collector, Birbhum

production by lending seed and money to the primary producer. They were
the men who could manipulate petite culture to raise the cash crops for
export far more successfully than either the zamindar or the planter. In
fact, they were already raising indigo for the planters, opium for the government and other cash crops for the big merchants and landlords in business.

The rent of the occupancy ryots could not be enhanced arbitrarily in
violation of the provisions of the Rent Act of 1859. A tenant was generally
not ousted if he had been holding the land for ten years and paying
whatever was demanded by his landlord.[83] The loss of a *kaimi* or resident
ryot was considered a more serious calamity than the loss of a year's rent.[84]
Mourasi pattas or permanent leases were also common. The importance
of the Rent Act lay therefore in its provisions for rent control to allow
capital formation and a growth of purchasing power at the grassroots
level. Thus, enhancement of rent was made conditional on the basis of
three factors. Rent could be enhanced (*a*) if *pargana* rate had risen
above it, (*b*) if the value of produce had risen since the last index of prices
and (*c*) if land had been added to the holding. A notice had to be given for
enhancement through the collector's office and rent suits were to be
decided in the revenue courts summarily by the collector.[85]

What the law achieved in effect, was to convert customary rent into
economic competition rent. As non-occupancy ryots were denied the
benefit of *pargana* rates they paid a competition rent fixed just short of
their subsistence. But this was then made the standard to determine the
pargana rate for the occupancy ryots.[86] The new ground for enhancement
with reference to a rise in prices made precise economic determinism a
feature of enhancement. It went to ludicrous lengths of input–output
analysis, as in the case of Hill vs Issur Ghose of 24 September 1862 in the
sadar diwani adalat when half the produce was awarded in the landlord's
favour in true Ricardian vein.[87] The third factor was, in fact, the codifica-
tion of old measurement methods.

---

83. P. P., vii (1857–58), J T Mackenzie, Q. 3741

84. *Mss. Eur. F. 86/161*, Temple Collection, Demi-official Enquiry into the
    Condition of Peasantry in Bengal (19875), E E Ravenshaw, commissioner,
    Orissa, 2 September 1875; also, J Mukherjee (A Lover of Justice), *The
    Permanent Settlement Imperilled, IOL Tract 508*, Calcutta, 1865, pp. 2–3

85. C D Field, *Introduction to the Regulations of the Bengal Code*, Calcutta,
    1863, pp. 120–30 for details of Acts X and XI of 1859

86. *Mss. Eur. F. 86/165*, C F Magrath, collector, Bogra, 15 July 1876

87. *Decisions under the Rent Laws of the Court of Sadar Dewani Adalat and
    of the High Court of Judicature*, Calcutta, 1865, vol. i, pp. 77 and 180

Landlord attitude and resistance to the Rent Act

Most of the landlords viewed the passing of the Act calmly. As Prosanna Kumar Tagore put it before the Indigo Commission, 'Generally speaking, the law is advantageous to both, perhaps more so in favour of ryots.' The skepticism about the benefit of the Act to the ryots could be measured from his later observation that the Act gave zamindars sufficient power to collect rent. The landlords were primarily concerned with the repeal of their summary power of summoning ryots to the *cutchery*. But Tagore felt that the poor ryots would still obey the summons of a *talabchitta* or zamindar summons even after the passing of the Act. 'The fat or rich ryot' however had never come to the *cutcherry* earlier either.[88] To Joykrishna Mukherjee, the Hooghly zamindar, the loss of his summoning power was not likely to prove difficult. But he voiced his protest against giving occupancy rights to squatters for 12 years. In his pamphlet, 'The Permanent Settlement Imperilled' (1865), he described the Act as an official mechanism to control affairs within the estate and a threat to the landlord's claim to absolute proprietory rights. The pamphlet was largely an exercise theoretically defending the landlord's position under the Permanent Settlement and its immunity from official intervention. But he admitted that the zamindar was still getting his way due to the ignorance of the people about the Act and its implications.[89] Another leading zamindar, Keshab-chandra Acharjya Choudhury of Mymensing, felt that the zamindars were still getting their rents solely because the ryots could not forget their old habits and associations. 'In spite of the rigour of the law,' he observed, 'zamindars still compel the attendance of their ryots and force them to clear out their accounts by criminal intimidations.' According to him, 85 per cent of the ryots submitted to it cheerfully. If some obstinate ryots sought protection under the new law, zamindars ruptured their unity by bribing the leaders. He narrated the story of one Sheikh Tamij who won a great victory against his zamindar in the law court and got his rent reduced. He also instigated other ryots to stop payment of rent. Tamij was called to the *cutcherry*. He was called ungrateful and disloyal but his father was praised as a good honest ryot of the *sarkar*. He was allowed to hold his tenure and pay his rent as admitted by him and decreed by the court. Around three or four days later he returned with all the other ryots. They agreed to pay their rents as before, and everything ended amicably.

---

88. R. I. C., P K Tagore, Q. 3768–76
89. J Mukherjee, *The Permanent Settlement Imperilled*, Calcutta, 1865

Keshabchandra also attacked the Rent Act for investing ryots with transferable occupancy rights. So they let out their lands to others at exorbitant rents at the expense of the actual cultivator of the soil. He challenged the *raison d'etre* of the measure and predicted that 'they will become a very merciless set of new landlords'.[90]

It is clear from the evidence of the three leading landlords of Rangpur, Hooghly and Mymensing that the Rent Act was only tangential in its impact on rent control. The last two testified strongly that the resident ryot or the *asullee proja* was never evicted. The tenants-at-will, who held tenures on a yearly basis were the ones subject to the most frequent charges. They now gained occupancy after 12 years by virtue of Act X. If they refused to pay higher rents, the question of eviction and coercion arose and the Rent Act could come to the aid of such aggrieved ryots. But in practice, the landlords had few confrontations with their ryots, as is evident from their own statements and official reports. In reply to a circular enquiring into rural indebtedness in 1876, most of the collectors reported that the distinction between occupancy and non-occupancy rights was hardly known and both groups paid virtually the same rent, as they had done before 1859.[91] The landlords had now the right to enhance rent on definite grounds which was to be decided by the collector summarily in case of a dispute. The collectors made quick work of such cases in the landlord's favour, as that facilitated the collection of revenue. This was an established practice in Bakarganj. In any issue relating to rent enhancements, the landlords seized the chance to take the matter to the law courts.[92] To lodge a complaint they had to pay an insititution fee of merely eight annas and have some hired witnesses at hand. The ryots preferred a compromise to the lodging of a complaint. False cases were brought up to harass ryots and exhaust their resources before they surrendered to the landlord's terms. A serious case of such oppression under

90. Keshabchandra Acharjya Choudhury, *The Rent Question in Bengal*, Calcutta, 1863, Enclosure from J Murdoch, *A Letter to the Right Hon'ble Earl of Elgin, Governor General of India on the Rent Question in Bengal*, Calcutta, 1863, pp. 15–22, 30

91. *Mss. Eur. F. 86/165*, W H Doyly, officiating collector, Rajshahi, C F Magrath, officiating collector, Bogra, E H Whinfield, collector, Burdwan, R H Pasey, officiating collector, Mymensing

92. *The Friend of India*, 26 May 1853, a letter by Anti-Humbug on spate of summary suits in Bakarganj; also, B. R. C., 17 May 1860, no. 69, E Latour, judge, 24 Parganas, 'Our summary suits in nine-tenths of the cases resorted to for some indirect purposes generally as a means of dispossession or enhancement of the proper rent'

legal cover was reported from Nadia by Commissioner Grote while pursuing a petition by the ryots of Rowtara to the lieutenant governor on 17 August 1859. The *patnidar* concerned had purchased a *patni* including that village from a zamindar at a very high price. He sought to realise the amount by raising rents. He brought 15 suits against the ryots in Nadia and various other places 'solely with a view to give the ryots distress and lastly to reduce them to obedience'. The ryots surrendered and agreed to pay the new rent.[93] This is corroborated by the evidence of one *jotedar*, Chandranath Sircar, before the Indigo Commission. He was unaware of the Act and besides he could not afford a plaint in any case. If a ryot of substantial means could be in such a predicament the fate of the ordinary ryots may be imagined.[94]

The Rent Act had taken away the power of distraint of a person but allowed the improvement to be neutralised by keeping the right to distrain crop and cattle. It was widely known in official circles that such cases of distraint were fictitious nine times out of ten and sought to ruin the ryot before he could fight his case. It was common practice to bribe the collector's peon and get him to serve the notice of arrears without the knowledge of the ryot. The right of distraint was granted *ex parte* as a result. A notice for arrears was like a notice of enhancement, as the former was caused by enhanced rent and abwabs.[95] Freshly instituted suits for arrears of rent for the month of September 1860 amounted to 3,964 cases and of the 3,858 cases disposed of, 1,074 were decided in favour of the plaintiff-landlord, 306 against him, 1,522 *ex parte*, 431 adjusted or withdrawn and 525 struck off on default. As could be expected, barring 306 cases, all the rest went in favour of landlords. The ryots had to pay or quit.[96]

Direct notices of enhancement were equally formidable in number. The indigo planters of six concerns in Nadia accounted for 22,000 out of 70,000–80,000 such notices in the district after the passing of the Act. The authorities viewed it as a revolution in an agricultural district.[97] The result was a rapid increase of rent in many districts after 1859. In Bakarganj, there was a comprehensive enhancement of rent following the

---

93. B. R. C., 17 November 1859, no. 15
94. R. I. C., Chandranath Sircar, Q. 695
95. B. R. C., 26 May 1859, nos 2–21 especially Latour and Glover; cf. W B Jackson, *Report of a Tour*, Calcutta, 1854, pp. 6–7
96. B. R. C., 26 November 1860, no. 224, Abstract Statement for the Month of September
97. B. J. C., February 1862, no. 41

Rent Act.[98] In Hooghly, the rate of rent of 1850 was virtually doubled by 1870 and the zamindars raised the rents again to prevent the growth of occupancy rights.[99] There were similar enhancements after the Act was passed in Mymensing and Dhaka.[100]

The Rent Act, as it may have been percived already, was a massive rise of abwabs or the consolidation of existing ones in the rent. In some districts like Bakarganj and Mymensing, the cesses were brought on a level with rent while the latter remained the same. The other method of doubling rents by false measurements showing excess land was also liberally used as in Rajshahi and Maldah, throughout the nineteenth century, since excess land in the holding had been made a special ground for enhancement in the Rent Act.[101]

Though the grant of an occupancy right did not seem to fortify the ryot's position against enhancement of rents the landlords took care to prevent the growth of such claimants to the right. In Rangpur, the practice of giving only short leases was ruthlessly adopted.[102] In Burdwan, similar care was taken to prevent the growth of occupancy rights.[103] In many districts, rent receipts were refused and kobuliyats forged to destroy evidence of occupancy.[104]

But the legal recognition of the *jotedar* had its effect. As few estates were available for sale, the educated *bhadralok* started infiltrating into jotes. Larmour, of the Bengal Indigo Company, talked to *committir* kortas or the new rural gentry in 1862 in Nadia, and Keshabchandra described deputy collectors and mukhtears appearing as occupancy ryots in Mymensing in 1863.[105] Apart from landholding, the mukhtears or the rural lawyers were a rising generation of professionals who sought a career in the *mofussil* by aiding and advising the rich peasants on the rent

---

98. J C Jack, *Bengal District Gazetteers, Bakarganj*, Calcutta, 1915, p. 73

99. W W Hunter, *SAB, Hooghly*, London, 1875–76, p. 356

100. *Ibid, SAB, Mymensing*, London 1875–76, p. 454 and *Dacca* p. 101

101. M V Carter, *Maldah Settlement Report*, Calcutta, 1938, pp. 70–71, 80; L S S O'Malley, *Bengal District Gazetteers, Rajshahi*, Calcutta, 1916, p. 98

102. *Mss. Eur. F. 86/165*, Glazier, 16 August 1876, para 47

103. *Ibid*, Whinfield, collector, Burdwan, 29 July 1876, Enclosure, Gopal-chandra Sen, deputy collector

104. B. R. C., 22 December 1859, no. 42; B. R. C., 26 November 1860, no. 224, Abstract of cases

105. R Larmour, *Notes on the Rent Difficulties in Lower Bengal and on the Proposed Amendment of Act X of 1859*, Calcutta, 1862, pp. 1–6; also, K A Choudhury, *The Rent Question in Bengal*, Calcutta, 1863; p. 15

question and taking 25 per cent less in fees from them to set up practice.[106] The Court of Wards report for 1875–76 refers to the emergence of bellicose ryots in many estates with mukhtears at their aid and ready to start a *dharmaghat* or strike at the slightest provocation.[107] The 1870s also saw the emergence of jute or the 'golden fibre' as a major cash crop, thanks to this class in Rajshahi, Dhaka and Pabna.[108] The Bengal Administration Report for 1874–75 noted the rise of this class with satisfaction.[109]

But it will be a mistake to assume that the rise was so spectacular as to eclipse the superior landlords. Their trial of strength was witnessed in the Pabna Uprising of 1872–73. The rate of rent in Pabna was traditionally low in order to induce reclaimers. The low rent was made up by abwabs which virtually formed part of an enhanced rent. The government measure to suppress abwabs in 1872 alerted the zamindars into consolidating the abwabs within rent rates. The Banerjees of *pargana* Yusufshahi thereby claimed a very high rent. They also undertook false measurements and forced the ryots to sign kobuliyats, agreeing to pay the enhanced rent and surrender their occupancy rights. The ryots fought a few cases in the munsiff's court with success. This motivated them to organise an agrarian league and begin a revolt like the indigo disturbances. They refused to pay anything but the old *pargana* rent. The landlords engaged lathials and bribed their headmen to gain their objective. The Tagores of Shajadpur and Sanyals of Salap reached a compromise but the Banerjees held out. They spent a fortune in rent suits until many of their opponents were exhausted in the legal battle. With the approach of the famine in 1873–74, the ryots began to play into their hands. Even the Tagores, who were prompt in showing amnesty, had won their law suits. But they refrained from enhancement and earned the gratitude of the paramaniks or the village headmen.[110]

106. *Mss. Eur. F. 86/165*, Whinfield, collector, Burdwan, 29 July 1876, Enclosure, Bagalananda Mukherjee, deputy collector

107. C. O. W. R. (1875–76), p. 12

108. *Hindoo Patriot*, 20 July 1874, Editorial

109. *Bengal Administration Report (1874–75)*, pp. 8–12

110. *Bengal Administration Report (1872–73)*, pp. 29–30; also W W Hunter, *SAB, Pabna*, London, 1875–76, pp. 315–25; *Mss. Eur. F. 86/165*, Pabna Uprising, W V G Taylor, officiating collector, Rajshahi, 9 July 1876; Enclosures, for various aspects of Pabna Uprising; Sir George Campbell 'Administration', *Hindoo Patriot*, 27 July 1874, News and Notes, for paramaniks expressing gratitude to Devendranath Tagore

Conclusion

It has been observed in the earlier sections that the ryots in 1876 were negotiating desperately with landlords for holdings in Nadia and Rangpur, even at the risk of encroaching on their bare subsistence. Hence, as Marshman put it, the landlords laughed at regulations like the Rent Act when nine-tenths of the population depended on agriculture and vied with each other for a foothold. The ryot hardly ever resorted to the law court to secure their rights under the new regulation for fear of being replaced by another land-hungry peasant while waiting for an uncertain verdict. Even an exceptional episode like the Pabna Uprising ended in the vindication of the landlord raj.

Seven

Conclusion

At the time of the Permanent Settlement, the alien government was primarily concerned with the security of revenue and the collection of it by the safest and cheapest agency, with minimum social disturbance. The landlords of the day were eminently qualified to be the official favourites. They emerged virtually unscathed from the initial rigours of the 1793 Sale Law with minor bruises here and there. By 1830, a new generation had succeeded them who benefited from official connections and enjoyed the best of both worlds.

Cornwallis thought of the problem of remittance and the need for agricultural development in 1793, but it was relegated to a secondary position at the time. This is clear from the government decision to arm the landlords with summary powers (Act VII of 1799 and Act V of 1812) for facilitating the collection of rent.

But the perpetual limitation on revenue demand caused alarming financial distress from the 1820s and virtually crippled the administration. Minimal government, which was a part of the official policy of non-interference, became the order of the day due to this pecuniary crisis. Worse still, it had to be at a time when interference had become a necessity.

The emergency was caused by the growing problem of remittance and the requirements of Free Trade after 1813. As imports to India were stepped up with no commensurate return of Indian produce, the government looked nostalgically back to Cornwallis' idea of improvement. India's value to England was once again measured in terms of her capacity to pay in kind. The economic programme of the Permanent Settlement which sought to lay the basis of capitalist farming in India on a large scale had been allowed to remain in abeyance for more than two decades since 1793 to safeguard revenue. It was given serious thought again in the changed context. The general agricultural development and promotion of cash crops mattered more than anything else to the government and the people in England. The government began looking for the entrepreneur who could deliver the goods.

In 1793, landlords were marked out for that role and the agricultural profits arising from perpetual limitation of the revenue demand was allowed as their incentive for the work of improvement. But it was too much to expect from them when they were given a free hand to negotiate with the tenantry. As the pressure of population on land mounted, the ryots lost their bargaining power and the landlords seized on the opportunity to maximise rents from ryots with undefined rights. The minimal government hardly worked as a restraining influence on them. All regulations were passed in favour of landlords, either defining their rights or arming them with summary powers. The patwaris and qanungos, the keepers of village records, were dismissed at the same time. Even the most energetic landlord was bound to become the most parasitic rent-receiver under such circumstances. Naturally, very few of them cared for agricultural development. Many of them only taxed the heads *ad infinitum* and were even blissfully ignorant of the acres they held.

The capital they amassed by increasing rents was enormous, especially in lightly assessed estates and most of it was invested in land speculation. This led to the formation of giant estates, spreading over several districts. This was the most lucrative business and as it called for a peculiar entrepreneurship they were almost wholly preoccupied with it. In the 1850s, the planters complained that all lands were bought by landlords who used their huge capital and local influence to monopolise the land market. Even small tenures and jotes were not spared. Clearly, the landlords were the most unlikely agents of improvement and the government had to find a substitute. Harrington's bill for the protection of the ryots in 1826 reflected this mood. The government was on the point of recognising the yeomanry as the ultimate agency of agricultural development. In the despatches to and from India, a sub-ryotwari settlement of *khas* mahals was seriously contemplated. But the bill had to wait until 1859 before it was made into a law. Meanwhile, the government and its new favourites, the planters, were to try their entrepreneurial skill.

The government had to subvert landlordism before it could begin its work of regeneration. Land resumption was the official instrument to break up the existing structure and build a new one. It was taken up seriously in 1819 with an assault on *taufir* or concealed wastelands in permanently settled estates. In 1836 *lakhiraj* or rent-free tenures and recent alluvial accretions were made the target. As we have already seen, these ostensibly charitable land grants had mostly been used for alienation of revenue as a safety valve against the rigours of British revenue demand between 1775 and 1793. By resumption the government hoped, at one stroke, to replenish the treasury, establish its right to intervene in agrarian relations and carry out its plans for a ryotwari settlement of resumed lands for the purpose of agricultural development. The landlords tried to thwart these plans by mobilising resistance on the spot. They tried to pressurise the government into submission by mobilising their community and the planters at the headquarters towards public agitation. They even carried the campaign to England. They attained considerable success in compelling the government to agree to a compromise. The measure was made harmless by the compromise thrust upon it. It was given up altogether after the government had helped itself to a portion of the landlords rental profits. The right of intervention was given up for the time being. The greater portion of the gain from alienations of government territory was, however, retained by the landlords. The agrarian structure did not break following resumption. The government failed in its attempts at a ryotwari settlement of the resumed land. Mismanagement, high expenses of collection, high taxation and landlord opposition made that experiment unworkable. The territory was resettled with the former proprietors in most cases. But the investigation enabled it to get an insight into the affairs of the estate. The government had a clear idea of the nature of agrarian relations, the rate of rent, assets of the land and the margin of profits for the landlords. The government's right to intervene in agrarian relations was vindicated. The right was not allowed to rust in future. It undoubtedly smoothed the passing of the Rent Act of 1859. But its chief significance lay in the monetisation of a semi-feudal economy.

The resumption operations can be seen in the broader perspective of the government resolve to tighten its grip on local administration. This was another way of subverting the landlord raj. A two-pronged policy was adopted for the purpose. An attempt was made to work through the local institutions. The landlords were enjoined by law to become errand boys of the government. They were to organise village watch, report crime and apprehend criminals. They were to help the magistrate, the marching troops and the surveyors on pain of heavy fine, recognisance and imprisonment.

On the other hand, the offices of collector and magistrate were united for a decade; the village watch was brought under its direct scrutiny. A new gradation of higher pay was introduced for darogahs. Deputy collectors and assistant magistrates were appointed. Munsiff's courts were created in the subdivisions to bring justice to the door. In the 1850s, a commission for suppression of dacoity was formed with its exclusive staff. The judges were sent on regular tours of inspection into the interior and the offices of collector and magistrate were united again.

All the measures were likely to ensure the rule of law, irrespective of caste, colour or creed. Equality before law was expected to sap the social and economic basis of exploitation. The courts and police stations called in a new balance of power in the countryside. Social engineering by regulation, it was thought, stood a fair chance of success.

But all these expectations faced only a partial fulfilment. The colonial government was, by its very nature, a weak government. Very little money was spared for ensuring a detailed and vigorous administration. The government suffered from chronic financial stringency caused by territorial expansion, large remittances and an expensive bureaucracy, apart from its fixed income from land revenue. The new administrative network was still hopelessly inadequate for governing the vast country at its disposal.

This was laid bare by the tactics of the landlords. They refused to be bullied into submission. They utilised the delegated authority over village watch and other officials to tighten their stranglehold on the countryside. The skeleton government stretched out over a vast territory of tortuous topography and was no match for the private militia of the landlords and their local influence. They took the law into their hands in areas virtually liberated from the British rule because of their great distance from the *sadar* station. Their lathials frequently overpowered the magistrate and his poorly paid, inefficient minions in pitched battles. At the same time, they subverted the government from within by bribery and infiltration. The law courts and police stations harassed people unnecessarily and proved to be expensive stations. Only the rich and the educated could avail of them. They were converted into engines of power for landlords. The threat of a suit was enough to bring a ryot to his knees.

The basic economic insecurity due to overcrowding in agriculture was the decisive factor in leading the oppressed peasant to avoid the law courts and police stations. While he waited indefinitely for an uncertain verdict he was sure to be replaced by a land hungry peasant willing to accept any terms. The limitation of a colonial government as an agency of social change was perhaps realised and the private agency of planters was especially sponsored as a better substitute for agrarian change. It was thought that they would be able to make more effective local inroads into the economic and political superstructure of landlords.

As the planters entered the field as landlords in their estates and under-tenures, the regulations protected their rights. The yeomanry lost the chance to become the official favourites. The landlords not only retained their rights as a result but also found a strong ally in the planters against official attempts at the subversion of their position.

The planters dominated the period as new economic messiahs who came to turn dust into gold. They were restless fortune seekers. They started with borrowed capital, expected an enormous profit on their transactions and got ready to depart the moment they had achieved their ambition. Such people were rarely good entrepreneurs.

At the initial stage, they entered into a collaboration with landlords for a foothold in the interior by paying large premia, high rent and forming a political alliance with them against government measures like land resumption.

They did not take the trouble of going all out for *nij* cultivation or capitalist farming. In that case, they would have commanded their own land, labour and capital and ignored landlords altogether. A major agricultural breakthrough may have resulted from such undertakings. Instead, they chose the easier, cheaper and more profitable way of manipulating the petite culture and appropriating the peasant's surplus. Even some early attempts at *nij* cultivation were given up in favour of ryoti since there was greater profitability and safer procurement of land and labour.

As long as there could be a fair division of the spoils between the landlord and the planter and no political and economic confrontation between them of any magnitude, the system worked to their mutual advantage, without causing any changes in the mode of production. The same old ryot with his same old primitive tools produced the required bundles of indigo plant in his small holding of 1–3 acres, under nominal advances from the planters.

Indigo ate into rice and affected the subsistence of the small peasants. As the market for indigo slumped in Europe, the planters resorted to a more ruthless kind of landlordism to maintain profit denying the peasants even the required price for the crop.

The strange bed-fellows, the landlord and the planter, began to fall apart as the storm over resumption subsided and the planters's investments dwindled considerably in the *moffusil*. The planters had, in the earlier stage ruined a number of native landlord-planters before they set up as virtual monopolists in the trade. But their brand of entrepreneurship needed so little ingenuity that they soon began to face competition from the landlords in the 1850s. The system of advance had a larger application in grain dealing and moneylending. The economic confrontation worsened due to the rise of prices of other cash crops. The cultivation of rice became more profitable than indigo and grain dealing landlords and their primary producers sought to abolish indigo cultivation. The political confrontation also became acute. The struggle for territorial influence was inevitable when two masters fought for authority over the same ryot. The official patronage of planters by protective legislation began to trench upon landlord rights. In the charged atmosphere of the Mutiny, mutual hatred soared high. The situation was made more explosive by two government measures which threatened to destroy the position of landlords in the countryside—the appointment of planters as honorary magistrates and the passing of Act X and Act XI of 1859.

The Indigo Revolt of 1859–1860 arose out of such inflammable materials. But it was not an agrarian revolution by peasants to liberate themselves from the landlords and the planters and bring a radical alteration in agrarian relations. As shown in Chapter 5, it was engineered by landlords to oust their bitterest rivals from the interior. The ryots did not follow suit out of a sense of feudal loyalty to the landlords. But it was their utter economic dependence on their patrons that accounted for their participation in the Indigo Revolt. Indigo was non-remunerative and its cultivation was forced under Indian and European landlords alike. So the ryots had a common grievance against both. But they joined the Indian landlords against the planters. The gradual decline of European enterprise in Bengal was soon followed by a spectacular multiplication of Indian factories. Both indigo and sugarcane were cultivated in full swing under the old system of advances. Jute became another major cash crop under indigenous supervision.

The planters failed to rally the primary producers to their side because they made no attempt to secure their commitment to the enterprise by allowing them a fair share in its profits. The government, perhaps, realised this. As the Free Traders pressed hard on the home government for a fuller utilisation of the empire for expansion of their trade, the planters' cause merged in it. The government had to think in terms of universal cultivation of the soil and production of a greater variety of cash crops than could be achieved by the planters.

The Rent Act of 1859 was the first direct intervention of the government in agrarian relations in favour of the ryot. It sought to rally him to the cause of agricultural development by attempting a fair distribution of agricultural profits between landlords and peasants. The government was acutely alive to the consequences of the protracted policy of *laissez-faire*.

It had led to polarisation of agricultural profits in favour of the rent-receivers. It had hindered capital formation at the grassroots level by giving landlords a free hand to mop up everything above the subsistence of the primary producers. The planters had toed the chosen line of the landlords by appropriating the peasant's surplus to the utmost. The planters were largely responsible for delaying the government intervention in the ryot's favour. They were again responsible for convincing the government of such a necessity in the 1850s. By helping capital formation at that level, the government could also hope to create massive purchasing power in the countryside.

The Rent Act of 1859 was not, however, a mandate for emancipation of the peasantry as a whole. The occupancy right was granted to ryots of ten years' standing. It included big jotedars who paid up to Rs 50,000 as rent to superior landlords but who were recorded as ryots in the rent roll of the zamindar. It excluded all non-occupancy ryots and *korfa* under-ryots who held jote under occupancy. They were by far the majority of actual cultivators. The government chose a select category of substantial jotedars who could act as small rural capitalists. The haoladars of Bakarganj or gantidars of Nadia and Jessore were really small capitalist farmers who were involved in grain dealing and moneylending on a small scale. They were undoubtedly entrepreneurs but seldom primary producers. They were instrumental in raising the huge quantity of cash crops in response to the market. They made their under-tenants and sharecroppers produce for them under nominal advances and left them with a scanty subsistence to keep the operation going. They were, in fact, petty landlords working in many cases as sub-contractors of their superiors.

Even the Rent Act failed to convert the occupancy ryots into rural entrepreneurs. It fizzled out like a damp squib. The right to sublet and transfer holdings under the Act allowed even the self-cultivating occupancy ryots to exploit the pressure of population on land to become rent-receivers and rivet the old structure of landlordism. But such vertical mobility was only marginal.

The majority of them were fleeced as usual by the superior landlords. The Rent Act converted customary rent into economic rent by conceding specific grounds of enhancement. There was a general enhancement of rent of more than 50 per cent in the years following the Rent Act. In the traditionally low rent areas, the lever of abwabs was used for similar enhancement. The rate of rent was irrelevant to those landlords who had no knowledge of the land possessed by their ryots. Their rent roll consisted of names of people and the amount paid by them. The area and the rate were seldom recorded. The abwabs and cesses were written as a separate account. It was common pratice to keep the rent account in arrears and adjust all payments against the cess. It was the head that paid, not the acre. A careful perusal of the settlement reports in the beginning of the twentieth century convinces the reader of the unabated supremacy of the big landlords and their power of exaction.

The contrast between the peasant's growing prosperity and the decline of the fortunes of landlords were, by and large, political shibboleths used by both the government and the landlords to criticise each other. It is true that the land was the only source of employment for the extended family of landlords. It resulted in overcrowding at the top as well as at the bottom of the agrarian structure. The distribution of agricultural profits among a numerous and highly differentiated people ruled out a very large surplus for any class. Legislation had only succeeded in effecting a slightly fairer distribution between the zamindar and the *jotedar* while the korfas and adhiars were allowed to be driven to serfdom. Peter had been partially robbed to pay Paul.

This sorry state of affairs can be interpreted in several ways. The *imperium* had obviously little concern for an agrarian change *per se* for the benefit of benighted Bengal. It had no particular animus against landlords. The policy of minimum interference remained the guide line of all rulers unless an emergency demanded intervention. The landlords, after all, collected the revenue from the masses and kept them quiet and loyal to alien rule. They surely deserved indulgence. They shared the burden of government with a handful of foreign rulers and could therefore stake a valid claim to a share of authority as well. The official pressures were not meant to reduce their power drastically or make them extinct as a class. The measures were calculated to restrain their excesses. The institution of the Court of Wards and its sincere efforts to salvage the most hopelessly encumbered estates like the Darbhanga Raj during the pro-underdog tide of the Curzon period illustrates the point. Much of the strength of the landlords was derived from their love–hate relationship with the government.

The weakness of a colonial government was inevitable. Its main purpose was not to govern for the sake of governing. Its object was to develop the conquered country for the requirement of the motherland. It had to run the administration at a minimum cost for a maximum profit. John Bright estimated in 1858 that the single city of Manchester spent a larger sum of money on water supply alone than the Company's government did on public works in the fourteen years from 1834 to 1848 throughout its vast possessions.[1] Still, British colonial rule was less commercial than its Dutch and French prototypes in southeast Asia. It is undeniably true that the second half of the nineteenth century saw more government activity than the first half. But this relative extension of authority was by no means a substitute for the vigorous government at home. The skeleton government that was set up in Bengal necessarily allowed free zones in many areas of difficult access. The few civilians, their ill-paid minions and corruptible courts could not cope with crafty landlords and their athletic lathials. Most of the regulations could not be enforced as a result. To account for the overwhelming territorial influence of the landlords simply in terms of weak and limited government is, however, to ignore their entrenched position before and after the Permanent Settlement. It is difficult to say if a strong government could or would have cut them to size. The theory was never seriously put to an objective test in Bengal. Even the experiment in Uttar Pradesh was given up after the Mutiny in favour of the taluqdars. The dexterity with which the Bengal landlords had drawn upon their traditional and modern sources of power to smother all pressures to upset the status quo, leaves the issue open to question. Their staying power was more than vindicated by their ability to meet force by force, and mobilise public opinion, through the press and the associations.

A strong government could solve the problem of law and order and enforce regulations to some extent. But that government needed a clear blue print for a radical social change. The *imperium* was not the congenial human laboratory for such experiments.

The inescapable conclusion seems to be that the government could at best erode the political base of the landlords' power but not its economic bastion, based on the multiplying pressure of population on land. As shown in Chapter 6, nine-tenths of the population depended on agriculture, in the absence of adequate industrial and urban outlets. The actual cultivators lost their bargaining power. By 1876, people were seen scrambling for land on terms of marginal subsistence. The great human surplus made the position of the peasants precarious. They capitulated to the demands of their landlords with no inclination to resort to the law. The fear of being supplanted by a fellow labourer neutralised peasant resistance. The fear was fed by the frequent demonstration of power by the landlords to victimise a recusant ryot.

The same adverse land–man ratio was responsible for the failure of early experiments in capitalist farming. Colebrooke noted in 1794 that the

---

1. J Strachey, *India: Its Administration and Progress*, London, 1903, p. 233

population at that time was optimum for the cultivation of all arable and
wasteland and the ratio was one acre of tillage per head on an average.[2]
Buchanan-Hamilton found in 1808 that the majority of holdings in Rangpur and Dinajpur in the hands of small peasants and sharecroppers was
less than five acres. Whoever owned 15 to 25 acres, invariably sublet for
a share-out.[3] R Davidson, a planter diagnosed that the 'altogether miser-
ably defective' nature of agriculture in India was due to 'extreme
sub-division of land and the want of accumulated capital' at the grassroots
level.[4] It was not surprising the Holt Mackenzie made the following
skeptical observation in 1832:

> . . . Whatever may be thought of the probable consequences of having
> the landed property of a country divided among a multitude of petty
> proprietors . . . it is certain that the existence of large zemindaries in
> Bengal has had no tendency to make farms large. And if in Ireland, we
> find that beggarly farms and a wretched people may be conjoined with
> domains of princely magnitude, still more may we look for poverty and
> distress under the zemindary system of India, so long at least as the
> people retain the remembrance of their rights and cling to their fields
> though rendered worthless by exaction.[5]

The fragmentation of holdings had gone to extremes by 1860. Of the
jotedars and gantidars who gave evidence before the Indigo Commission,
Mir Ramzan Ali of Jhenidah, Jessore, had a *jumma* of Rs 70, let out to
20–25 *koljama* under-ryots; Ameer Mullick, a *gantidar* of Khanpur,
Nadia, had a *jumma* of Rs 58 distributed among 170 under-ryots; Badan
Choudhury of Tribela, Nadia, having 99 bighas, was thinking of subletting.
Even at a *pargana* rate of 8 annas per *bigha* the unit of cultivation of the
actual cultivator under the parent holding would be less than 10 bighas.
Badan illustrates the tendency to sublet.[6] The Road Cess Returns in 1876
revealed that in the supposedly prosperous districts of Dhaka, Faridpur
and Tripura, three-fourths of the ryoti holdings did not exceed one acre.[7]

---

2. H T Colebrooke, *Remarks*, Calcutta, 1806, p. 27
3. *Mss. Eur. D. 75*, Buchanan-Hamilton Papers on Rangpur, p. 102;
    F Buchanan-Hamilton, *Dinajpore*, Calcutta, 1833, p. 236
4. P.P. vi (1830), p. 259
5. P.P. xi (1831–32), pp. 308–9
6. R.I.C, Ramzan Ali, Q. 3234, Ameer Mullick, Q. 1037, Badan Choudhury,
    Q. 3225–6
7. Quoted in K K Sengupta, 'Agrarian Disturbances in Nineteenth Century
    Bengal' in *IESHR*, vol. viii (1971), no. 2, p. 194

With population soaring, even the reclaimed areas were fragmented into small peasant holdings. Those who grabbed more land, lacked the capital to cultivate it all. They began to sublet it until the units of cultivation became a few acres again. Bakarganj provides the best example of such proliferations.[8] It was difficult to get untenanted large holdings for capitalist farming. It was economically more profitable to sublet than invest a fortune in an enterprise of doubtful returns. The absence of protective legislation for ryots added to the temptation of becoming a rent-receiver to ensure large profits.

Bengal began to foster a petite culture from the time of the Permanent Settlement. There was an exploitable surplus of people to whom estates could be handed down in fragments to fetch more profits than could be gained by capitalist farming. It was no wonder then, that the beneficiaries of the Permanent Settlement did not become improving landlords. Planters like W G Rose of Ramnagar factory, Murshidabad, were major capitalist farmers of large plantations in 1841.[9] By the 1850s, they had given up the farm and there was a rapid swing from *nij* to ryoti or manipulation of the petite culture for its greater profitability and scope of expansion. As Durup de Dombal, a planter who favoured *nijabad*, testified in 1860, it was extremely rare to find large, unoccupied holdings suitable for indigo in Nadia.[10] The planters even stopped making advances and held arrears of rent as the whip to goad ryots into cultivating the dictated crop. They became absorbed, body and soul, into landlordism.

The rising population even corrupted many of the occupancy ryots with holdings of more than six acres. They indulged in social climbing by subletting their holdings to the large army of *korfa* under-tenants and sharecroppers.

The thrust of commercialisation only brought about sharecropping as the final upshot. The landless agricultural labourer on wages was, by and large, the supplementary wage earner of a family of resident ryots.[11] Some determined Sunderban grantees and planters had to import migratory tribal labour or offer tenancy rights to unwilling ryots, to retain supply of

8. J C Jack, *Bakarganj Settlement Report*, Calcutta, 1915, pp. 47–52

9. B. J. C., 30 March 1841, no. 48

10. R.I.C.,Dombal, Q. 741

11. *Mss. Eur. F. 86/165*, Temple Collection, Answers to Circular regarding, Substantive Law for Determination of Rent (1876), E G Glazier, magistrate, Rungpore to commissioner, Rajshahi, Observations on Adhiars of Rungpore, a district given to sharecropping

labour.[12] Even the railway constructions in the mid-1850s failed to attract marginal farmers and sharecroppers.[13] The prospect of industrial labour must have been less attractive than sharecropping at home, with its many collateral advantages. The tension generated by official and non-official pressures on rural Bengal did not end in a crisis. It subsided in a social equilibrium. Efforts towards industrialisation and urbanisation would perhaps have upset the equilibrium. But it was difficult to come from within. The over-populated fertile plains of Bengal were detrimental to such a process. Much depended on the state initiative in the matter. But it was idle to expect this from an imperial government with its built-in limitations.

Meanwhile, the landlord raj was securely cushioned against all pressures threatening to undermine it.

---

12. R.I.C, Morrell, Q. 2383–5, Dombal, Q. 730, R P Sage, Q. 562 and 544, Larmour, Q. 1939–41
13. H Ricketts, *A Few Last Words on the Rent Difficulties in Bengal*, no. 3, London, 1864, pp. 8–9

Glossary

abwab	taxes imposed under the Mughals in addition to the regular assessment on the land; miscellaneous cesses, imposts and charges levied by zamindars and public officers
adhiar	a person sharing half the crop with the landlord
aima	a Muslim religious endowment of rent-free land
amin	a commissioner; an Indian judicial and revenue functionary
amlah	the collective head Indian officers of a judicial or revenue court under the European judge or collector
asullee proja	original tenant
badmash	a disreputable person; a rogue
bastu	homestead
baze zamin	miscellaneous lands, especially *lakhiraj*
be-ilaka	beyond one's jurisdiction
benami	fictitious or fraudulent
benamidar	a person holding such tenures
bhadralok	gentry
bhatottar	a Hindu religious endowment of rent-free land to priests
bigha	a measure of land, varying in extent in different parts of India; the standard *bigha* of the revenue surveys in the United Provinces was equal to five-eighth of an acre; in Bengal, it was equal to 1,600 square yards or a little less than one-third of an acre

brahmottar	a Hindu religious endowment of rent-free land to priests
brajabashi	upcountryman
boona	forester
bukeya	balance of revenue arrears
burkundaze	a guard or watchman armed with sword and shield
cazee	a Muslim judge to administer Muslim law; also spelt *kazi/kazee/qazi*
chakran	service land
chitta	a rough note or account
chowkidar	watchman
chur	alluvium
cutcherry	office of a zamindar or a public office
darogah	head of a police station
devottar	dedicated to god
dewan	a head officer of any revenue or financial department; the term applied to managers of zamindaris; also spelt *diwan*
dharmaghat	strike
duftar	Public Record Office
durpatni/-putni	a subordinate or sub-leased tenure
durpatnidar/ -putnidar	a sub-lessee
faridar/pharidar	head of a police outpost
ferazees	a Muslim religious sect established by Sharatatullah in Dhaka in 1828; Doodoo Mean was its celebrated leader in the 1840s
ganti	a hereditary under-tenancy of land at a fixed and permanent rent
gantidar	its occupant
ghatwal	a ferryman or a person in charge of a mountain pass; a kind of tenure in Birbhum for such persons.
goala	a cowherd or milkman
gola	a granary
gomasta	a steward; an officer employed by zamindars to collect rent
gram-saranjami	the requisite establishment for the business of a village

hajut/hajjot	need or necessity
haoladar	a holder of land, an intermediate tenure
hustabuds	a comparative account showing the present and past produce of an estate; rent roll or declared statement of assets
ijmali	joint
ilaka	jurisdiction
imam	keeper of a mosque
istimrari/istemrari	perpetual lease
izara/ijara	a lease
izaradar	a lease-holder
jajmani	patron–client relationship, especially in religious service
jagir/jaghir	service land under Mughal government granted to military and civil officers
jemadar/jamadar	an officer of police, next to the *darogah*
jote	tenure of a cultivator
jotedar	a cultivator or a holder of a *jote*; very often the non-cultivating owner of that holding
jumma	aggregate or total amount of rent payable to zamindar by an under-tenant or revenue payable by the zamindar to the government
jungleboori/ jungleburee	jungle *mahal* or lease of land having jungle
kabul beshi	voluntary excess paid
kabuliyat/kobuliyat	document in which the payer of rent agrees to pay the amount assessed on his land; from ryot to zamindar
kaimi	long-settled
kazee/kazi/qazi/ cazee	a Muslim Judicial official of the local court
khamar	land belonging to zamindar and let out at a grain rent; originally waste
khas	private land
khas mahal	land held and managed by the government directly without any intermediary
khasra	a field-book
khatadar	a ryot; more specifically a head ryot

khudkasht	a resident cultivator, cultivating hereditary lands at a fixed rate
koljama	a ryot holding from a ryot; an under-ryot; an under-tenant
korfa/kurfa	a sub-tenure, primarily in West Bengal, which the occupant holds from a hereditary tenure
koss	1–2 miles; also spelt *coss*
lakh	one hundred thousand
lakhiraj(-dar)	rent-free tenure and its holder
lathi	stick, club or bludgeon
lathial/lattial	club-men or bludgeon-men
lotdar	the holder of a division or allotment of reclaimed land in lots
mahajan/mahajani	
mandal/mondal	headman; moneylender; moneylending
mahal	a revenue division in a district or an estate
mal	revenue bearing land
malik	proprietor
matbar	village headman
mathot	an additional cess imposed on the cultivators under some incidental pretext; literally, per head
mofussil	country as opposed to *sadar* or the headquarters
mohurir	a clerk or a writer attached to any court or office
mollah/mullah	a Muslim priest
moulavee/moulvi	a Muslim priest or learned man
mourasi patta	permanent lease
mouza	area surrounded by a cluster of huts
mukarrari	tenures having fixed rent
mukhtear	an attorney; a legal agent
munshi	clerk
munsiff	an Indian civil judge of the lowest rank
mutsuddi	broker
naib	a deputy, generally in a zamindari establishment
nawab	ruler
nawarra	barge; revenue of land assigned for the support of the flotilla under the Mughal government
nazir	a revenue official
nerikbundy	measurement records

nij	land cultivated by proprietors themselves for their own benefit; also, private land of zamindar directly under his supervision
nul/nal/null	a measuring rod, usually 400 cubits in Bengal
pahi	temporary tenant or peasant
paik	a footman
paikasht, pahi	a non-resident ryot
paramanik	barber; clever man; usually headman of the village
pargana	a revenue district consisting of several villages
patni(-dar)	perpetual immediate under-tenure of a zamindari; a holder of such under-tenure
patta	a deed of lease from zamindar to ryot
patwari	a village accountant
peshkar	a subordinate Indian officer in a judge's or collector's office, next to *sheristadar*
peshki	money paid in advance as deposit for rent
prodhan	headman
proja	subject or ryots of an estate
pucca	brick-built
qanungo	record-keeper
rubakari	order
ruqba/rukba	area of a holding
russom(-oti)	customary payments
ryot/raiyat	cultivator paying cash rent; also *raieut*
ryoti	belonging to a ryot; a ryot's holding; cultivation of their own holdings by ryots under advances
ryotwari	a land settlement with ryots as in Madras
sadar/sudder	headquarter or principal station of a town
sadar amin/sudder amin	empowered to try cases to the extent of Rs 1000 from whom an appeal can be taken to the principal *sadar amin*, who can decide suits to an unlimited amount
salami	perquisite or bonus, apart from rent or loan
sali	arable plain land
sanad	a grant or deed
sarkar	zamindar or his representative in an estate; government
sayer	miscellaneous local taxes allowed to be levied by zamindars other than revenue or rent; frequently, illegal duties including toll duties

sezawal/sazawal	a bailiff or receiver of an attached or escheated estate on behalf of government
sheristadar	a registrar or record-keeper; head Indian officer of a court or collector's office
sicca	silver rupee
soona	high land
tahsil(-dar)	a tract of land of one or more parganas; an Indian collector of rent under zamindar or state for such units
taidad	a document of authority; a deed of lease
talabchitta	summons
taluq/taluk	part of a zamindari under a zamindar; a tenure under a zamindari paying rent to zamindar or paying revenue to government through zamindar
taluqdar	holder of a *taluq*
taufir	concealed land
tauzi/tauji	rent roll or revenue roll.
thak-bast	boundary delimitation (surveys)
thana	police station
thani	a resident hereditary cultivator
thikadar	contractor
tuccavi	loan of assistance by government to cultivators
vakeel	a legal agent who can plead in the court; zamindar's legal representative in the *sadar*
vritti	land grant to priests and other professionals
zamindar/zemindar	holder of an estate
zamindari	estate paying revenue directly to the state in Bengal
zillah	district

Bibliography

1. Manuscript sources

A. *British Museum, London*

Earl of Auckland Papers in Additional Manuscripts
Addl. Mss. 37711
Hastings Papers: Amini Commission Report
Addl. Mss. 29086–88
Also, Additional Manuscripts 21548 and 7450/14

B. *India Office Library (Commonwealth Relations Office), London*

Bengal Revenue Consultations
Bengal Judicial Consultations
Bengal Criminal and Judicial Consultations
Bengal Political Consultations
Indian Revenue Consultations
Home Miscellaneous Series, vols 381, 530 and 859
European Manuscripts:
    Mss. Eur. D. 72–75: Buchanan-Hamilton Papers
    Mss. Eur. G. 11: *Ibid*
    Mss. Eur. F. 86/161–165: Sir Richard Temple Collection
    Mss. Eur. F. 78/79: Sir Charles Wood Collection and letters

> Mss. Eur. D. 700: Letter Book of Lieutenant Governor Grey
> (1869–70)
> Mss. Eur. F. 95/1: Kyd Papers
> Mss. Eur. C. 97/I-III: Prinsep Papers: Typescript: Three Genera-
> tions in India
> Fort St George Revenue Consultations

C. *Public Record Office, London*

PRO/30/11/150: Cornwallis Papers
PRO/30/12/19: Ellenborough Papers

D. *Scottish Record Office, Edinburgh*

GD/45/6: Dalhousie Muniments

E. *Archives of the Centre of South Asian Studies, Cambridge*

Samuel Wauchope Papers
Scott-Moncrieff Papers (in microfilm)
S N Mukherjee Collection (in microfilm)

F. *University Library, Cambridge*

F C Brown Papers

2. Printed official sources

Bengal Administration Reports (1872–76)
Decisions of Zillah Courts of the Lower Provinces (1846–1854), Volumes
on Sylhet, Dinajpore, Rungpore, Tippera, Hooghly and 24 Parganas
Decisions under the Rent Laws of the Court of Sadar Diwani Adalat and
of the High Court of Judicature, vol. i, Calcutta, 1865
East India Company, Reports and Documents Connected with the
Proceedings of the East India Company in Regard to the Culture and
Manufacture of Cotton-wool, Raw Silk and Indigo in India, London,
1836
Extracts from Regulations and Correspondence Relative to Permanent
Settlement, Calcutta, 1884
Fifth Report of the Select Committee of the House of Commons, London,
1812

Papers Relating to the System of Police in the Bengal Presidency, London, 1857

Parliamentary Papers, Cited Volumes

Police Reports for the Lower Provinces of Bengal 1841–1854 (available volumes)

Police Committee Report on the Reform of Mofussil Police (1838) with Minutes of Evidence

Proceedings of the Controlling Council of Revenue at Murshidabad, vol. vi, Calcutta, 1919–24

Proceedings of the Legislative Council of India, vols ii–v (1856–1859)

Report of the Commissioner for Suppression of Dacoity in Bengal (1854–1857)

Report of the Survey Operations of the Lower Provinces (1852–53), Calcutta, 1853

Report of the Rent Law Commission, Calcutta, 1880

Report on the Revenue Administration of the Lower Provinces (1849–1860)

Report of Proceedings at a General Meeting of the Inhabitants of Calcutta on the 15th of December 1829, Calcutta, 1830 (or Report of the Meeting in Support of Colonisation, 1829)

Report on the Wards' and Attached Estates of the Lower Provinces (1874–79)

Selection of Papers from the Records of the East India House Relating to Revenue, Police, Civil and Criminal Justice under the Company's Government in India, vol. i, London, 1820

Selections from the Records of the Government of Bengal, vol. xvi, W B Jackson, Report of a Tour of Inspection, 1854

Selections from the Records of the Government of Bengal, vol. xxx, Parts I–III, Papers Relating to Indigo Cultivation in Bengal, Calcutta, 1860

Selections from the Records of the Government of India, vol. xix (PWD), Report of Greathead, 1855

Trial of Doodoo Mean and His Followers, Calcutta, 1847

Final Report on the Survey and Settlement Operations in the District of:

Bakarganj	(1900–1908)		Jack, J C, Calcutta, 1915
Bankura	(1917–1924)		Robertson, F W, Calcutta, 1926
Burdwan	(1927–1934)	vol. i	Hill, K A L, Calcutta, 1940
		vol. ii	Banerjee, P N, Calcutta, 1940

Dacca	(1910–1917)	Ascoli, F D, Calcutta, 1917
Dinajpur	(1934–1940)	Bell, F O, Calcutta, 1941
Hooghly	(1904–1913)	Certain Government and Temporarily Settled Estates and Zamindary Estates, Gupta, M N, Calcutta, 1914
Jessore	(1920–1924)	Momen, M A, Calcutta, 1925
Khulna	(1903–1908)	The Phulhatta Estate, Mukherjee, S C, Calcutta, 1908
Maldah	(1928–1935)	Carter, M V, Calcutta, 1938
Midnapore	(1907–1913)	Minor Settlement Operations, Sanyal, B, Calcutta, 1914

Bengal District Gazetteers:

Bakarganj	Jack, J C, Calcutta, 1918
Bankura	O'Malley, L S S, Calcutta, 1908
Birbhum	O'Malley, L S S, Calcutta, 1910
Hooghly	O'Malley, L S S, and M Chakrabarty, Calcutta, 1912
Jessore	O'Malley, L S S, Calcutta, 1912
Midnapore	O'Malley, L S S, Calcutta, 1911
Murshidabad	O' Malley, L S S, Calcutta, 1914
Mymensing	Sachse, F A, Calcutta, 1917
Nadia	Garrett, J H E, Calcutta, 1910
Pabna	O'Malley, L S S, Calcutta, 1923
24 Parganas	O'Malley, L S S, Calcutta, 1915
Rajshahi	O'Malley, L S S, Calcutta, 1916

3. Newspapers and periodicals

The Bengal Hurkaru (daily)	for year	1830–1860
The Hindoo Patriot (weekly)	"	1854–1874
The Englishman (daily)	"	1835–1860
The Friend of India (weekly)	"	1835–1860
The Calcutta Courier (daily)	"	1835–1840
The Reformer (weekly)	"	1833, 1836–1837
The Indian Field (weekly)	"	1858–1862
The Calcutta Review (monthly)	"	1844–1876
The Bengal Spectator	"	1842
The British Friend of India (quarterly)	"	1842

The Asiatic Journal (bi-annual)   "   1835–1840
Sambad Probhakar (daily)
   in vernacular   "   1846–1852
Sambad Purnochandroday (daily)
   in vernacular   for year 1852
Sarbatattwadipika (monthly)
   in vernacular   "   1830–1831
Bharatbarsha (monthly)
   in vernacular   "   1326 B.S. (Jan–Feb 1920)

4. Proceedings of public meetings and associations

Report of Proceedings at a General Meeting of the Inhabitants of Calcutta on the 15th of December 1829, Calcutta, 1830

Report of a Public Meeting held at the Town Hall, Calcutta on the 24th of November 1838, London, 1839

Great Non-Exemption Meeting (1857), Calcutta, 1857

Landholders' Society, Rules, Regulations and Report of Proceedings for the first six months, (in vernacular), *India Office Library Vernacular Tracts*, no. 1900, Calcutta, 1838

British Indian Association, Reports (monthly and annual) (1851–62), Calcutta, 1852–63

British Indian Association, Petitions, Calcutta, 1852–60

Indigo Planters Association, Central Committee Proceedings, Calcutta, 1856

The Landholders and Commercial Association of India: Memorial to Sir Charles Wood, Secretary of State for India, London, 1861

5. Unpublished secondary works

A. Unpublished Theses of London University

Akhtar, S   The Role of Zamindars in Bengal (1707–1772), Ph.D., 1973

Haraksing, K   An Economic and Administrative Study of the Sylhet District (1765–1793), Ph.D., 1973

Islam, M M   Agricultural Development in Bengal: A Quantitative Study (1920–46), Ph.D., 1972

Islam, M S   The Permanent Settlement and the Landed Interests in Bengal (1793–1819), Ph.D., 1972

Mahmood, A B M   The Land Revenue History of Rajshahi Zamindari (1765–93), Ph.D., 1966

Mohsin, M H   A Study of the Murshidadad District (1765–1793) Ph.D., 1965

Serajuddin, A M   The Revenue Administration of Chittagong (1761–85), Ph.D., 1964

Wahiduzzaman, A M   Land Resumption in Bengal (1819–1846), Ph.D., 1969

B. Calcutta University

Saha R   British Administration in a Bengal District—Nadia (1785–1835), Ph.D., 1973

C. Oxford University

Choudhury, B B   Agrarian Relations and Agrarian Economy in Bengal (1858–85), Ph.D., 1968

D. Cambridge University

Ray, R   Change in Bengal Agrarian Society: A Study of Select Districts (1760–1850), Ph.D., 1974

6. Published secondary works

Ahmed, A F S   *Social Ideas and Social Change in Bengal, 1818–1835*, Leiden, 1965

Ali, M M   *The Bengali Reaction to Christian Missionary Activities, 1833–57*, Chittagong, 1965

Anon   *An Enquiry into the Alleged Proneness to Litigation of the Natives of India*, London, 1830

Baden-Powell, B H   *Land Systems of British India*, vols i–iii, Oxford, 1892

Bagal, J C   *Peasant Revolution in Bengal*, Calcutta, 1954

Banerjee, B N, (ed.)   *Sambad Patre Sekaler Katha* (in vernacular), *Selections from Samachar Darpan (1818–1830)*, Calcutta, 1344 B.S. vol. i

Banerjee, Rev K M   *A Few Facts and Memoranda with Reference to the Early Career of the Late Hon'ble P C Tagore, CSI*, Calcutta, 1870

Banerjee, P N   *A History of Indian Taxation*, London, 1930

Banerjee, T D   Zemindar and Ryot in Bengal, *India Office Library Tract 507*, Calcutta, 1863

Bayley, H V   *Report on the Settlement of the Majnumutha Estate in the District of Midnapore (1844)*, Calcutta, 1884

Bayley, H V   *A History of Midnapore*, Calcutta, 1902

Bell, J H   *British Folks and British India Fifty Years Ago*, London, 1891

Beveridge, H   *The District of Bakarganj: Its History and Statistics*, London, 1876

Boeke, J H   *The Structure of the Netherlands Indian Economy*, New York, 1942

Boeke, J H   *Economics and Economic Policy of Dual Societies*, Haarlem, 1953

Bose, G C   *Sekaler Darogar Kahini*, (in vernacular), Dhaka, 1295 B.S.

Boserup, E   *The Conditions of Agricultural Growth*, London, 1965

Bottomore, T B   *Elites and Society*, Penguin, 1971

Boulger, D C   *Maharaj Debi Sinha of Nasipur Raj*, London, 1912

Buchanan, D H   *The Development of Capitalist Enterprise in India*, New York, 1934

Buchanan-Hamilton, F   *A Geographical, Statistical and Historical Description of the District or Zillah of Dinajpore in the Province or Soubah of Bengal (1808)*, Calcutta, 1833

Buckland, C E   *Bengal under the Lieutenant Governors*, vols i and ii, Calcutta, 1902 (second edition)

Buckland, C E   *Dictionary of India Biography*, London, 1906

Campbell, Sir George   'Administration', *Hindoo Patriot*, Calcutta, 1874

Chakrabarty, S C, (ed.)   *Autobiography of Devendranath Tagore* (in vernacular), Calcutta, 1962

Chandra, Bipan   Towards a Re-interpretation of Nineteenth Century Indian Economic History, (Seminar Report) *IESHR*, March 1968, vol. v, no. 1, pp. 1–18

Choudhury, B   *The Growth of Commercial Agriculture in Bengal*, vol. i, Calcutta, 1965

Choudhury, K C   *History and Economics of the Land Systems in Bengal*, Calcutta, 1927

Chaudhuri, K N   *The Economic Development of India under the East India Company*, Cambridge, 1971

Clarke, R   *Regulations of the Bengal Government Respecting Zemindary and Lakhiraj Property*, London, 1840

Clarke, R   *The Regulations of the Government of Fort William in Bengal*, vols i-iii, London, 1854

Colebrooke, H T   *Remarks on the Husbandry and Internal Commerce of Bengal*, (first published, 1795), Calcutta, 1806

Cooke, C N   *The Rise, Progress and Present Condition of Banking in India*, Calcutta, 1863

Cotton, H J S   *Memorandum on the Revenue History of Chittagong*, Calcutta, 1880

Crawford, D G   *Hooghly*, Calcutta, 1903

Deane, P   *The First Industrial Revolution*, Cambridge, 1967

Desh-U-Lubun Ocharik of Calcutta, Letter to the Author of 'View of the Present State and Future Prospects of the Free Trade and Colonization of India', *India Office Library Tract 36*, London, 1830

Drake-Brockman, E G   *Notes on the Early Judicial Administration of the District of Midnapore*, Midnapore, 1904

Dumont, L   *Religion, Politics and History in India*, Paris, 1970

Field, C D   *Introduction to the Regulations of the Bengal Code*, Calcutta, 1863

Firminger, W K, (ed.)   *The Fifth Report of the Select Committee of the House of Commons on the Affairs of India (1812)*, vols i-iii, Calcutta, 1917

Frykenberg, R E   *Guntur District, 1788–1848*, Oxford, 1965

Frykenberg, R E, (ed.)   *Land Control and Social Structure in Indian History*, Wisconsin, 1969

Furber, H J   *Company at Work*, Cambridge, Mass, 1951

Furnivall, J S   *Colonial Policy and Practice*, Cambridge, 1948

Gastrell, J E   *Geographical and Statistical Report of the Districts of Jessore, Fureedpore and Bakergunge*, Calcutta, 1868

Geertz, C   *Agricultural Involution*, California, 1963

Ghosal, H R   *Economic Transition in the Bengal Presidency, 1793–1833*, Patna, 1950

Ghose, L N   *The Modern History of the Indian Chiefs, Rajahs, Zemindars*, Calcutta, 1881

Ghose, R G   *Some Remarks on the So-called Black Acts*, Calcutta, 1851

Ghose, S   *Indian Sketches*, Calcutta, 1898

Glazier, E G   *Further Notes on Rungpore Records*, Calcutta, 1876

Grant, C   *Rural Life in Bengal*, London, 1860

Grant, J   *A View of the Revenues of Bengal*, Appendix 5 to the Fifth
    Report to the House of Commons, 1812
Guha, R   *A Rule of Property for Bengal*, Paris, 1963
Gupta, M N   *Land System of Bengal*, Calcutta, 1940
Gupta, M N   *Analytical Survey of Bengal Regulations*, Calcutta, 1943
Habib, I   *The Agrarian System of Mughal India*, London, 1963
Harnetty, P   *Imperialism and Free Trade: India and Lancashire in the
    Mid-Nineteenth Century*, Manchester, 1972
Harrington, J H   *Minute and Draft of Regulation on the Rights of Ryots
    in Bengal*, Calcutta, 1827
Hartwell, R M   *The Cause of the Industrial Revolution in England*,
    London, 1967
Hobsbawm, E, (ed.)   *Karl Marx: Pre-Capitalist Formations*, London, 1964
Hunter, W W   *Statistical Account of Bengal*, vols i–xx, London, 1875–76
Hunter, W W   *Annals of Rural Bengal*, seventh edition, London, 1897
Hutchins, F G   *The Illusion of Permanence: British Imperialism in
    India*, Princeton, 1967
Huttman, G H   *Revised Tables of Routes and Stages through the Terri-
    tories under the Presidency of Bengal*, Calcutta, 1838
Jack, J C   *The Economic Life of a Bengal District*, Oxford, 1916
Jenks, L H   *Migration of British Capital to 1875*, New York, 1927
Kaye, J W   *The Life and Correspondence of Charles Metcalfe*, London,
    1854
Khan, P   *The Revelations of an Orderly*, Calcutta, 1857
Kling, B   *The Blue Mutiny*, Philadelphia, 1966
Kumar, D   *Land and Caste in South India*, Cambridge, 1965
Larmour, R   *Notes on the Rent Difficulties in Lower Bengal and on the
    Proposed Amending of Act X of 1859*, Calcutta, 1862
Leach, E and S N Mukherjee   *Elites in South Asia*, Cambridge, 1970
Lees, W N   *Land and Labour of India*, London, 1867
Leibenstein, H   *Economic Backwardness and Economic Growth*, New
    York, 1962
Majumdar, B B   *Indian Political Associations and Reform of Legis-
    lature (1818–1917)*, Calcutta, 1965
Majumdar, B B   *History of Indian Social and Political Ideas*, Calcutta,
    1967
McNeille, D J   *Report on the Village Watch of the Lower Provinces of
    Bengal*, Calcutta, 1866
McNeille, D J   *Memorandum on the Revenue Administration of the
    Lower Provinces of Bengal*, Calcutta, 1873

Misra, B B   *The Indian Middle Classes*, Oxford, 1961

Mishra, G   'Indigo Plantation and Agrarian Relations in Champaran during the Nineteenth Century', *IESHR*, vol. iii, no. 4, December 1966

Mitra, A, (ed.)   *Midnapore District Records (New Series), 1777–1800*, Calcutta, 1962

Mitra, A and R Guha (ed.)   *Burdwan District Records (New Series), 1780–1800*, Calcutta, 1956

Mitra, K C   *Memoirs of Dwarakanath Tagore*, Calcutta, 1870

Mitra, L   *History of the Indigo Disturbances in Bengal*, Calcutta, 1903

Morris, M D   Towards a Re-interpretation of Nineteenth Century Indian Economic History, (Seminar Report) *IESHR*, March 1968, vol. v, no. 1, pp. 1–18

Mukherjee, A   *The Annals of British Land Revenue Administration in Bengal from 1698 to 1793*, Calcutta, 1883

Mukherjee, J   *The Permanent Settlement Imperilled*, Calcutta, 1865

Mukherjee, J   (A Lover of Justice), *India Office Library Tract 508*

Mukherjee, P   *Opinions of Mofussil Landholders on the Bengal Tenancy Bill*, Calcutta, 1883

Mukherjee, R K   *The Dynamics of a Rural Society*, Berlin, 1957

Mukherjee, R K   *The Rise and Fall of the East India Company*, Berlin, 1958

Mukherjee, S   'A Note on Lakhiraj Lands', *Indian History Congress Proceedings*, 1958, pp. 425–30

Mullik, K M   *Brief History of Bengal Commerce from the Year 1814 to 1870*, Calcutta, 1871

Murdoch, J   A Letter to the Right Hon'ble Earl of Elgin, Governor General of India, on the Rent Question in Bengal, Calcutta, 1863; with the valuable pamphlet: Keshabchandra Acharjya Choudhury, *The Rent Question in Bengal*, Calcutta, 1863

Pargiter, F E   *A Revenue History of the Sunderbans from 1765 to 1870*, Calcutta, 1885

Pavlov, V I   *The Indian Capitalist Class*, New Delhi, 1964

Phillimore, R H, (ed.)   *Historical Records of the Survey of India*, vol. iv (*1830–43*), Dehradun, 1959

Price, J C   *Notes on the History of Midnapore*, Calcutta, 1876

Reid, W M   *The Culture and Manufacture of Indigo*, Calcutta, 1887

Ricketts, H   *A Few Last Words on the Rent Difficulties in Bengal*, London, 1864

Rostow, W W   *The Stages of Economic Growth*, Cambridge, 1969

Roy, K C   *Kshitishavamsabalicharita* (in vernacular): *A History of the Nadia Raj*, Calcutta, 1932

Roy, K C   *Autobiography* (in vernacular), Calcutta, 1956

Roy L M   *Degradation of Bengal Zemindars*, Calcutta, 1893

Roy Choudhury, S K   *Mymensinger Barendra Brahman Zamindars* (in vernacular): *Zamindars of Mymensing*, vols i and ii, Calcutta, 1911

Roy Choudhury, T   *Bengal under Akbar and Jehangir*, Calcutta, 1953

Schultz, T W   *Transforming Traditional Agriculture*, New Haven, 1964

Seal, A   *The Emergence of Indian Nationalism*, Cambridge, 1971

Sen, R S   *Report on Jhenidah, Magura, Bagirhat and Sunderban Sub-divisions in District Jessore*, Calcutta, 1874

Sengupta, K K   Agrarian Disturbances in Nineteenth Century Bengal, *IESHR*, 1971, vol. iii, no. 2

Sherwill, J L   *A Geographical and Statistical Report of the Dinajpore District*, Calcutta, 1865

Singh-Roy, S and B P   *History of Chakdighi Singh-Roy Family*, Calcutta, 1971

Singh-Roy, P N   *The Chronicle of the British Indian Association*, Calcutta, 1965

Sinha, B K   Attitudes of the Christian Missionaries towards Land Problems of Bengal in the first half of the Nineteenth Century, *Journal of Indian History*, 15 August 1968

Sinha, N, (ed.)   *Who's Who in Freedom Movement in Bengal*, Calcutta, 1968

Sinha, N K   *Economic History of Bengal*, vols i and ii, Calcutta, 1962 and 1970

Smart, R B   *Geographical and Statistical Report on the District of Tipperah*, Calcutta, 1866

Smyth, Major R   *Statistical and Geographical Report of the 24 Parganas District*, Calcutta, 1857

Stokes, E T   *The English Utilitarians and India*, Oxford, 1959

Strachey, J   *India: Its Administration and Progress*, London, 1903

Taylor, J   *A Sketch of the Topography and Statistics of Dacca*, Calcutta, 1840

Thompson, E M L   *English Landed Society in the Nineteenth Century*, London, 1963

Thorner, D   'Marx on India and the Asiatic Mode of Production', *Contributions to Indian Sociology*, vol. ix, 1966

Thorner, D and A   *Land and Labour in India*, Bombay, 1962

Torrens, R   Letter to Right Hon'ble R V Smith, *India Office Library Tract 508*, London, 1856

Toynbee, G   *A Sketch of the Administration of the Hooghly District from 1795 to 1845*, Calcutta, 1888

Tripathi, A   *Trade and Finance in the Bengal Presidency, 1793–1833*, Calcutta, 1956

Walsh, J H T   *A History of Murshidabad District*, Calcutta, 1902

Weber, M   *The Religion of India*, Glencoe, 1958

Westland, J   *A Report on the District of Jessore*, Calcutta, 1874

Whitcombe, E   *Agrarian Conditions in Northern India*, vol. i, *The United Provinces under British Rule, 1860–1900*, Berkeley, 1972

Wilson, H H   *Glossary of Revenue and Judicial Terms*, London, 1855

Wilson, M   *History of the Behar Indigo Factories*, Calcutta, 1908

Wittfogel, K   *Oriental Despotism*, New Haven, 1957

Wylie, M   *The Commerce, Resources and Prospects of India*, London, 1857

Appendix A

Return of haats or village bazars in two subdivisions of
in rural

Return of Haats—Sub-Division

No	Name of hat	Name of thannah wherein situated	On what river situated	Name of proprietor	Annual rent at which leased out to ijaradar
1	Amtolah	Bargirhat	Kamarkhali Khal	Mohima C. Roy	Rs
2	Amtolah	Rampal	Dhaitkhali	Goburdanga Est.	...
3	Bagirhat	Bagirhat	Bhairab	Mohima C. Roy and others	...
4	Badhal	Morrellgunge	Bishkhali	Nakuleswar Roy	100
5	Baliaghatta	Bagirhat	Bhola	Durga P. Roy	...
6	Baonta	Ditto	Bhairab	Goburdanga Est.	...
7	Banagram	Morrellgunge	Banagram Khal	K. K. Chow-dharani	5
8	Basurhat	Bagirhat	Mater Khal	Mudan M. Bose and others	...
9	Baluibunia	Morrellgune	Pangoochi	R. T. Biswas	5
10	Charakhali	Bagirhat	Goalbathan	Mohima C. Roy and others	...
11	Chaksri	Rampal	Dhaitkhali	Goburdanga Est.	50
12	Chamar's Hat	Bagirhat	Jugikhali	H. P. Chowdhary	15
13	Chandpai	Rampal	Chandpai	S. S. Dasi and others	...
14	Chitalmari (c)	Bagirhat	On the confluence of the Madhumati and Chitra	Abdool Rohim and others	200
15	Chingrakhali	Morrellgunge	Chingrakhali Khal	Jan Ali Khan	...
16	Choolkati	Bagirhat	Choolkati Khal	D. P. Roy Chowdary	...
17	Dhalchaka	Ditto	Dhalchaka Khal	Goburdanga Est.	...
18	Dhaighata	Rampal	Inland	Maharaj Sing	...
19	Daibagnakati	Morrellgunge	Sankarikati Khal	R. T. Biswas	100
20	Depara	Bagirhat	Taleswar Khal	G. N. Sarkar	100
21	Fakirhat (d)	Ditto	Bhairab	P. N. Ghosh	...
22	Fakirhat	Ditto	Ditto	Kali P. Roy and others	500
23	Fatehpur	Ditto	Ditto	R. S. N. Ghoshal	42
24	Goakkhali	Ditto	Boata Khal	M. C. Roy	...
25	Ghose's Hat	Ditto	Joukhali Khal	Goburdanga Est.	...
26	Gilatola	Rampal	Gilatola Khal	Ditto	35

(c) Signifies that the place is also a cattle market

Jessore district in 1873 as a measure of market organisation
Bengal

Bagirhat, District Jessore

On what day held	Approx. no. of attending persons	Chief articles sold	Remarks
Tues, Sat	150	Rice, paddy, fish, vegetables, cloth, salt, oil, tobacco, betel leaf, betel nut, &c.	
Wed, Sat	200	Salt, oil, tobacco, cocoanut, arecanut, &c.	
Sun, Wed	1,000	Rice, paddy, cloth, cocoanut, arecanut, poultry, tobacco, salt, oil, betel leaf, fish, &c.	Middle class school, post-office, zemindary cutcherry, moonsif's court, Sub-divisional Court, police station.
Sun, Thu	500	Paddy, rice, salt, tobacco, arecanut, &c.	Guru patshala.
Sun, Wed	25	Fish, salt, oil, vegetables, &c.	
Mon, Fri	30	Fish, vegetables, betel leaf &c.	
Mon, Fri	100	Tobacco, betel nut, paddy, rice, oil, salt.	Letter-box, middle class school zemindary cutcherry.
Tues, Sat	250	Fish, oil, betel nut, betel leaf, cloth, paddy, rice, &c.	
Wed, Sat	100	Paddy, rice, fish, oil, salt, vegetables, oil, &c.	
Wed, Sun	50	Fish, vegetables, oil, &c.	
Tues, Fri	300	Betel nut, paddy, salt, oil, &c.	
Mon, Wed	200	Fish, vegetables, &c.	
Mon, Thu	200	Paddy, rice, vegetables, cocoanut &c.	
Sat, Wed	3,000	Rice, paddy, cloth, matswood, timber, arecanut, cattle, &c.	
Mon, Fri	150	Fish, vegetables, rice, paddy	Guru patshala.
Ditto	25	Fish, salt, oil, tobacco, &c.	
Ditto	200	Ditto	
Tues, Fri	100	Rice, salt, oil, &c.	
Wed, Sat	400	Paddy, rice, fish, vegetables, &c.	
Sun, Thurs	600	Ditto	
Daily Bazar	...	Fish, vegetables, &c.	
Wed, Sun	800	Arecanut, tamarind, pottery, rice, cloth, salt, cocoanut, &c.	Police out-post, post-office
Mon, Thurs	400	Fish, oil, salt, cloth, rice, &c.	
Mon, Fri	250	Ditto	
Ditto	70	Fish, oil, salt, &c.	
Mon, Thurs	60	Oil, salt, fish, betel leaf, &c.	

(*d*) Signifies that the place is also a daily market.

Return of Haats—Sub-Division

No	Name of hat	Name of thannah wherein situated	On what river situated	Name of proprietor	Annual rent at which leased out to ijaradar
					Rs
27	Gourrumbha (c)	Rampal	Bhola	K. P. Roy Chowdhary	100
28	Jatrapur (d)	Bagirhat	Bhairab	Gobardanga Est.	...
29	Jhan Jhania	Rampal	Daitkhali	D. N. Ghosh	...
30	Kaliganj	Bagirhat	Bhairab	S. N. Dutt	...
31	Kaliganj	Rampal	Kumerkhali	Goburdanga Est.	...
32	Katali	Ditto	Katali Khal	D. N. Ghosh and others	...
33	Katakhali	Bagirhat	Bhairab	B. Datta	40
34	Kachua	Ditto	Ditto	A. M. Dasi	200
35	Karamara	Ditto	Ditto	Gobardanga Est.	...
36	Lakpur	Ditto	Jugikhali	P. C. Roy and others	50
37	Mandara	Ditto	Talessur Khal	A. N. Roy and others	62
38	Mansa (d)	Ditto	Bhairab	P. Ghosh	12
39	Magra	Ditto	Rohimabad Khal	K. K. Roy	15
40	Morrellgunge (d) (c)	Morrelgunge	Panguchi	Morrell & Lightfoot	3000
41	Mukherjee's Hat	Bagirhat	Mater Khal	Goburdanga Est.	12
42	Noapara	Ditto	Noapara Khal	H. N. Ghosh	...
43	Panighat	Ditto	Bhairab	Gobardanga Est.	4
44	Phailarhat	Rampal	Dhaitkhali	K. P. Roy Chowdhary	10
45	Rampal	Ditto	Ditto	H. N. Ghosh	36
46	Rakhalgachi	Bagirhat	Rakhalgachi Khal	P. C. Nag and others	...
47	Shukdeb Roy's Hat (c)	Ditto	Ichhamati	H. Roy Chowdhary	120
48	Shib's Bazar (d)	Ditto	Bhairab	N. Datta and others	...
49	Shonakhali	Ditto	Ditto	Ditto	...
50	Shonatali	Rampal	Baliaghatt Khal	P. Ghosh	...
51	Sholkhali	Morrellgunge	Sholkhali Khal	K. K. Chowdharani & others	50
52	Taleswar	Bagirhat	Bhairab	M. C. Roy	300
53	Umajuri	Ditto	Inland	K. N. Biswas	25

(d) Signifies that the place is also a daily market.

Bagirhat, District Jessore

On what day held	Approx. no. of attending persons	Chief articles sold	Remarks
Mon, Thurs	700	Paddy, rice, salt, and 10 or 15 cattle in the months of Choit and Baisak.	Letter-box, zemindary, cutcherry.
Tues, Sat	600	Paddy, rice, betel nut, fish, vegetables, cocoanut, &c.	Post-office letter-box, zemindary, cutcherry.
Wed, Sat	200	Paddy, rice, oil, salt, &c.	
Tues, Sat	250	Rice, cloth, salt, betel nut, &c.	
Ditto	125	Oil, salt, fish, betel leaf, &c.	
Wed, Sat	350	Paddy, rice, cloth, &c.	A zemindary cutcherry.
Mon, Fri	300	Rice, cloth, salt, oil, &c.	
Mon, Thurs	1,000	Rice, salt, cocoanut, betel nut, oil, fish, vegetables, &c.	Post-office, Police out-post
Mon, Fri	80	Rice, paddy, &c.	
Tues, Fri	300	Salt, fish, rice, &c.	
Mon, Fri	400	Fish, rice, paddy, &c.	
Daily Bazar	300	Paddy, rice, fish, vegetables, &c.	Zemindar's cutcherry, middle class school.
Mon, Thurs	500	Cloth, rice, paddy, cocoanut, betel nut, fish, salt &c.	Narail Zemindar's cutcherry.
Mon, Fri	1,500	Paddy, rice, cloth, cocoanut, arecanuts, cattle, &c.	Port, sub-registrar's office, post-office, police station, Messrs. Morrell and Lightfoot's zemindary cutcherry.
Ditto	60	Oil, fish, salt, vegetables, &c.	
Thurs, Sun	100	Fish, vegetables, &c.	Middle class school, post-office.
Tues, Sat	25	Fish, salt, vegetables, &c.	
Thurs, Sun	60	Rice, salt, oil, fish, &c.	
Tues, Fri	500	Paddy, rice, cloth, &c.	Police-station, post-office, zemindary cutcherry.
Thurs, Sun	50	Fish, salt, oil, tobacco, &c.	
Tues, Sat, daily bazar.	1,000	Paddy, rice, cloth, cattle, &c.	
Wed, Sun	50	Fish, vegetables, &c.	
Tues, Sat	60	Ditto	
Mon, Thurs	150	Rice, salt, oil, &c.	
Wed, Sun	300	Paddy, rice, fish, &c.	
Tues, Sat	1,200	Rice, salt, cocoanut, arecanut, vegetables, small boats, &c.	Post-office letter-box.
Wed, Sat	300	Paddy, rice, &c.	

(*c*) Signifies that the place is also a cattle market

APPENDIX A

Return of Haats—Sub-Division

Name of hat	Name of thannah wherein situated	On what river situated	Name of proprietor	Annual rent at which leased out to ijaradar
				Rs
Abaipur	Soelkopa	Kumar	Babu N. Sikdar	...
Aladikhali (c)	Hurinakunda	Ditto	Mrs Sherrieff	40
Atlia	Jhenidah	Inland	Babu K. N. Acharjee	250
Bijalia (c)	Soelkopa	Kumar	Mrs Sherrieff	700
Bakri	Ditto	Nabagunga	Babu C. K. Roy	400
Bajukhali	Ditto	Kumar	Babu G. D. Mazumdar	...
Baidanga (Gilapol)	Jhenidah	Nabagunga	Babu B. R. Gossyami	450
Benipur	Soelkopa	Kaligunga	Babu C. K. Roy	250
Bhatue	Ditto	Public road	Babu M. M. Mazumdar	150
Bhabanipur (c)	Hurinakunda	On a canal issued from Kumar	Babu C. K. Roy	1,200
Bashdebpur	Soelkopa	Nabagunga	Mr C. Tweedie	60
Bisaikhali	Jhenidah	Bang Nudi	Babu C. K. Ray	200
Chandipur	Ditto	Inland	Mr W. Sherrieff	60
Dhantala	Ditto	On road to Chuadanga	Babu K. N. Acharjee	190
Durgapurkuti	Ditto	Inland	Mr W. Sherieff	60
Dantia (Malitha) (c)	Soelkopa	Gorae	Babu B. C. Ghose	125
Fulhari	Ditto	Kumar	Babu K. C. Chakravarti	100
Fazilpur Hat	Ditto	Ditto	Babu G. C. Ghose	90
Garakholla	Ditto	Ditto	Babu Gurudas Roy	80
Gangutia (Abaipur)	Ditto	Ditto	Babu N. Sikdar and others	1,000
Gopalpur (c)	Jhenidah	Nabagunga	Mr C. Tweedie	500
Harinakunda (c)	Harinakunda	Bangar	Babu C. K. Roy	500
Gobindapur (c)	Jhenidah	Nabagunga	Babu H. N.Bose	60
Joradaha	Harinakunda	Kumar	Mr J. Sherrieff	1,000
Jhenidah (d)	Jhenidah	Nabagunga	Babu C. K. Ray and others	1,250

Jhenidah, District Jessore

On what day held	Approx. no. of attending persons	Chief articles sold	Remarks
Thurs, Mon	50	Rice, dall, oil, dhan, salt, tobacco, vegetables	Middle-class English school, post-office letter-box.
Wed, Sun	60	Ditto and cows	Silk manufactory.
Sat, Wed	300	Ditto, excepting cattle	... ...
Thurs, Sun	1,000	Ditto and cattle	Indigo factory, zemindary cutcherry, post-office letter-box.
Fri, Tues	600	Ditto, ditto	Post-office, letter-box, zemindary cutcherry,
Mon, Fri	...	...	... ...
Sun, Thurs	500	Ditto, excepting cows	Zemindary cutcherry, post office letter-box, patshala
Mon, Fri	400	Ditto and cattle	Post-office letter box, patshala, indigo factory, zemindary cutcherry.
Wed, Sun	300	Ditto, excepting cattle	Ditto
Mon, Fri	706	Ditto and cattle	... ...
Tues, Fri	200	Rice, paddy, vegetable, clothes, salt, fish	Patshala.
...	100	Ditto ditto	Post-office letter-box.
Sun, Wed	50	Rice, paddy, vegetables	... ...
Fri, Mon	200	Ditto	... ...
Sun, Wed	70	Fish, tarkari	Indigo factory.
Mon, Thurs	200	Rice, tobacco, fish, salt, cows, clothes, &c.	Patshala.
Sun, Thurs	250	Ditto, excepting cows	Post-office, letter-box, patshala.
Ditto	200	Ditto, ditto	Patshala.
Ditto	150	Ditto, ditto	Ditto.
Tues, Fri	2,500	Ditto, ditto	Post-office, letter-box, middle class school, patshala, zemindary cutcherry.
Sun, Wed	500	Ditto, cows and many others	Indigo factory, post-office letter box, zemindary cutcherry.
Sat, Wed	400	Ditto, excepting cows	Middle-class English school, patshala, post-office letter-box.
Wed, Fri	50	Fishes, tarkari, &c.	... ...
Tues, Satur	700	Ditto and cows	Indigo factory.
Sun, Thurs	700	Rice, sarika, vegetable, fish, billet, oil, salt.	Middle-class English school, indigo factory, sub-divisional Small Cause Court, Moonsiff's Court, police station, cutcherry, head chakla of Nurrail zemindars, post-office letter-box.

APPENDIX A

Return of Haats—Sub-Division

Name of hat	Name of thannah wherein situated	On what river situated	Name of proprietor	Annual rent at which leased out to ijaradar
				Rs
Katlagari (d)	Soelkopa	Gorae	Babu C. K. Ray	40
Kotchanpur	Kotchandpur	Kabotarko	Babu G. N. Mazumdar	675
Kalicharanpur	Jhenidah	In the interior	Babu W. K. Guha	175
Katlamari	Ditto	Nabagunga	Mr W. Sherrieff	...
Khulumbari	Soelkopa	Gorae	Babu C. K. Roy	25
Nangalband	Ditto	...	Babu B. C. Ghose	...
Madur Hat	Jhenidah	Nabagunga	Babu U. C. Singh	60
Madhupur	Ditto	Ditto	Mr C. Tweedie of Madhupore	200
Makrampur	Soelkopa	Kumar	Babu G. D. Roy	90
Nagirat	Ditto	Ditto	Ditto	100
Noalidanga (d)	Jhenidah	Bang	Babu O. C. Debraj	...
Nagarbathan (c)	Ditto	Nabagunga	Babu C. K. Roy	400
Porahati	Soclkopa	Kumar	Ditto	1,000
Rayra	Ditto	Ditto	Mr W. Sherrieff	...
Salimanpur (c)	Chandpur	Kabadak	Babu B. N. Mukherjee and others	60
Suadi	Ditto	Inland	Babu S. C. Roy	250
Soelkopa	Soelkopa	Kumar	Babu C. K. Roy	400
Sakaridaha	Ditto	Interior	Mr W. Sherrieff	100
Sibnagar	Chandpur	Chitra	Babu M. Biswas	...
Talsar	Ditto	Ditto	Babu S. Ghose	60
Tribeni	Soelkopa	Kaligunga	Not known	250
Tikri	Jhenidah	Sanchaie	Babu P. C. Ganguly	200

Source: R.S. Sen: *Report on Jhenidah, Magura, Bagirhat and Sundarban Sub-divisions in Jessore*, Calcutta, 1874.
Appendix 7 for Bagirhat and Appendix D for Jhenidah.

Jhenidah, District Jessore

On what day held	Approx. no. of attending persons	Chief articles sold	Remarks
Ditto	100	Ditto	Zemindary cutcherry.
Sun, Thurs	4,000	Fishes, vegetables, tobacco, chillies, earthen-pots, spices	Post-office letter-box, police station, middle-class English school, zemindary cutcherry, sugar factory.
Wed, Fri	200	Ditto and cattle	... ...
Wed, Sat		... ...	... ...
Tues, Sat	50	Ditto, excepting cattle	
Wed, Sun			
Sun, Thurs	50	Ditto	
Mon, Fri	300	Ditto	Patshala, indigo factory, post-office letter-box.
Sun, Wed	100	Ditto	Patshala, indigo factory, zemindary cutcherry.
Mon, Fri	300	Ditto	Post-office letter-box at Buxipur on the opposite side.
Sat, Tues		... ...	Post-office letter-box, zemindary cutcherry.
Tues, Sat	500	Ditto and cattle	Indigo factory.
Sun, Thurs	2,500	Ditto, ditto	Post-office letter-box, indigo factory.
Wed, Sat		Ditto, excepting cattle	... ...
Sat, Wed	200	Ditto, with cattle	Patshala, zemindary cutcherry.
Sat, Wed	400	Rice, pan, supari, fish	Zemindary cutcherry.
Sat, Tues	450–500	Rice, paddy, vegetables, spices, dall, &c.	Post-office, police station, zemindary cutcherry, English middle school, indigo factory.
Mon, Fri	300	Ditto, ditto	Zemindary cutcherry, post office letter-box.
Wed, Sun	...	Vegetable, oil, salt, &c.	... ...
Mon, Fri	200	Ditto	Post-office letter-box, patshala, zemindary cutcherry.
Tues, Sat	300	Ditto	Indigo factory.
Ditto	300	Rice, vegetable, pan, &c.	... ...

Index